In an era when institutional conflict has seemingly become the norm in EU affairs, this book is a must read. Theoretically, instead of pulling existing work 'off the shelf', Norman develops an innovative constructivist account of the social mechanisms shaping institutional change. Methodologically, he demonstrates how interpretive process tracing can be used to study such dynamics. The result is a book that not only tells us important things about the EU, but also contributes to central debates over theory and method.

**Jeffrey T. Checkel**, *Simon Fraser University, Canada,*
*and Peace Research Institute Oslo, Norway*

Norman has produced an outstanding reflection on the dynamics of institutional conflict within the EU institutional framework. By linking new theoretical insights derived from international relations constructivism with empirical investigations in highly interesting case studies, the book makes a substantial contribution to our understanding of both the institutional dynamics and the political role of EU institutions. It is highly recommended for anyone interested in European security or European studies more generally.

**Christian Kaunert**, *Professor of International Politics,*
*Director of the European Institute for Security*
*and Justice, University of Dundee, UK*

This is a conceptually sophisticated, empirically rich, and theoretically meaningful contribution to the study of EU institutional dynamics. It can be read as an innovative constructivist approach at interpretive process tracing, an inductive account of the underexplored influence of EU-level legal services (Council, Commission, EP) in shaping integration discourse, and as a nuanced story of how JHA and CFSP have 'communitarized' from humble intergovernmental origins. The impressive research design uses empirical triangulation and engages in alternative explanation testing in ways that few studies actually deliver on, and thus contributes to the growing interest at moving beyond either/or debates between rational institutionalists and constructivists.

**Jeffrey Lewis**, *Cleveland State University, USA*

# The Mechanisms of Institutional Conflict in the European Union

How institutional conflicts arise in international political orders and the conditions shaping the outcomes of such conflicts has become the object of considerable contemporary focus.

This book considers the dynamics of institutional conflict and institutional change in international organizations, specifically focusing on the European Union, the most highly integrated international political order on the globe. In a world where political decision making increasingly takes place above the nation state level, it theorises the social mechanisms that lead to the point at which these tensions become explicit and the customary functioning of international political orders tips into outright conflict between different organizational entities. Taking a constructivist approach, it examines two in-depth case studies – in the field of Justice and Home Affairs (JHA) and the EU's Common Foreign and Security Policy (CFSP) – to explain the dynamics of the processes that lead up to institutional conflicts and provide some explanation for their final outcomes.

This text will be of key interest to fields of and European Integration, EU Politics and more broadly International Relations.

**Ludvig Norman** is Researcher and Lecturer in the Department of Government, Uppsala University, Sweden.

**Routledge Studies on Government and the European Union**
Edited by Andy Smith, University of Bordeaux, France

# The Mechanisms of Institutional Conflict in the European Union

**Ludvig Norman**

Routledge
Taylor & Francis Group

LONDON AND NEW YORK

First published 2017
by Routledge
2 Park Square, Milton Park, Abingdon, Oxon OX14 4RN

and by Routledge
711 Third Avenue, New York, NY 10017

*Routledge is an imprint of the Taylor & Francis Group, an informa business*

*British Library Cataloguing in Publication Data*
A catalogue record for this book is available from the British Library

*Library of Congress Cataloging-in-Publication Data*
Names: Norman, Ludvig, 1976–
Title: The mechanisms of institutional conflict in the European Union /
    Ludvig Norman.
Description: New York, NY : Routledge, 2016. | Series: Routledge studies
    on government and the European Union | Includes bibliographical
    references and index.
Identifiers: LCCN 2016007795 | ISBN 9781138963092 (hardback) |
    ISBN 9781315658995 (ebook)
Subjects: LCSH: European cooperation. | Intergovernmental
    cooperation—European Union countries. | Law enforcement—European
    Union countries. | Justice, Administration of—European Union
    countries. | Judicial assistance—European Union countries. | Common
    Foreign and Security Policy. | European Union countries—Foreign
    relations. | National security—European Union countries.
Classification: LCC JN30 .N677 2016 | DDC 341.242/2—dc23
LC record available at https://lccn.loc.gov/2016007795

ISBN: 978-1-138-96309-2 (hbk)
ISBN: 978-1-315-65899-5 (ebk)

Typeset in Times New Roman
by Apex CoVantage, LLC

# Contents

# Illustrations

**Figures**

**Tables**

# Acknowledgments

The author would like to thank the Swedish Royal Academy of Sciences, the Anna-Maria Lundin Stipend fund, the Borbos Hansson fund and the Swedish Network for European Studies for generous support enabling the fieldwork on which the study in this book is based. Thanks also to the Centre for European Policy Studies (CEPS) and Michael Emerson for generously providing a workspace in Brussels when conducting interviews. Thanks to Jeremy Richardson and Taylor and Francis for the permission to reproduce parts of my article originally published in the *Journal of European Public Policy* 22(5): 630–649 on which parts of Chapters 4 and 6 are based. Thanks also to *Acta Universitatis Upsaliensis* for kind permission to reproduce parts of the text. The author gratefully acknowledges the insightful comments and suggestions from series editor Andy Smith as well as those from two anonymous reviewers. Special thanks go to all interviewees who took the time to share their insights and experiences with me. Substantially, many people contributed along the way: advisors, colleagues and students with insightful comments, suggestions and critique which helped significantly improve the final product. I owe you all my most profound gratitude.

# Abbreviations

| | |
|---|---|
| ACP | African, Caribbean and Pacific states |
| AFSJ | Area of Freedom Security and Justice |
| CDPC | European Committee for Crime Problems |
| CFSP | Common Foreign and Security Policy |
| COHOM | Council Working Group for Human Rights |
| COREPER | Committee of Permanent Representatives |
| CSDP | Common Security and Defence Policy |
| DG | Directorate General |
| DG DEV | Directorate General for Development Cooperation and relations with ACP countries |
| DG ENV | Directorate General for Environment |
| DG JLS | Directorate General for Justice Liberty and Security |
| DG RELEX | Directorate General for External Relations |
| EDF | European Development Fund DI discursive institutionalism |
| EEAS | European External Action Service |
| EEC | European Economic Community |
| EC | European Community |
| ECJ | European Court of Justice |
| ECOWAS | Economic Community of West African States |
| EPA | Economic Partnership Agreement |
| EPC | European Political Cooperation |
| EPPO | European Public Prosecutor's Office |
| ESDP | European Security and Defence Policy |
| EU | European Union |
| HI | historical institutionalist |
| IR | international relations |
| IMF | International Monetary Fund |
| JHA | Justice and Home Affairs |
| OECD | Organisation for Economic Co-Operation and Development |
| PSC | Political and Security Committee |
| SALW | Small Arms and Light Weapons |
| TEU | Treaty on the European Union |
| TFEU | Treaty on the Functioning of the European Union |
| UNDP | United Nations Development Programme |

# 1 Dynamics of institutional conflict in the European Union

## Introduction

How institutional conflicts arise in international political orders and the conditions shaping the outcomes of such conflicts have become the object of considerable contemporary focus. In a world where political decision making increasingly takes place above the level of the nation-state, tensions between different levels are becoming ever more pronounced. These dynamics are perhaps most clearly manifested in the European Union, one of the most highly integrated international political orders on the globe. Political decisions taken within the framework of the EU have wide-ranging implications in both national and international settings. With deeper integration in a seemingly ever-expanding catalogue of policy issues, the distribution of decision-making competencies across organizational entities has become increasingly salient. This general problematique is addressed by theorizing the social mechanisms that help us better understand at which point these tensions become explicit. It explains the turn from day-to-day functioning of international political orders to outright conflict between organizational entities representing different levels of decision making. It also engages with questions regarding what happens after the outbreak of institutional conflicts, and explains the dynamics of such conflicts and how they may contribute to shifts in the distribution of decision-making competencies.

The points of departure here are two landmark cases of institutional conflict in the European Union, the *small arms case* and the *environmental crimes case*. In these two cases the European Commission (Commission) brought legal action against the Council of the European Union (Council) and the Member States to the European Court of Justice (the Court). The outcome of these legal actions involved moving two issues of principal importance from the intergovernmental area of EU decision making into its supranational framework. These were instances where conflicts between the organizational entities of the EU resulted in the reconfiguration of institutional boundaries. In-depth engagement with these cases is used here for further developing our understanding of institutional conflict and institutional change in international political orders.

In the first case, and against the explicitly stated preferences of a vast majority of Member State governments, the Community gained the competence to impose on Member States the enforcement of Community law with the use of criminal sanctions. The Commission had challenged a 2003 Council decision that had as its aim the protection of the environment through criminal law, and argued that this decision should be replaced by a Directive based on what was then Community law.[1] The competence to equip Community legislation with criminal sanctions had until this point been exclusively dealt with in the intergovernmental Justice and Home Affairs (JHA) area.[2] In the ensuing legal battle before the Court, no less than eleven Member States of the then fifteen members intervened in support of the Council. The final judgment was extremely controversial and sent shockwaves through the European political system.[3] In this case, the so-called *environmental crimes* case,[4] it was clear that most Member State governments at the time were intensively opposed if not openly hostile to the idea that the EU would have criminal sanctions at its disposal for the implementation of Community legislation. The final ruling of the Court, however, affirmed the position of the Commission. In the decision, it did point out that 'neither criminal law nor the rules of criminal procedure fall within the Community's competence'. Nonetheless, in the very next paragraph it went on to argue that this

> does not prevent the Community legislature, when the application of effective, proportionate and dissuasive criminal penalties by the competent national authorities is an essential measure for combating serious environmental offences, from taking measures which relate to the criminal law of the Member States which it considers necessary in order to ensure that the rules which it lays down on environmental protection are fully effective.
>
> (Court 2005a: paragraph 47–48)

Thus, through this decision the Court effectively moved a competence in the field of criminal law out of the control of the Member States and up to the supranational level. The political significance of the decision at the time was considerable. National systems of criminal law are generally regarded as an expression of highly ingrained societal norms defining what should be considered reprehensible behaviour. While states often cooperate on law enforcement issues, the ultimate decisions on which kinds of behaviours are reprehensible enough to be treated within the framework of criminal law have traditionally been carefully guarded from outside involvement. The decision to criminalize a certain form of behaviour is thus not only the final means of the state for upholding order, but is also a highly symbol-laden area of policymaking. Its move into the supranational framework of EU policymaking against the will of most Member States thus signified an important break with these conceptions.

In the second case, the Commission gained the right to enact measures in the field of non-proliferation and disarmament of small arms and light weapons (SALW) within the framework of the Community's development policy. Institutional conflict broke out over a Council decision in the Common Foreign and Security Policy (CFSP), a decision with the aim of making a financial contribution to the Economic Community of West African States (ECOWAS) in the field of SALW. Preceding the outbreak of institutional conflict over the decision of the Council, the issue of SALW had been exclusively dealt with through the strictly intergovernmental procedures of the CFSP.[5] The Commission's legal action against the Council, and the subsequent decision of the Court in 2008 in the so-called *small arms* case[6] brought the issue within the supranational framework. The Member States and the Council expressed that the issue could not be regarded as anything but an issue of security. The ruling of the Court, however, stated that

> certain measures aiming to prevent fragility in developing countries, including those adopted in order to combat the proliferation of small arms and light weapons, can contribute to the elimination or reduction of obstacles to the economic and social development of those countries.
>
> (Court 2008: paragraph 68)

Based on this definition of the aims of the EU's anti-SALW policies, the Court ruled in favour of the Commission's position. For the Council and many of the Member States this was intrinsically an issue of international peace and security. Nonetheless, through the decision of the Court, SALW was moved into the supranational framework of Community development policy.

Similar to issues of criminal law, the field of international security is commonly regarded as an area of politics which nation-states are least likely to surrender to the control of others. External security policies belong to the 'high politics' of states and represents an area of political decision making where states are traditionally reluctant to commit to far-reaching formal cooperative arrangements. The fact that an important aspect of this intergovernmental policy field slipped through the fingers of the Member States and was moved into the supranational framework of the EU thus warrants a closer look at the dynamics of the case.

All of this raises pressing questions. Why did the Commission initiate these institutional conflicts? How was it able to move two issues of such principal importance from these respective areas into a supranational framework against the explicit stated preferences of a majority of the Member States? And what can these cases tell us more generally about institutional conflicts over decision-making competencies in the EU? That an international administrative body, like the Commission, and an influential international Court like the ECJ will at times develop different perspectives on particular issues than Member States is not in itself an event that is likely to raise eyebrows. However, the fact that this international body was able to do so in these core areas of national sovereignty stands out even in the context of a well-institutionalized environment like the EU.

## The unexplored potential of constructivist theories

These cases touch on the very core problematique of European integration theory: the tension between national sovereignty and supranational decision making. This much reiterated theme in EU studies has structured academic debate in this field since the inception of the European project itself (Haas 1964). More recently, debates have centred on questions such as when it is likely that the Commission will challenge the Council and the Member States over competence issues, and to what extent supranational organizations such as the Commission and the Court actually serve as the 'engines of integration' (Pollack 2003a).

This general theme of EU studies incorporates a broad array of theoretical and meta-theoretical approaches, drawing on a highly diverse set of research traditions. However, when it comes to the more specific issue of institutional conflict and institutional change, rationalist perspectives have come to more or less dominate the scholarly field. The notion of supranational organizations as 'competence maximizers' (Héritier and Moury 2012), as utility-maximizing actors which strive for larger budgets and more influence over the policy process, lies at the heart of these approaches and has often served as an influential shorthand for understanding such processes. This book challenges such a view in two ways, the first by highlighting the extent to which these perspectives fall short in providing an adequate understanding of both the triggers and outcomes of institutional conflicts in the EU. Secondly, and perhaps more importantly, it explores and demonstrates the potential of constructivist perspectives to offer more nuanced, accurate and meaningful explanations.

The two selected conflicts are treated here as crucial cases in relation to rationalist theories of institutional conflict, each brought from what was at the time the two intergovernmental policy areas of the EU, the JHA and the CFSP. They are crucial in that they ostensibly conform well to the expectations of existing explanatory models built on the notion of the Commission as a 'competence maximizer': cases where it is conventionally deemed likely that rationalist approaches would be able to provide an exhaustive explanation. In this sense they represent the very home turf for rationalist perspectives on institutional relations in the EU. Engaging with the limits and possibilities of rationalist perspectives in relation to these cases allows something more broadly to be expressed regarding the pertinence of these perspectives to deal with the issue of institutional conflict. Conversely, this also paves the way for asking questions regarding the possibilities of constructivist perspectives to make a contribution in this theoretical field. There has been a curious absence of constructivist scholars explicitly addressing this issue, and yet while there is considerable potential in constructivist perspectives to deal with these questions, this potential has gone largely unexplored.

The constructivist field of research in EU studies has been largely devoted to theorizing the mechanisms through which actors' self-understandings and preferences converge at the European level. More concretely, these accounts have paid less attention to processes through which agents' self-understandings and preferences become increasingly more disparate. In spite of their considerable contributions to our understanding of the institutional dynamics of the EU, constructivist perspectives seem to harbour an apparent inability to explain at which point latent tensions of the European project become not only explicit but also the object of open conflict between different organizational actors such as the Commission and the Council. Similarly, they have rarely engaged with the actual dynamics of institutional conflicts once they have commenced. From this perspective, it seems as if constructivists have often mistakenly accepted the division of work as defined by those rationalist scholars who tend to argue that once preferences are distributed in a dichotomous fashion, ideational factors will have little or no impact. This is the well-rehearsed move through which ideational or 'cultural' components are thought to only shape social interaction when agents are in basic agreement on particular issues (cf. Goldstein and Keohane 1993).[7] From this perspective, a constructivist approach would, by definition, have little to contribute when understanding the dynamics of conflict. As will be fleshed out in subsequent chapters, while many constructivist scholars seem to have accepted such a division of labour, this is far from true. That said, there are certain aspects of constructivist understandings of institutions and agents that have tended towards explaining stability and continuity rather than processes of seemingly sudden institutional change. Defining how these concepts can help us capture the dynamics of institutional conflict in international political orders like the EU is an important aim of this book.

The two cases offer a promising starting point to engage with the broader question of institutional conflict in the European Union. Empirically, they open up for an in-depth account of crucial processes through which the EU is actually governed, and do so in two policy areas which have moved to the very centre of European politics in recent decades. Theoretically, the study serves as a way to discuss the limits of rationalist approaches to level fruitful explanations of these types of cases, and more importantly, to explore the potential for constructivist approaches to make a contribution to our understanding of this aspect of the EU, and international political orders more broadly. To more clearly specify why, a first assessment of the cases is provided here, highlighting to what extent they present rationalist theories with puzzles.

## The two cases: a preliminary assessment

At first glance, the two cases seem to conform to rationalist expectations regarding international organizations, such as the Commission and the Court, as 'competence maximizers' (Héritier and Moury 2012: 1320; cf. Pollack 2003a: 35). From this perspective, it is expected that given a number of auxiliary factors, supranational institutions exert a more or less stable pressure to gain control over the policy process and expand their institutional turf. The fact that institutional conflict broke out in these two cases should thus not come as a surprise. For rationalist institutionalists (RI), the fundamental reasons for why the Commission would challenge the Council over a certain issue are assumed *a priori*, and as such need little further explanation, as they form part of the underlying assumptions of the analysis. The Commission's actions in the *small arms case* and the *environmental crimes case* become understandable in view of the anticipation that taking the Council to Court in these instances would likely result in the expansion of its influence over the policymaking process.

Underlying this characterization of the Commission is the notion that it nurtures more or less stable pro-integration preferences. As Tallberg (2002) notes, there is close to scholarly unanimity on the pro-integration nature of supranational institutions' preferences (Garrett and Tsebelis 2001; Pollack 2003a; Tallberg 2002: 44–45).[8] From this perspective the Commission will work to increase institutional turf and expand its budget as well as influence over the policy process. It is posited that the Commission can generally be expected to promote policies that entail 'More Europe' (Ross 1995). The governments of Member States then will be expected to prefer those options which entail a minimum loss of sovereignty, all else being equal. International organizations, such as international courts and bureaucratic institutions, are expansionist by nature (cf. Alter and Hefler 2010). As Pollack states:

> [R]ational-models of regulatory agencies generally assume that such agencies are unitary actors with exogenously given and fixed utility functions which they attempt to maximize within the constraints of the principal-agent relationship.
>
> (Pollack 2003a: 35)

However, the analytical purchase gained from positing that Member States protect their sovereignty while supranational actors like the Commission and the Court hold stable 'More Europe' preferences is not self-evident, particularly not in relation to the two cases. Both cases were preceded by the adoption of several very similar legislative measures, but where there were no indications of institutional conflict. Previous to the Framework Decision on the protection of the environment through criminal law that sparked institutional conflict in the *environmental crimes case*, several legislative acts had been adopted as intergovernmental measures in the field of criminal law, such as within the field of money laundering (Council 1991a, 2001d), the protection of the euro (Council 2000b), and regarding EU immigration policy (Council 2002c, 2002d). Similarly, in the years previous to the adoption of the Council decision on SALW, several measures in this policy field had been adopted under the intergovernmental CFSP without any sign of protest from the Commission (Council 1999d, 2002a, 2002b, 2004c). If we assume that the Commission nurtures stable 'More Europe' preferences, then it must be asked why the Commission had not challenged the Council previously on the adoption of any of these measures.

The likelihood of institutional conflict, it is argued, changes with certain conditions which form the opportunity structures facing strategic actors. Farrell and Heritiér (2007a) identify the history of rulings by the ECJ in a particular policy area as an important factor which affects the ability of the actors to use the threat of legal action in cases of disagreement (Farrell and Héritier 2007a: 238–39; cf. Tallberg 2002: 34). Similarly, a weak formal role for the Commission in a particular policy field will lessen its propensity to initiate conflict. Finally, if the Commission faces strong opposition from Member States, it will be expected to refrain from such actions for fear of long-term costs, such as the reversal of changes in subsequent treaty revisions (Farrell and Héritier 2007: 240). These conditions thus feed into the assessment by the Commission or its sub-units of the viability of mobilizing internal and external support for their position and initiating legal actions against the Council to expand its competencies. The Commission's bargaining strength will, for example, be much more extensive in policy fields where the ECJ has a history of handing out rulings in favour of the Community. Farrell and Héritier comment:

> In situations where the ECJ has previously consistently ruled to support an interpretation of procedure that favours one party, and does not favour the other, we may expect the former party's bargaining strength to be substantially increased vis-à-vis the latter's.
>
> (Farrell and Héritier 2007a: 238–239)

Quite simply, if the Court has a long and well-established history of handing out pro-integration rulings in a particular area, this will signal to the Commission that it can take a firmer stance against the Council and the Member States in negotiations on legislation. Under such conditions, Member State representatives will also be likely to be more responsive to the Commission's position. Consequently, in such cases it will also appear more rational for the Commission to actually take the Council to Court in cases of disagreement.

It is important in this context to note that the formal institutional setting remained largely unaltered across the adoption of these different legislative acts. That is, changes in the formal position of the Commission in relation to the Council that might have explained the Commission's more active approach to the Framework Decision on the environment and the Decision on SALW were absent. An important aspect of these cases was precisely the fact that the jurisprudence of the Court was *not* well established in the respective areas in which institutional conflict erupted. The Court was largely excluded from these intergovernmental fields of policymaking under the Amsterdam Treaty and the Nice Treaty.[9] Formally, the role of the Commission in CFSP and JHA at the time was correspondingly weak. Thus, the conditions as posited by RI that would need to be in place to enable an active pro-integration approach by the Commission were largely absent in these cases.

Even if those conditions would have been present, it would of course be unreasonable to expect that the Commission would take legal action against the Council on every issue where there are uncertainties on the issue of the delimitation of competencies. That is, there might have been less visible aspects of the previous measures in criminal law and SALW that prevented the Commission from challenging the Council. From a rationalist perspective, there are other considerations on the part of the Commission that will condition decisions to block legislative measures or take the Council to Court. The short-term benefits to getting a legislative act adopted at all, even if there are doubts regarding the choice of legal basis on which it is adopted, might outweigh the possible benefits for the Commission associated with instigating a controversial legal action against the Council and the Member States (cf. Farrell and Héritier 2003: 584). Moreover, from the RI perspective, the continued maintenance of institutions is due to the utility that agents expect that continued support for institutions will generate. Thus, the Commission could choose not to engage in conflict in the interest of safeguarding continued long-term cooperation with Member States on particular issues.

However, the outbreak of institutional conflict in both of these cases was preceded by not one but several very similar legislative acts. Not only did the Commission refrain from going to Court in these previous cases, it also refrained from issuing any formal statements or declarations that would indicate it did not approve of the position of the Council. The fact that the Commission eventually brought the Council to Court on the basis of the Framework Decision on environmental criminal law and the Council Decision on SALW raises questions regarding what separated these measures from the previous ones in the eyes of the Commission officials involved. In seeking to answer those questions, it is not obvious that assumptions regarding the inherent pro-integration leanings of the Commission will be of much help.

As for the second aspect of these cases, the final decisions of the Court which effectively formalized the decision-making competencies led to a similar set of empirical discrepancies. Rationalists explain the ability of the Court to further integrate through its jurisprudence with reference to three important factors: (1) its inherent pro-integration preferences; (2) the formal institutional structures in which it is embedded; and (3) the widespread legitimacy it enjoys. Similar to the Commission, it is conventionally argued that the European Court of Justice has a general pro-integration leaning (Alter 2009; Blauberger 2014; Weiler 1991).[10] As Conant notes, scholarly consensus has emerged on the finding that the Court, when ruling on cases involving the institutional entities of the EU, is most likely to agree with the legal analysis of the Commission (Conant 2007: 53). From this perspective, the outcomes in the *environmental crimes case* and the *small arms case* in favour of the Commission's pro-integration alternative are consonant with the expectations of existing research. In terms of formal institutional structures, it is conventionally argued that the Court has been highly resistant to any efforts by the Member State governments to limit its powers, since it is largely protected by what is commonly known as the 'joint decision trap' (Tallberg 2002: 32). In most cases, treaties have not been amended *ex post* to regain losses of decision-making competencies. This joint decision trap limits Member States' ability to control or re-legislate as a response to unwanted Court rulings. Treaty amendments require unanimity among the Member States and are, as such, not a credible threat to the Court (Alter 2009: 124; Scharpf 2006: 853). It has learned to count on the support of at least one Member State to block the treaty revisions that would otherwise limit its powers (Tallberg 2002), making it more or less immune to sanctions and effective control. Finally, in terms of its legitimacy, as Kelemen (2012) points out, broad public support for the Court makes it less likely that the ECJ's 'activism' will be curtailed. From this perspective, the long-term political costs associated with derogating from the rulings of the Court act as constraints on dissatisfied Member States. Thus, while individual Member State governments might be disgruntled by particular Court rulings, the Court's enjoyment of a high level of legitimacy often shields it from more thorough-going attempts to limit its powers. However, it is also commonly held that to preserve this legitimacy, the Court can only exert its influence within certain limits. Garret et al. (1998), for instance, argue that

> the Court's legal legitimacy is contingent on its being seen as enforcing the law impartially by following the rules of precedent. On the other hand, the Court cannot afford to make decisions that litigant governments refuse to comply with or, worse, that provoke collective responses from the EU governments to circumscribe the Court's authority.
>
> (Garret et al. 1998: 174)

In this context, Farrell and Héritier (2007a) go even further as they state that in relation to conflicts over comitology procedures between the Council Commission and Parliament:

> In some cases of conflict the actors have turned to the European Court of Justice to solve the conflict, but the ECJ has been highly reluctant to go against the member states' wishes, given the sensitivity of the issue area and the lack of treaty text to interpret.
>
> (Farrell and Héritier 2007b: 410)

If these constraints act as a moderating force on the 'activism' of the Court, it is far from clear what prompted its decisions in the two cases. Rationalist approaches usually argue that an agent's ability to pursue its own agenda is greatest when the principal's preferences are weak or unclear (Da Conceicão-Heldt 2011; Garrett and Tsebelis 2001; Pollack 2003a; Tallberg 2002). While this statement might seem reasonable enough, the cases herein point in a completely different direction. In the *environmental crimes case*, more than two thirds of the Member States actively intervened in support of the Council in front of the Court. As regards struggles over decision-making competence, such a level of mobilization among the Member States in defense of national sovereignty is highly uncommon. In the *small arms case*, the Member States that intervened were not as numerous. However, the intensity of the conflict as brought out by, in particular, the written interventions of France and the United Kingdom bear witness to the locked positions of these Member States and Council on the one hand and the Commission on the other. In light of the intensity of the conflict between the Commission and the Council in these cases and the lack of any clear precedents, the controversial decisions of the Court seem to contradict the theoretical expectations of rationalist approaches regarding its behaviour.

It should also be noted that in research on the ECJ, constructivist and rationalist institutionalist explanations tend to converge considerably. Burley and Mattli (1993) and Mattli and Slaughter (1998) have argued in this context that the Commission's reputation for being the provider of impartial information, and as such of being an apolitical actor, makes it easier for the ECJ to take sides with the position of the Commission than that of the Council or individual Member States in struggles on the delimitation of competencies (Burley and Mattli 1993: 43). Similar to how rationalists view the Court as being constrained by its need to maintain its legitimacy as an impartial judiciary, constructivists regard the conduct of the Court as constituted by its institutional identity. Consequently, if the Commission is able to level arguments in a way that permits the Court to maintain these self-understandings, then it will be more likely to lend its support to the Commission.

This also means that in legal conflicts between the Commission and the Council, the Court will be able to affirm the Commission's position rather than that of the Council and the Member States if the Commission has a well-institutionalized position in a particular policy field. In such cases, the argument goes, the Court is able to act in line with its self-understanding as an impartial judiciary body, thus allowing it to maintain its 'mask' of legal formalism (cf. Burley and Mattli 1993: 72). It is less clear how we should understand intense legal conflicts where large numbers of Member States intervene in support of the Council. It is thus not immediately obvious how the Court would be able to issue more controversial rulings while at the same time maintaining its identity of impartiality and legal formalism. Specifics of the two cases also indicate that there might be reasons to question the strength of these explanations.

In the *small arms case* only a few years previously, the ECJ had delivered a ruling in which it stated explicitly that it did *not* have the jurisdiction to rule on matters relating to the CFSP (Court 2007). Similarly, in a previous case in the mid-1990s, the Court had ruled against the Commission in a case concerning the delimitation of competencies between the Community and the JHA pillar (Court 1998). Importantly, the interest from the Member States in these cases was far more limited. Thus, if the Court is assumed to be nurturing more or less stable pro-integration preferences, the question arises as to why it did not act on these previous occasions. Especially in the previous case concerning the JHA, it appears that the Court could have advanced the scope of the Community in JHA, as it later did in the environmental crimes case, but with far less controversy.

It thus seems as if there are important discrepancies between the expectations of rationalist approaches and the specifics of these cases. Obviously, we cannot discard rationalist explanatory models on the basis of this first assessment of the cases. On closer inspection, there might be other aspects of these cases, not immediately obvious, that lend support to rationalist perspectives. However, this assessment does offer an indication of the extent to which these cases present conundrums for rationalist approaches. Consequently, this assessment also provides compelling reasons to explore whether these cases could be dealt with more effectively by alternative perspectives. It thus serves as a cue to engage more intimately with these cases, and in line with the general ambition of this book, to explore the potential of constructivist theories to offer more comprehensive explanations of their outcomes.

## Reconsidering research questions

The preliminary assessment of the two cases prompts a general and more open-ended reflection on the dynamics of institutional conflict in the EU. As a result of the general lack of engagement from constructivist scholars with this issue, there is no immediately available tool box upon which we can draw in order to make more sense of these cases. The apparent difficulties of existing approaches to address these cases prompt reflection on their underlying assumptions in terms of producing knowledge on the dynamics of European integration, and more specifically, institutional conflicts over decision-making competencies. In this sense, this book picks up the thread from Allison's seminal and multi-perspective analysis of the Cuban Missile Crisis, wherein he states:

> Not only do lenses lead analysts to produce different explanations of problems that appear, in their summary questions, to be the same. Lenses also influence the character of the analyst's puzzle, the evidence to be assumed relevant, the concepts used in examining the evidence, and what is taken to be an explanation. . . . [D]ifferent conceptual lenses lead analysts to different judgments about what is relevant and important.
> (Allison and Zelikow 1999: 387–388)

To clarify, the discrepancies between rationalist approaches and certain aspects of the two cases do not necessarily mean that rationalist theories are unable to level explanations of the *environmental crimes case* and the *small arms case*: in fact, they do. As was suggested above, the move by the Commission and the Court on these policy issues into a supranational framework is largely consistent with the expectations of rationalist institutionalists. From this perspective it is of little consequence, it could be argued, whether the prior processes in these cases exhibit unpredicted elements. The most important point is that the actions of the agents in the final instance are broadly consistent with the assumptions regarding agents' motives as 'competence maximizers'. However, and most significantly, the question concerns the extent to which these explanations actually tell us something meaningful regarding when and why institutional conflicts arise and how they end.

The discrepancies with rationalist perspectives that were identified only by widening the temporal perspective ever so slightly seem to indicate that these explanations exclude important factors that might lead to a more comprehensive explanation of what caused these outcomes. This directly leads to observing how the discrepancies of the cases thus prompt us to take equifinality seriously – after all, different explanations can be consonant with the same outcomes. However, applying a different perspective also has the potential to provide an explanation that is more exhaustive, nuanced and comprehensive than existing ones. It is on this basis that the more general potential of a particular theoretical perspective can be evaluated.

The first assessment of the two cases and the empirical anomalies that were uncovered in relation to existing approaches leaves us with the two main empirical research questions which this book intends to answer. The first is why institutional conflict broke out in both cases, and the second concerns why the ECJ subsequently took its decisions in favour of the Commission.

## A constructivist approach

The analytical approach used in engaging with the two cases relies on broadly defined constructivist assumptions and is applied through an interpretive variant of process tracing. It is based on a notion of social action which sees intentionality and preferences as emergent rather than fixed properties of agents and organizations. With this in mind, action is seen as being fundamentally conditioned by the contextually defined self-understandings of agents. Secondly, the analytical framework conceptualizes institutions as having *both* constitutive and regulative elements. Institutions are associated with constitutive effects as they shape collective norms, identities and practices. These aspects serve as the starting point for a constructivist analysis. However, this does not exclude that institutions can also at times produce regulative effects. Rather, it is argued here the relative degree of these elements changes over time, and conditions different logics of action which can help explain the occurrence of conflict. Thirdly, these two elements necessitate an explicit concern with time in terms of the theoretical importance of the sequence and timing of specific processes, as developed in historical institutionalism. The explicit preoccupation with time is based on the assumption that extending the time frame studied will help us understand how specific institutional preferences emerge and why they emerge in particular social settings and at particular points in time. An in-depth engagement with how longer-term processes unfold to produce specific outcomes will thus be a central element of the effort to make sense of the cases. By themselves, the analytical categories defined draw on widely embraced theoretical commitments in constructivist theorization in IR and EU studies. However, this book demonstrates more clearly how they can be put to use in explaining the dynamics of institutional conflicts in international political orders, and in the EU more specifically.

### *Interpretive process tracing and constructivist analysis*

In line with the commitment to these broad analytical dispositions, an interpretive variant of process analysis is further elaborated. I draw on recent discussions on process tracing and social mechanisms and engage more specifically with the emerging attempts in this field to link inductive and interpretive work with causal statements (cf. Bennett and Checkel 2014; Guzzini 2012; Norman 2015b; Pouliot 2014). When preferences are seen as emergent properties tied to agents' contextually defined self-understandings, rather than *a priori* assumptions, there is a need to proceed both inductively and interpretively in efforts to identify the central mechanisms of a particular process. Inductively, because even as we invariably enter the specific cases with certain theoretical assumptions, the aim of the analysis is not to test for the occurrence of already hypothesized mechanisms. Rather, the aim is to identify the social mechanisms that we have not previously acknowledged. The analysis needs to retain an interpretive quality for similar reasons. When preferences are posited to flow from contextually defined self-understandings and when such self-understandings are seen as a result of the constitutive aspects of institutions, then it is necessary to pose questions regarding how agents view themselves in relation to specific contexts. This prompts an interpretive approach to the process in the sense of trying to map the agents' understandings of themselves and their roles in relation to specific points in the process.

Process tracing is commonly associated with efforts to identify the social mechanisms that operate in a particular case. Mechanisms are defined here as contextually specific causal patterns that let us unpack how macro-level institutional developments create dispositions for agents to act in certain ways, and how such actions feed back into the shape and form of institutions on the macro-level. This conception of mechanisms represents a way in which we can identify the specific characteristics of the relation between institutions and agents in particular settings. The use of process tracing and the specification of mechanisms thus serve as a way to make the findings more distinct. It allows us to define clearly what explains particular outcomes and, crucially, prompts us to continually entertain alternative explanations and to contrast the findings with the case-specific observable implications of alternative approaches (cf. Parsons 2010).

As discussed subsequently, among the main findings are the identification of two social mechanisms derived from the analysis of the two cases. One explains the outbreak of institutional conflict and is termed the *rupture mechanism*. A second explains the final outcomes of the cases, and more particularly, what conditioned the final decision of the Court in these cases, and is termed the *discursive lock-in mechanism*. Rather than front loading the account by defining the mechanisms *a priori* as is customary in much case study work that is proceeded by hypothesis testing, these mechanisms will be discussed in light of the process tracing evidence. They are then theorized in more detail and related to broader typologies of similar mechanisms.

## Sources and structure

In order to ensure a firm empirical foundation and to be able to develop the social mechanisms, the selected case studies relied on a combination of interview data and official documents and legislation. The interview data are drawn from a total of fifty-four semi-structured interviews conducted with officials from the European Commission and the European Council and permanent representatives of the Member States to the European Union. This part of the data responds to the need, prompted by the focus on social mechanisms, to investigate how macro-level developments play out on the level of agents. It thus aims to capture both the proximate and more distant factors that contributed to the outbreak of institutional conflict in the two cases. A large number of documents were drawn from in order to trace the process through which certain ideas and practices emerged in the respective policy fields. It is argued that this enables the identification of the mechanisms that explain why institutional conflict broke out. It also allows us to approach the question of what made the conflicts end in favour of the Commission. Answering the question of what explains the rulings of the Court involves an analysis of the complete written submissions to the Court by the participating actors in the conflicts.[11]

### Structure of the book

There are three main parts to this work, the first part including discussions on theory, analytical framework, and research design, and comprising two chapters. Its second chapter further develops the discussion on the existing theories and in particular the ways in which constructivist theorization on international institutions could contribute to our understanding of institutional conflict and institutional change. It also elaborates on the analytical framework. Chapter 3 examines an interpretive variant of process tracing and clearly defines the role of social mechanisms for the investigation. It makes an argument for a typological theorization in which social mechanisms can be ordered in inductively derived taxonomies of general theoretical problems.

In Part II, the separate processes that led to the outbreak of explicit institutional conflict between the Commission, the Council and the Member States are analyzed. The first process covered is in the field of EU Justice and Home Affairs for the *environmental crimes case*, and the second involved the EU's Common Foreign and Security Policy for the *small arms case*. In Chapter 6, consonant with the interpretive bottom-up approach, the insights from the processes analyzed are drawn together and a general social mechanism, the *rupture mechanism* that helps to explain the outcomes, is proposed. The mechanism is theorized on the basis of the two cases, examined in its component parts and finally related to a broader typology of 'crisis mechanisms' in IR and EU studies.

Part III focuses on the institutional conflict itself. It thus seeks an answer to the second empirical research question: what explains the final move of these intergovernmental issues into the supranational framework? Again, as in the previous part, it is demonstrated in Chapters 7 and 8 more clearly just what the analytical framework permits us to see in relation to rationalist approaches. Thereafter the analysis highlights the specific factors that help us to explain the final outcomes. In Chapter 9, insights from the previous two chapters are brought to a higher analytical level by theorizing the central social mechanism that is crucial for explaining the outcomes. The social mechanism theorized is that of *discursive lock-in*, which is discussed in its component parts and related to a typology of similar lock-in mechanisms. The empirical part of the book thus mirrors the inductive research design and the overarching aim of theory development. The mechanisms are identified as a *result* of the in-depth engagement with the cases. Their more general definition and theoretical implications are thus discussed after the engagement with the processes. In the concluding chapter, the main claims are summarized and further discussed, in particular relating to their implications for our understanding of the EU and international political orders more generally.

### Notes

1  For comprehensive accounts of the organizational bodies of the EU, see Naurin et al. (forthcoming) on the Council and Nugent and Rhinard (2015) on the Commission. On the European Parliament, see Corbet et al. (2011).
2  The case arose prior to the entry into force of the Lisbon Treaty in 2009. At this point cooperation in the framework of the JHA was still largely governed through intergovernmental procedures.

3 For commentary from the European legal community provoked by the case, see Apps (2006), Dawes and Lynskey (2008), Herlin-Karnell (2007) and Wasmeier and Thwaites (2004).
4 Case C-176/03 *Commission v Council*.
5 This meant that the Council takes its decisions via unanimous votes and that the Commission does not have the right to initiate legislation. Furthermore, the Court lacks jurisdiction in this area.
6 Case C-91/05 *Commission v Council*. See Hillion and Wessels (2009) and Van Ooik (2008) for legal commentaries of the *small arms* court case.
7 See Gofas and Hay (2010) for a discussion.
8 See also Duina and Kurzer (2004) and Elinas and Suleiman (2011).
9 The Amsterdam Treaty entered into force May 1, 1999 and the Nice Treaty entered into force February 1, 2003. Both treaties largely kept the institutional divisions between Community policy, JHA and the CFSP.
10 For other contributions along these lines, see also Alter and Helfer 2010; Burley and Mattli 1993; Garrett et al. 1998; Mattli and Slaughter 1998; Scharpf 2012; Schmidt 2012.
11 A more detailed account of data gathering and processing can be found in the methodological appendix to this book.

# Part I

# 2 Institutional conflict and change in international political orders

The reasons that constructivist approaches to the EU have often refrained from asking questions on institutional conflict and rapidly unfolding institutional change are not self-evident. To explore the potential of these approaches to deal with these questions, a more in-depth discussion is needed. It will clarify why the division of work between rationalist and constructivist approaches in EU studies is largely unfounded. It furthermore points to how constructivist conceptualizations of how institutions and agents interact over time can help supply vital clues regarding how new preferences arise, how cooperation breaks down and how institutional boundaries are redrawn.

A key claim in recent debates is that constructivist approaches have an analytical bias towards explaining institutional continuity rather than change. Indeed, the constructivist field of research on international institutions, particularly in the EU, has devoted considerable energy to theorize the mechanisms through which collective identities and common norms emerge in the framework of international political orders. Furthermore, mechanisms underlying socialization and the development of norms of appropriate action have an important self-reinforcing element (Barnett and Finnemore 2004; Beyer 2010; Checkel 2005; March and Olsen 1998; Neyer 2006). Once established, they are expected to become increasingly ingrained. Many scholars have noted that this poses a challenge for attempts to capture institutional conflict and, more generally, institutional change (Mahoney and Thelen 2010: 5; Rittberger and Stacey 2003; cf. Schmidt 2008). As Immergut (2005) states, 'if institutions socialize actors and thus endogenize preferences . . . then it is difficult to explain why these actors would suddenly prefer a new set of institutions' (Immergut 2005: 90, quoted in Héritier 2007). Constructivist research on international political orders have thus paid less attention to processes through which agents' self-understandings and preferences become increasingly more disparate (Norman 2015a). As Michalski and Norman (2015) have argued, this point also extends to constructivist perspectives on European security cooperation, where the emergence of common norms and practices are often emphasized to the detriment of a clear engagement with often irregular and seemingly unpredictable patterns of cooperation. Instead, changes in formal and informal institutional arrangements resulting from broad ideational shifts have been described by 'sociological' variants of historical institutionalism (HI) as predominantly occurring in subtle steps, characterized by the absence of conflict (Hall 2010: 216). In EU studies, constructivist perspectives seem to harbour an apparent inability to explain at which point latent tensions of the European project become not only explicit but also the object of open conflict between different organizational actors such as the Commission and the Council.

From the perspective of these approaches, institutions are able to shape self-understandings and preferences through various forms of knowledge production and social interaction rather than simply acting as possibilities and constraints on actors with predefined utility functions (Checkel 2005; March and Olsen 1998; Wendt 1999); prevalent shared understandings and agents' understandings of themselves exist in a mutually reinforcing relationship. Central mechanisms for these approaches are persuasion, social learning and socialization, all of which seem to leave aside an analysis of the deterioration of social relations into explicit and intense institutional conflict.

Rationalist perspectives, in contrast, rely more or less on a Dahlian conception of power based on the idea of capabilities and clearly defined preferences of the parties involved (Dahl 1957). It is perhaps this feature that makes them more apt prima facie at capturing conflict. The notion that the EU is built around a fundamental tension between politics on the European level and politics on the level of its Member States has served as a useful starting point for much research on the EU. On an aggregate level, the Commission as well as the Court have indeed been organizations that have worked towards more integration among the Member States of the EU rather than less, and the Council, as the organizational unit where Member States congregate, has tended to resist such pressures, all else being equal. Assigning general pro-integration preferences to its supranational organizations, such as the Commission and the Court, might thus be a useful shorthand to capture its general dynamics. However, as the initial assessment of the *environmental crimes case* and the *small arms case* has indicated, it is not entirely clear how acknowledging institutional tensions in general helps to explain specific instances when these latent tensions become explicit and result in conflictual dynamics.

This chapter turns to a discussion of the reasons why addressing this question has been particularly complicated for constructivists. The chapter's second half considers the conceptualizations of institutions and agents, which, widely held in the field of constructivist research and contrary to critics, can serve as useful analytical tools. This is especially so in bringing concerns with institutional conflict and institutional change to the centre of constructivist theorization in both EU and IR studies.

## Social practices and institutional change

Of course, constructivists are not oblivious to the fact that conflicts occur. The issue of conflict is addressed both in deliberative approaches as well as by scholars emphasizing the importance of more highly ingrained social institutions. The question, rather, is a more general one and concerns that of understanding change as well as continuity. For the increasing number of scholars in IR, EU studies and beyond who focus on how social practices structure interaction among actors the question of change has become highly pertinent (Adler and Pouliot 2011; Bueger and Gadinger 2015; Hopf 2010; Pouliot 2008; cf. Reckwitz 2002). Practices, it is argued, supply the generally taken-for-granted rules and boundaries within which conflicts occur. Such social institutions define the scope of rationality and supply particular agents with an immediate sense of what constitutes reasonable and rational action in a particular context. They shape preferences, and even emotions, and supply interpretive frameworks for acting and reacting (Reckwitz 2002). Social practices can thus dispose agents to engage in peaceful *as well as* in conflictual behaviour towards other agents.

As Mitzen (2006) demonstrates in discussing the concept of ontological security in IR, conflictual relations with particular others can become an important part of a state's identity, and as such exhibit a considerable degree of stability. Hopf similarly points to the stability and indeed habitual aspects of conflictual relations between the US and the Soviet Union during the Cold War (Hopf 2002). Applied to the EU, highly institutionalized organizational identities are sometimes assigned to different administrative bodies, most commonly the Commission and the Court, to explain their actions, which might at times be in obvious contradiction to the preferences of Member States. It is thus a mistake to make an intrinsic connection between constructivist frameworks that emphasize socialization and harmonious social interaction (Beyer 2010: 912; cf. Checkel 2014), in the same way that it would be a mistake to make an intrinsic connection between realist theoretical frameworks in IR and conflict.[1] Neither realists nor constructivists are wedded to any specific empirical outcomes, whether for instance violent or peaceful, but supply different, often competing, explanations to both conflict and peaceful interaction. This being said, constructivist research has made fewer efforts to explain instances where social interaction – for instance, between organizational units of an international political order – degenerates into conflict from a previous state of relative harmony.

In relation to the EU, the notion of social practices has rather been used as theoretical tool to understand how shared understandings develop (Bicchi 2011; Bremberg 2015). The problematique, rather than being exclusively about conflict as such, concerns explanations of institutional continuity and change. In this regard, it is fair to say that the theoretical tools to explain continuity have been more developed than those that would explain change (cf. Bueger and Gadinger 2015: 455).[2] Routinization of social action, and the importance of habits and taken-for-granted ways of doing things are at the centre of many recent accounts focusing on practices. Emphasis is placed on the unreflected and habitual aspects of social action.

The problem of how to conceptualize change in view of these fundamental assumptions has prompted theorists to point to how agent-level dynamics can help explain change. While shared understandings and taken-for-granted practices do tend to produce patterned social behaviour, they do not, it is argued, determine individual conduct. Practices instantiate themselves in social life in often unpredictable ways. For instance, the standard operating procedures of a particular organization, such as the Commission bureaucracy, provide scripts and self-understandings that dispose agents to act in particular ways. However, in the context of social interactions and faced with often complex situations, such general dispositions produce outcomes in ways that are not always easy to foresee and which can, it is argued, alter established social structures. In the reproduction of social structures, there is always a certain degree of 'wiggle room' allowing for agency (Adler and Pouliot 2011: 6). Complex situations faced by particular agents are often characterized by a degree of what Reckwitz calls 'interpretive indeterminacy' (Reckwitz 2002: 255). This actualizes the creativity and innovativeness of reflexive agents who can subvert established practices and engender institutional change. However, in light of the general analytical commitment to routinization and taken-for-granted background knowledge and recurrent assertions that practices produce patterned social action, we are left uncertain as to how, more precisely, we can expect to identify instances where patterns and routines are broken rather than reproduced. A clearer specification of when and why we can expect agency to trump structure, when reflexivity and creativity become more important than routinization, would be needed to address this issue.

### Deliberative approaches

For approaches to international institutions emphasizing the importance of deliberation, conflict is in a sense the very starting point of the analysis. From this perspective, change becomes an intrinsic part of the analytical framework. In addition, frameworks emphasizing deliberative dynamics are explicitly formulated as attempts to theorize how social interaction characterized by utility maximization, as situations where actors pursue their interests instrumentally, evolve through deliberative dynamics into a process of broader institutionalization. At the end state of this, common norms are more or less taken for granted (cf. Risse et al. 1999). For instance, some writers have argued that the members of committees and working groups in the EU more commonly strive for consensus rather than safeguarding specific interests (Joerges and Neyer, 1997; Neyer 2006; cf. Risse 2000).[3] Social interaction from this perspective is characterized 'by persuasion, argumentation and discursive process rather than command, control and strategic action' (Blom-Hansen and Brandsma 2009: 722). Similar to practice theory, then, deliberative approaches assume that agents learn and internalize common norms through social interaction (cf. Bueger and Gadinger 2015: 453). When norms are contested, uncertain or in conflict, actors, rather than thinking instrumentally, adjudicate between them by arguing (Risse 2000: 6):

> Argumentative rationality . . . implies that the participants in a discourse are open to being persuaded by the better argument and that relationships of power and social hierarchies recede in the background.
>
> (Risse 2000: 7)

So, even if agents might enter deliberative settings with certain preferences, repeated interaction, especially in relatively insulated arenas of interaction, tend to bring forth other social dynamics than those implied by instrumental rationality.

Common interests and shared preferences are discovered through interaction with others.[4] What the process would look like when these common interests and shared preferences dissolve into conflicting factions is, however, more rarely discussed.

The mechanisms of social change that deliberative approaches rely on are echoed more broadly in constructivist theorizing on institutional change and connected forms of social authority which emphasize legitimacy and socialization. Bids for institutional change or certain policy solutions are awarded with legitimacy by reference to, for instance, formal precedents or their previous use in national settings and in other organizations. Dominating professional practices are thus spread and deployed in new settings.[5] As sociological institutionalists have suggested, new organizations tend to imitate already existing ones and use these as templates (Meyer and Rowan 1977; Powell and DiMaggio 1993). A related way to formulate such processes is that new policy frames of elites and 'epistemic communities' (Haas 1992; 2004; cf. Radaelli 1999) can come to replace older ones as a consequence of the wider 'social legitimacy' of such frames (Stone Sweet et al. 2001: 16).[6] In addition, it is through learning that

> policymakers can absorb new meanings and interpretations of reality, as generated in intellectual, bureaucratic, and political institutions, and therefore can change their interests and adjust their willingness to consider new courses of action.
>
> (Adler and Haas 1992: 385)

Professional authority and expertise on specific issues lend weight to new ways of framing policy issues. This is in line with Edelman (1977), who notes that the reliance on expertise enables representations of issues which are not perceived as being political at all, but simply flowing from the authority of widely recognized professions (Edelman 1977: 136). Deliberative approaches, then, have elaborated on the mechanisms through which tensions and disagreements are overcome but have had less to say about instances when cooperation breaks down.

### *Agency-based constructivism*

Recently researchers in the broader constructivist field have identified the lack of attention to agency in constructivist theorizing as one of the principal reasons for its shortcomings (cf. Carstensen and Schmidt 2016; Schmidt 2008). In particular in the EU studies field, many scholars have turned to how policy entrepreneurs project influence through the strategic use of their expertise and framing. In the EU the Commission as well as the secretariats that are set up to assist the Council and the Parliament are often seen as wielding this sort of influence. As Stone Sweet et al. (2001) argue in a seminal contribution to this research field:

> Skilled actors are crucial for institutional change because of their ability to generate and manipulate frames that make sense of institutional or policy problems and offer persuasive solutions. Frames can help mobilize

cooperation among diverse actors by linking their interests and identities to a set of ideas – symbols, theories, models – that allow for further institutional development.

(Stone Sweet et al. 2001: 12)

For instance, such actors can help to break the deadlock in negotiations or open up new ways to formulate issues that allow new actors to become engaged in the policy process.[7] Several studies have also indicated that bureaucratic authority of supranational organizations plays a role even in the sensitive areas of the CFSP and JHA (Christiansen and Tonra 2004; Howorth 2007; Stetter 2007; Tonra 2000).[8] By mobilizing specific policy frames, agents can define 'problem ownership' in the sense of establishing themselves as recognized authorities 'on essential questions of causes, consequences and solutions' (Rochefort and Cobb 1994: 9; cf. Baumgartner and Jones 1993; Saurugger 2013). Mörth has shown how new frames emerge from broad professional fields and may enable new and resourceful actors to enter the policy process (Mörth 2003). Importantly, Mörth also captures how different policy frames originating in different professional fields can create conflictual relations, internally, between different parts of the Commission.[9] Extended to relations between the Commission and the Council, these discussions might supply an opening to understand how conflicts over decision-making competencies arise. However, some of these perspectives also move their conceptions of institutional conflict and change closer to the turf of rationalist institutionalism in ways that do not necessarily help address the problems of constructivist approaches.

In rationalist institutionalism, the Commission is also often credited with harbouring considerable expertise on technical matters on the jurisprudence of the European Court of Justice and the functioning of the EU policy process. This is a level of expertise that is difficult for most Member States to match. The resulting conceptualization of the Commission's influence is thus not entirely separate from constructivist theorization in its agency-based form. The Commission, it is argued, tends to have a clearer view of the policy process and is thus able to design its strategies more efficiently in relation to the other actors that participate in the policy process. This contributes to its considerable agenda-setting powers (Pollack 1994; Princen and Rhinard 2006; cf. Stone Sweet and Sandholtz 1998). In short, the Commission is able to mobilize considerable organizational capabilities in its interactions with Member States. It is the extent to which it is able to do so in relation to a specific policy issue that will help explain the likelihood of institutional conflict.

Many scholars within the rationalist field have also emphasized the internal dynamics of supranational organizations, and in particular the Commission, to explain its actions. Supranational policy entrepreneurs, in particular directorates, and sometimes with portfolio-specific agendas rather than general pro-integration preferences, can seek to instigate change (cf. Cram 1994). As Pollack also points out, the Commission is structured vertically, with the Commissioners who are appointed directly by Member State governments on one level, and beneath them, on another level, the corresponding services. This vast bureaucratic organization is also divided horizontally into various Directorate Generals (DGs), all with their own agendas in relation to specific issues, 'and their own sense of mission' (Pollack 2003a: 36; cf. Rhinard 2010: 25).

The ability of such actors to mobilize support for particular issues is sometimes identified as one of the most important factors in explaining how the Commission unifies around a particular position (Carbone 2007: 21; cf. Kaunert 2011; Kingdon 1995). These arguments tie into rationalist variants of HI theorization, where agents of change form coalitions that may unsettle otherwise deeply institutionalized orders. The allocation of resources inherent in any institutional arrangement shapes preferences of such agents and drives change (Mahoney and Thelen 2010: 11; cf. Pierson 2004). In the context of the EU, such resource allocations often translate into the distribution of decision-making competencies, institutional turf or control over the policy process.

Agency-based constructivism has sought to address the issue of institutional change and can thus be seen as contributing to our understanding of how institutional conflicts break out. However, there is a tendency to use the role of norm entrepreneurs or framing agents as a solution to the problem posed by the notion of self-reinforcing social institutions in ways that leave the fundamental problem unsolved. By avoiding the problem of structure and instead focusing on how ideas are deployed strategically by particular agents, they also risk reproducing the problems associated with rationalist institutionalism, effectively excluding explanations of why agents would formulate particular strategies in the first place. Awarding more room for agency does not automatically solve the problem of change in a theoretically coherent or convincing way. For these scholars, instead, the problem becomes a mirror image to that of practice theorists. The emphasis on agency and the strategic deployment of norms begs the question as to what explanatory power is awarded to the social institutions themselves.

One of the strengths of constructivist theorizing in general is its attention to how social structure shapes action, which includes attention to the process through which particular identities and preferences emerge. The notion that ideas are employed strategically by purposive and skilled actors to attain certain ends, for instance by placing a certain issue on the agenda or expanding a policy domain, seems to circumvent the problem of institutional change rather than dealing with it head on. It brings constructivist reasoning and the logics of social action on which it is based into a narrower choice-theoretic explanatory model which, although not without merit, is likely to face similar problems as are rationalist institutionalist models (cf. Nexon and Jackson 2013). There is thus a need to define more carefully the analytical dispositions that would help explore the potential of a more sustained engagement from constructivists with issues of institutional conflict and change.

## Agents, institutions, time

The occurrence of institutional conflict over issues of decision-making competence has hitherto clearly been the home turf of rationalist institutionalism. As the discussion above demonstrated, broadly defined constructivist approaches on their part have encountered difficulties in supplying coherent theoretical tools for understanding sudden ruptures in established institutions. The emphasis on norm internalization, routinized practices and deliberative logics of social interaction makes it difficult for these approaches to account for instances where latent tensions, such as those around which the European political project has been built, would erupt in explicit institutional conflict. More agency-based approaches, on the other hand, do not necessarily alleviate these problems and instead reproduce many of the shortcomings of rationalist institutionalist frameworks. In this section of the chapter, a general analytical framework is defined, focusing on three central concepts: agents, institutions and time. An argument is made for how a constructivist understanding of these concepts can help explain institutional conflict and change in ways that have hitherto received less attention.

### *Agents*

The analytical framework relies on the assumption, widely held in constructivist theorization, that agents are meaning-making animals rather than primarily carriers of different attributes and properties. Investigating how shared understandings and agents' understandings of themselves evolve as part of particular processes is key to understanding sudden shifts in modes of social interaction. From this point of view, agents act in accordance with their contextually defined self-understandings and in accordance with socially produced, shared understandings of particular events. Importantly, this does not exclude instrumental action. However, it subsumes instrumental action in a theoretical framework which allows for the analysis of the emergence of actorness and the formation of preferences (cf. Bennett 2013; Jupille et al. 2003).[10] The self-understandings of agents in particular social and institutional contexts shape their interpretation of events and consequently the actions that agents find meaningful to engage in.[11]

This fundamental stance towards human action forms the basis of the analysis. Even scholars who do not necessarily accept a maximalist definition of Weber's *Verstehen* approach and the singular focus on contextually defined meanings will, as Hall argues, find it difficult to 'explain most actions (or identify the causal mechanisms associated with them) without reference to such meanings' (Hall 2013: 5). From this perspective, an interpretation of how actors understand themselves and their role in specific contexts is a necessary element of explaining their actions. Actorness, understanding oneself as a purposeful actor, is defined as an emergent property of agents, groups or organizational entities. The development of actorness connotes the process through which agents, groups or organizations develop intentionality and purposiveness in relation to some aspect of the social world. Intentional and purposive behaviour is thus not necessarily the starting point of social and political analysis but the result of specific processes, the component mechanisms of which need to be identified (cf. Whitford 2002). This is a view that resonates with broadly held constructivist assumptions but which differs from agency-based constructivism in that it retains a specific focus on the mechanisms through which agency emerges rather than positing its exist-ence from the start. Furthermore, unlike many approaches to socialization and deliberative dynamics, it does not necessarily start from reflected or instrumental action and move towards the internalization of norms and shared understandings.

In essence, assigning meaning to behaviour is also what rationalist scholars do when they identify preferences of actors as a way to give a causal account of their actions (cf. Davidson 1963). The important difference is that the analytical framework argued for here is not locked into a single theory of human action as instrumental defined *a priori*. That is, prior to the analysis, it is not decided how agents understand themselves and their contexts. Instead, this is something that is learned about during the course of conducting the investigation. The extent to which actors actually reflect on their self-understandings or their actions, act stra-tegically or act habitually according to well-defined rules and roles is ultimately an empirical question. The inductive study of particular processes will allow us to address questions regarding how such logics change, something which, it can be argued, is of crucial importance to investigating the eruption of institutional conflicts.

The framework posits that actorness, and hence agency, is context depend-ent and situational. At certain points in time agents may act habitually or in accordance with the logic of appropriateness, while at other times agents may act strategically according to explicitly formulated preferences. The aim of the investigation is to understand when and why such shifts occur and why latent institutional roles and identities suddenly become salient. This particular point, and its potential for capturing sudden institutional changes, has thus far not been sufficiently explored.

In relation to the EU, assumedly very much in line with the conventional con-structivist story, Commission and Council officials often act pragmatically and interact through deliberative practices (Blom Hansen and Brandsma 2009; Neyer 2006). Moreover, it is posited that these organizational bodies are permeated by professional practices that are in many aspects taken for granted and reproduced habitually in everyday actions and interactions. However, when they encounter sit-uations which resist these practices, latent but highly ingrained institutional roles are activated. The Commission's roles can be associated with the concrete policy issues dealt with, connected to professional practices and self-understandings (Hooghe 2012: 104). When procedural, they tend to be based on agents' principled conceptions of the Commission as the 'Guardian of the Treaties' (cf. Ripoll-Servent 2013; Schafer 2014). Roles can be expected to differ across different parts of the Commission. Roles associated with professional identities tied to substantive policies dominate in DGs dealing with the often complex technical aspects of policy issues. Conversely, officials in its legal service are commonly perceived as nurturing procedural roles related to formal tasks of guarding the institutional boundaries between different policy areas. In the Council, when the Commission's position on a particular issue is perceived as explicitly challenging the formal institutional order, then Member State representatives are more likely to abandon their otherwise often pragmatic stance. Their role as defenders of the principle that the EU should only be allowed to evolve as a result of the competencies explicitly conferred in Treaty revisions will come to the fore.

This argument contrasts with the notion that when norms are contested, agents promote ideas strategically that resonate with their 'perceived power interests' (Marcussen et al. 1999: 631). It also differs from the assumptions underlying RI, as these general institutional roles do not represent stable pressures for expanding or guarding competencies. The conception of agents argued for here is one which posits that agents' actorness is activated by particular processes, that it is an emergent property of agents. Institutional identities and shared understandings matter in different ways at different points in time depending on the tensions that arise in the process of moulding particular policies. The character of such tensions, and the factors that contribute to making them explicit, can be more clearly defined by engaging with the concept of institutions.

### Institutions

Institutions are conceptualized here as *relatively stable sets of norms, rules and practices associated with constitutive as well as regulative effects*. This conceptualization relies on standard definitions in constructivist theorization on international institutions (Duffield 2007; Finnemore and Sikkink 1998) but also emphasizes two specific aspects that are not always made explicit. Firstly, in addition to norms and rules, it also includes practices. This is important, as it also captures the unreflected 'ways of doing things' that arguably characterize more or less structured social and political settings. Secondly, the analytical framework builds on the assumption that institutions *produce* regulative as well as constitutive effects, and not that institutions *are* by themselves primarily regulative or constitutive. It is also posited that institutions are not just social facts that regulate the behaviour of agents, but that agents, through the way that they 'transpose' these institutions in particular situations, reshape them in various ways (cf. Adler and Pouliot 2011; Wiener 2004).

This conception of institutions can thus be contrasted with that of rationalist institutionalists, who, rather than awarding any independent explanatory power to institutions, emphasize the primacy of instrumental rationality. Actors will pursue the interpretation of a particular rule which is most likely to help realize their preferences, and exploit ambiguity and rule tensions to achieve what they want. They conceptualize institutions as 'institutional rules' (Héritier 2007: 6) primarily acting as possibilities and constraints for purposive actors (Crawford and Ostrom 1995; North 1990; Ostrom 1986; cf. Keohane 1984). Rationalist institutionalists are not unaware of the costs that come with the formulation of institutions in this narrow sense. However, as Héritier (2007) argues, these are the costs we need to pay for methodological reasons. She argues:

> To focus on all possible dimensions of institutions simultaneously would overload the explanatory design of institutional change by trying to accommodate too many variables at the same time.
>
> (Héritier 2007: 7)

The constitutive function of institutions, as emphasized by constructivists and by which social institutions are internalized and shape identities, is disregarded in favour of a conceptualization of institution as opportunity structures. The emphasis of these approaches is then to sort out how organizational actors are able to back up their interpretation of particular rules in various ways, and how the structure of the system of formal and informal institutional rules award respective actors with bargaining capabilities which can be deployed in relation to actors with other preferences.

At the centre of rationalist institutionalist approaches and apart from the rule-like, regulative side of institutions, constructivists emphasize their constitutive elements. Institutions are not only thought to regulate behaviour but are also seen as the source of more thoroughly internalized norms, shared understandings and taken-for-granted practices. The problem that emerged from the theoretical discussion above is that the exclusive focus on the evolution of common norms, shared understandings and practices has impeded constructivists from developing the necessary tools for explaining rapid changes and seemingly sudden outbreaks of institutional conflict. This has resulted in arguments, such as those by Hall (2010), that rationalist frameworks are better equipped to capture conflict and rapid institutional change, while constructivists are more apt at explaining broader, incremental changes of general norms and ideas. In spite of what this division of work between rationalists and constructivists might lead us to think, the dividing line between institutions as regulative on the one hand or constitutive on the other does not line up neatly with the analytical divisions of these perspectives. Rather, from a constructivist perspective it is important to keep open the possibility that the constitutive and regulative aspects of institutions dominate at different points in time and that they might coexist in different configurations.[12] Parallel to the understanding of agents, defining institutions in this way helps identify when and why either of these effects are prevalent and how this plays into an understanding of the outbreak and subsequent dynamics of particular institutional conflicts. This position assumes that agents tend to act according to different logics of action, for instance instrumentally, or according to the logic of appropriateness, as a result of different configurations of institutions' constitutive and regulative aspects. This is also related to issues of informal and formal institutions. As Duffield (2007) suggests, highly formal rules can in some instances be combined with weak and non-existent norms, and conversely, that widely held norms and taken-for-granted practices are not necessarily accompanied by formal rules. This duality of institutions and the initial uncertainty regarding to what extent a particular institution, formal or informal, produces mainly regulative or constitutive effects at a given point in time is a necessary element of this analytical framework.

This actualizes the question of the internal tensions of institutions. Scholars on international norms have supplied fruitful starting points for thinking about norm contestation and change in light of such tensions. As was demonstrated above, rationalist and constructivist approaches converge around the general notion that institutions are tension ridden and ambiguous and often conflict with the specificity of concrete experience, whether conceptualized as a set of rules or more internalized norms and practices (Sandholtz 2008). Tensions such as inconsistencies between different sets of rules or internal ambiguities open up space for contestation that may lead to change. For instance, O'Mahoney argues that rule ambiguity, questions regarding whether or not a rule applies to a certain set of actions, is likely to produce disputes with the outcome of changing the scope of the rule (O'Mahoney 2014: 841). Sandholtz's cycle of normative change posits that such tensions push actors to engage in argumentative practices, the results of which alter the normative structure (Sandholz 2008; cf. Risse 2000). However, these arguments do not deal sufficiently with the mechanisms that explain why tensions generate conflicts in some instances and not in others. Tensions, it is argued, are a prevalent feature of all institutions, whether it be international law (Hansen 2016), international norms regarding the conduct of war (O'Mahoney 2014; Sandholtz 2008) or international norms on gender equality (Krook and True 2012).[13] Similarly, the very point of departure for this book is that the European polity is structured around fundamental tensions between different levels of decision making, manifested in its organizational structure and decision-making procedures. But if this is the case, then this raises the question about why these tensions are sometimes, or even most of the time, dealt with pragmatically, while at times being the object of seemingly unbridgeable conflict. The fact that rules are ambiguous, imprecise or inconsistent does not in itself explain the outbreak of institutional conflict. What is needed is an understanding of how institutions shape the self-understandings of particular agents in ways that make them perceive particular tensions as unbridgeable. The definition of institutions as having regulative *as well as* constitutive effects offers the possibility to do this.

Thus, different configurations of the constitutive and regulative elements of institutions can be expected to predispose agents to act in certain ways. The perhaps most clear example of this is when there is a high discrepancy between widely held intersubjective understandings and formal rules. Depending on the inflexibility and "stickiness" of formal rules and, one would assume, the zealousness with which they are enforced, such discrepancies can be expected to give rise to important social and political tensions. Such tensions will not only take on the character of logical inconsistencies but will have the potential to contradict the very identities of particular agents. This opens the door for more clearly understanding the reasons why agents would regard some tensions as bridgeable, activating deliberative practices, while others would give rise to conflict. Formal rules that are not supported by widespread norms and self-understandings but which are scrupulously applied will be more likely to create such tensions. Consequently they can also be expected to give rise to instrumental behaviour, as part of the social world will be perceived in terms of clearly defined constraints. It can also be assumed that the characteristics of an institution, in terms of the degree to which it produces regulative and constitutive effects, change over time. Indeed, understanding the processes through which such changes occur seems crucial if the eruption of conflict is to be explained.[14]

In sum, the definition of institutions argued for here allows for a study of processes where the specific character of institutions is not determined *a priori*. This means that an investigation is not entered into with a fixed idea regarding the character of institutions as primarily regulative or constitutive. This allows a study of how the quality and intensity of tensions, as perceived by the agents that inhabit particular institutions, change. Thus it is possible to remain open to how institutions shape the actions of agents, as well as how the actions of agents might induce institutional change.

## *Time*

Within this analytical framework it is vital to elaborate more clearly on the aspect of time that is implied in the definitions of both agents and institutions. Strictly speaking, time does not constitute an independent analytical category, but instead, and drawing on HI insights, the *process* elements of agents and institutions are further drawn out. The initial motivation of extending the time frame of the analysis is aptly captured by Pierson, who argues that the factors which are most temporally proximate and act as triggers to a specific outcome can sometimes be of minor significance (Pierson 2004: 102). Instead, applying a long-term perspective can reveal the mechanisms through which agents develop particular self-understandings and ways of interpreting particular situations.[15] It also allows us to theorize the extent to which institutional arrangements can exhibit important lock-in effects, crucial for understanding the dynamics and outcomes of particular conflicts once they have erupted.

The motivation for this analytical move is thus not to capture the infinite complexity of the social world (as if this would be possible) as an end in itself, but to enable the identification of mechanisms that a shorter perspective seems to exclude.[16] The idea that 'history matters' is thus not a general call for widening the temporal perspective in terms of including material from different points in time. It is rather a theoretical perspective that in line with the formulation of agents and institutions posits *inefficient histories* (March and Olsen 1998: 958).[17] This is the idea that neither institutions nor the preferences of agents that act within them are the result of a series of effective adaptations to environmental pressures and where institutions are constantly updated and reformed to accommodate changes in such pressures. There is no determinate match between institutions and exogenous circumstances (March and Olsen 1998: 955), in the same way as there is no determinate relation between such exogenous circumstances and individual action. Instead, consequences of previous events come to shape the social and political institutions in which actors find themselves, often in unpredictable ways.

In keeping with the notion that institutions can produce both constitutive and regulative effects and predispose actions in certain ways, the *order* in which institutions develop particular characteristics is crucial. The notion that the effects of certain exogenous events are shaped in different ways if they occur before or after certain institutions have been formalized is well established in HI[18] and appears important for the investigation here. Agents' interpretations of specific exogenous events are contingent on their institutional outlook. The point at which a specific event takes place in the trajectory of institutional development will thus be important for how such an event is perceived by particular agents.

This perspective also paves the way for an investigation into how particular processes are initiated and how the dynamics of such beginnings might shape the subsequent process in important ways. That is, it encourages investigation into how different types of path dependencies shape particular outcomes. In the cases selected for analysis in this book, it is hypothesized that identifying the specifics of the early dynamics of the particular processes might supply important insights as to why institutional conflict broke out in the respective policy fields when they did, and what eventually made it possible for the Court to rule in favour of the Commission. This is in line with the notion that seemingly insignificant, largely random events can set in motion self-reinforcing processes if they occur at a specific point in time. 'Insignificant circumstances become magnified by positive feedbacks that "tip" the system into the actual outcome "selected". The small events of history become important' (Arthur 1989: 127; cf. North 1990: 104).

While this part of the analytical framework draws heavily on ideas developed in HI, it is important to note that it seeks to move beyond the rather restricted conception of agent-level dynamics that characterize most path dependency accounts. The notion of the recursive relationship between agents' self-understandings and institutional contexts opens up for the definitions of path dependencies in situations which are not primarily driven by the stakes that actors have in specific institutional arrangements. Instead, the notion of increasing returns that in conventional path dependence arguments account for the 'stickiness' of institutions can be reformulated along interpretive lines to capture the process through which certain interpretations of policy problems and their solutions become increasingly plausible. This in turn can shape the self-understandings of agents and make them redefine their roles in specific settings.

From this point of view, it can be posited that new practices and shared understandings may well become institutionalized as long as they enter the policymaking process under the radar of currently salient political divides and as commonsense solutions to widely held problems. Furthermore, it is not obvious that tensions that may arise in a particular institutional context will be immediately apparent to particular agents. Instead, tensions – for instance, between shared understandings and a formal system of codified rules – may accumulate over time.

The framework argued for here enables the researchers to be sensitive to the process through which preferences, or indeed actorness as such, develop as part of specific institutional developments. At some point it might be fruitful to talk about how specific actors are *constrained* by institutions, connoting an intentional agent with clear preferences which the agent is able or unable to pursue. At other times no such preferences will be in evidence, and it will be more fitting to talk about how institutions produce habitual action, logics of appropriateness or internalized identities, thus emphasizing their constitutive aspects. So rather than approaching a particular process with a single assumption regarding the basic logic of action, the cases are instead approached in a more open-ended way. The assumptions outlined here point to the need to draw out the longer-term processes and identify the component mechanisms of those processes that will help explain the outcomes of particular cases. To do this, a reconceptualization of process tracing and the theorization of social mechanisms along interpretivist lines are needed. This concerns in particular the extent to which interpretive process tracing can offer causal explanations of institutional change.

## Notes

1 For a criticism against IR constructivism for not engaging enough with 'the dark side of politics', see Checkel (2014). Checkel is correct in identifying a lack of engagement among IR constructivists in how socialization dynamics can produce violent outcomes. However, I would argue that rather than a theoretical question, this is instead a question of applying already established theoretical tools in new empirical settings. Socialization mechanisms, whether producing violent or peaceful outcomes, are bound to have the same general structure in terms of processes through which norms and ways of doing things are internalized, and eventually taken for granted in particular social settings.

2 Bueger and Gadinger identify the question regarding continuity and change as one of the most disputed ones in practice theory.

3 This is in contrast to rational institutionalists and public administration theorists, who view the system of Committees in the EU as mechanisms through which Member States can control the Commission (Pollack 2003a).

4 Joerges and Neyer, writing almost two decades ago, even go as far as to argue that persuasion, argument and discursive process have come to largely supplant hierarchical modes of policymaking characterized by strategic interaction in the EU (1997: 620).

5 Many of the approaches discussed here work in the revived tradition of neo-functionalism (cf. Haas 1964; Lindberg 1963).

6 As Barnett and Finnemore have argued, bureaucratic organizations are able to 'use discursive and institutional resources to induce others to defer to their judgment' (Barnett and Finnemore 2004: 29).

7 The idea of the framing activities of policy entrepreneurs is formulated as tools to 'persuade others that innovations suit their interests and are normatively appropriate' (Stone Sweet et al. 2001: 20; cf. Carbone 2007; Kaunert 2011; Rhinard 2010). Rein and Schön's seminal work on framing also emphasizes the ability of frames to help solve seemingly intractable policy conflicts (Rein and Schön 1994).

8 See also Smith's (2004) seminal work on the early developments predating the CFSP in the framework of the European Political Cooperation (EPC).

9 See also Egeberg (2006) for an account of how roles condition specific lines of conflict in the College of Commissioners (cf. Egeberg 2012).

10 A more comprehensive discussion of different ways in which IR theorists have conceptualized the relations between rationalist and constructivist frameworks lies slightly beyond the scope of this book. For different takes on this topic, see, Checkel (2012); Fearon and Wendt (1999); Gofas and Hay (2010); Jupille et al. (2003); March and Olsen (1998). See also Johnson (2002) for an excellent discussion on the issue of pluralism.

11 Hacking refers to the recursive dynamics between self-understandings and institutional context as 'looping effects' (Hacking 2000: 105).

12 This distinction between regulative and constitutive aspects of particular institutions is thus different from the idea that some rules are constitutive while others are regulative (Rawls 1955; Ruggie 1998; Searle 1995).

13 As Krook and True (2012) point out, ambiguity and vagueness are often conditions for the diffusion of norms, since it allows them to encompass a range of different

meanings. This parallels the argument of interpretative indeterminacy of social practices (Reckwitz 2002).

14 This leaves the question of the difference between 'institution' and 'organization', a question often complicated by the everyday usage of the term *institution* in the sense of political organization. This is especially the case in the context of the EU, where the Commission, Council and European Parliament are commonly referred to as the 'institutions of the EU' (cf. Peterson and Shakleton 2012). I will not delve into this matter further beyond stating that institutions are not organizations. For instance, an organization like the Commission is constituted and regulated through a range of rules, norms, and practices but can also be regarded as an actor or a collective actor, which rules, norms and practices are not. That is, institutions condition, regulate and predispose actions, as do organizations, but organizations can also be seen as actors in their own right.

15 Pierson adds that the connection between triggers and deeper, more long-term causes also indicates that what is sometimes perceived as rival explanations might often be complementary (Pierson 2004: 102).

16 For discussions regarding the possibilities to establish complex causal narratives which are at least potentially open to mechanisms from different research traditions, see Checkel 2012; Checkel and Zürn 2005; Fearon and Wendt 1999; Finnemore 1996; Risse et al. 1999.

17 The issue of time has been awarded an especially prominent position among researchers within the broader field of historical institutionalism, which has most often been coupled with rationalist models. This is most obviously the case in institutional economics (cf. Arthur 1989; David 1985; North 1990) In IR, see Fieretos (2011). The close link between some historical institutionalist accounts and rationalist models is made clear by Kassim and Menon (2003), who treat Pierson's (1996) article as a variant of Principal-Agent theory (Kassim and Menon 2003: 129–31).

18 See, for instance, David (1985); Gryzmala-Busse (2011); Hacker (1998); Pierson (2000; 2004); Skocpol (1973). For instance, Skocpol's critique of Barrington Moore's *The Social Origins of Democracy and Dictatorship* relies on an alternative theory that emphasizes how a sequence of events explains particular outcomes. She argues that in England, the weakly developed bureaucracy and the fact that a standing army had yet to come into existence made harsh repression as a response to bourgeois demands for democracy impossible (Skocpol 1973: 22).

# 3 Explaining institutional change

## The role of interpretive process tracing

As the initial assessment of the two cases indicated, there is a need to rethink how processes leading up to sudden breakdowns in cooperation are studied. If we depart from static assumptions regarding institutional effects and actors preferences, different tools are needed to capture the social dynamics that explain institutional change. This point gains further weight in light of the conceptualization of agents and institutions in processual terms as fleshed out in the preceding chapter. How can these conceptualizations be put into practice to produce well-grounded explanations of particular institutional outcomes?[1]

Interpretive process tracing seeks to incorporate an in-depth understanding of intersubjective social worlds with a slightly more structured analysis geared towards explaining particular outcomes (cf. Guzzini 2012; Norman 2015b; Pouliot 2014). Process tracing, interpretive or otherwise, is intrinsically entwined with attempts to specify the *causal* element of particular processes. Rather than leaving the causal forces of interpretive arguments implicit, or at the meta-theoretical level and beyond the scope of the actual investigation, causality is placed front and centre. For this approach the point of interpretation is thus not only, as Geertz argues, 'to aid in gaining access to the conceptual world in which our subjects live' (1973: 24) but also to help us capture the processes through which such worlds change and how these changes condition the emergence of specific social and political effects (Norman 2015b: 4). Indeed, interpretive process tracing answers precisely the need to investigate the interface between what is taken for granted by particular agents and what is not; between habitual action and other logics of action; how routinized social action is unsettled, and how taken for granted ways of thinking and acting suddenly come to appear as possibilities and constraints. Interpretive process tracing is thus a tool which enables us to capture the complex relations between constitutive and regulative aspects of social institutions as they play out over time at the level of agents.[2]

This is an approach that differs from process tracing that proceeds largely deductively and that emphasizes the primacy of theory testing to adjudicate between different mechanisms in a specific case. In this sense it also departs slightly from the recently formulated best practices as formulated by Checkel and Bennett (2014), and more clearly from some of the ways in which similar best practices have been formulated and applied by others[3] (Beach and Pedersen 2013; Bennett 2010; Collier 2011; Jacobs 2014; Mahoney 2012; Waldner 2014).

Starting with areas of common ground, however, general guidelines regarding the need to be generous and open to alternative explanations are embraced here. This includes the need to draw out the case-specific implications of applicable theories to be able to discriminate between different explanations, as well as to employ different and independent sources of data to verify different steps in a process. However, the penchant towards deductive styles of reasoning in many recent contributions tends to, mistakenly, make such guidelines synonymous with the *a priori* definition of a set of competing mechanisms that are subsequently tested against the process tracing evidence (cf. Bennett 2010; Jacobs 2014; Schimmelfennig 2014). In contrast, interpretive process tracing investigations take their point of departure from more general analytical dispositions, such as those discussed in the previous chapter.

Trying to make sense of the complex and multifaceted beginnings of a certain process is an intrinsic part of the investigation. It is part of the process to be traced, what we expect to learn, and not something we know before the analysis. Crucially, this also extends to the definition of the outcomes, that is, the eruption and outcome of institutional conflict. The meaning of these outcomes for the participating agents are, for rationalist institutionalists, set from the beginning. They were struggles over the distribution of decision-making competencies and control over the policy process at the European level. For the interpretive framework, a final statement of what these conflicts were actually about is left partially open. This also means that a formulation of the relevant mechanisms can only be achieved after a more in-depth engagement with the actual cases.

## Social mechanisms and causal explanations

Social mechanisms are conceptualized here as a structured way to answer the question, why did he/she/they do that? (Elster 1998). As I have argued elsewhere, this allows us to specify the patterns of action and interaction that link the *explanans* to the *explanandum*. Similar to many central concepts in the social sciences, there has yet to emerge any widespread consensus regarding the meaning of the concept of mechanism.[4] For the purposes herein we seek to identify such causal patterns to enhance our understanding of broad and complex processes and their outcomes, specifically by theorizing how different levels of analysis, macro and micro, are related to each other. A focus on mechanisms allows us to open the much referred to 'black box' of broad institutional changes and seemingly revolutionizing events such as the outbreak of institutional conflict and institutional change; it forces us to establish how they are related to processes at the level of agents. To quote Stinchcombe,

> Mechanisms in a theory are . . . bits of theory about entities at a different level (e.g. individuals) than the main entities being theorized about (e.g. groups) . . . serve to make the higher-level theory more supple, more accurate, or more general.
>
> (Stinchcombe 1991: 367)

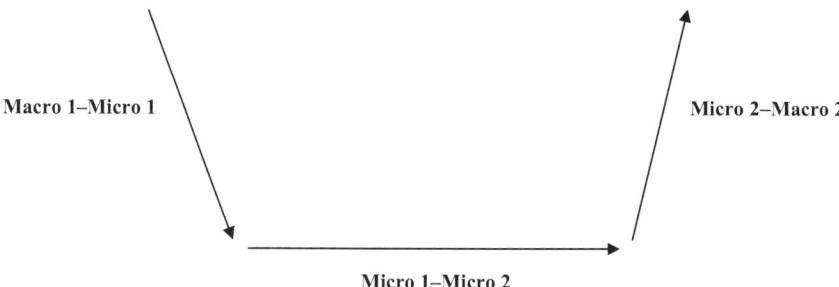

Macro 1–Micro 1

Micro 2–Macro 2

Micro 1–Micro 2

*Figure 3.1* Adaptation of Coleman's boat model of the relations between micro and macro in social mechanisms (Coleman 1990: 8)

Commonly, mechanisms are formulated as capturing more fine grained, more specific aspects of a given case, residing on a lower level of analysis (Stinchcombe 1991). The set of different micro-macro connections are illustrated in Figure 3.1 by the simple model of mechanisms as supplied by Coleman (1990: 8).

This actualizes the question of whether we are in fact talking about constitutive relations rather than causal ones. Constitutive explanations are defined by Wendt (1998, 1999) as answering questions regarding how something was made possible in relation to the structure in which it happened (cf. Ylikoski 2013). While the analytical framework indeed operates with a conception of agents as highly embedded in their social contexts, the careful tracing of a particular process seeks to answer questions of why they acted the way they did at a particular time. This thus tends towards addressing causal questions which 'inquire into the antecedent conditions or mechanisms that generate independently existing effects' (Wendt 1998: 105; 1999: 373). As Wendt also argues, we will need to refer to both constitution and causality in the context of a single investigation (cf. Lebow 2009; Ylikoski 2013).

For the analysis of processes that lead to the outbreak of institutional conflict and change, this means firstly to map changes in the broader institutional setting in which agents find themselves. Secondly, the way in which such changes reconstitute the self-understandings of agents and give rise to particular actions needs to be established. That is, we need to know how changes in collective understandings play out at the agent level. In a last step, the analysis is brought back to the macro-institutional level to explain the specific outcomes.

Admittedly, the meta-theoretical position of much constructivist work makes it challenging to separate macro and micro, due to the recursive relations posited between agents and institutions. However, the detailed engagement with a particular process facilitates the investigation of particular junctures where triggers in that set of particular mechanisms can be identified. This is particularly the case if explicit attention is devoted in the concrete research process to timing and sequence as discussed in the previous chapter, whereby we remain attentive to how different phases of institutional development are related to each other and how each phase potentially alters the positions and self-understandings of particular agents. An important point here is that interpretive process tracing is out to establish the *causal* relation between two broadly defined events, rather than just mapping how particular social institutions make some actions possible. The aim of interpretive process tracing is thus to establish the relation between changes in a particular social system with particular outcomes. In establishing that link, the mechanism connecting *explanans* to *explanandum* supplies the explanation. The mechanism in our theoretical account thus works as an analytical construct that *explains* a specific set of actions and their relation to certain macro-phenomena, and in the two cases that would be the eruption of institutional conflict and the movement of two intergovernmental issues into the supranational framework.

### Situating mechanisms of institutional change: typological theorizing

A remaining question concerns to what extent mechanisms identified through interpretive process tracing can have bearing beyond the confines of a particular case. Some have argued that mechanism-based explanations, especially when not explicitly confined to a specific research tradition, may prevent cumulative theoretical knowledge and instead give rise to 'proliferating lists of variables and causal mechanisms', mid-range theories that are not embedded in any theoretical whole (Checkel 2014: 92). The question concerns the logic of generalizations and cumulativity.

The notion of typological theorization has often accompanied discussions on process tracing, connected as it is to the move towards middle-range theories and the more careful specification of scope conditions for particular mechanisms (Bennett 2013; Elman 2005; George and Bennett 2004). However, despite its potential to retain contextual richness while being open to thinking about knowledge cumulation, the use of typologies has not been explicitly discussed in relation to interpretive forms of process tracing. I would argue that the establishment of theoretically informed inductive typologies are well suited to specify the ways in which interpretive process-tracing accounts can generate more general theoretical statements. As a way to situate the insights derived from a particular case study in a broader research field, inductive typologies also facilitate evaluation of the contributions made by the definition of particular mechanisms, and help define the empirical domains and research fields in which they have been identified.

Bennett and George (2004) succinctly define the goal of creating inductive typologies as an instrument 'to identify the variety of causal patterns that can lead to the outcome of interest and determine the conditions under which these patterns occur' (Bennett and George 2004: 244). A typological theory from this perspective revolves around a more or less well defined social phenomenon, with the ultimate goal of specifying more carefully the multiple possible pathways that can lead to this phenomenon. It is thus a clear move away from the notion that each social phenomenon is associated with one principal cause. Typological theory not only addresses equifinality as a problem but embraces it. Seeking to specify the scope conditions that make some mechanism more important than others in particular cases, it highlights such efforts as one of the principal tasks of social science research. The concept of inductive typologies as developed here also captures how particular mechanisms, while exhibiting a common structure, might result in *different* outcomes, depending on the empirical setting.

This form of typology is by definition open-ended in the sense that it is not possible to say with any certainty that all 'boxes' in a particular typology are filled. It thus differs from explanatory typologies, the purpose of which is to define all the types that flow logically from a particular theory and then go about testing in which of these categories a particular empirical case should be placed (Elman 2005; Bennett 2013). Instead, inductive typologies address an important aspect of knowledge cumulation by establishing a framework wherein new studies can be positioned in a slightly more structured way than is usually the case for interpretative studies. The logic behind this argument is not novel in the sense that it largely conforms to the criteria in which theoretical contributions of research, including those of constructivists, are regularly evaluated in IR studies and political science. Inductive typologies help us map the differences and similarities of different mechanisms, and highlight the distinctive characteristics of patterns of social interaction in the particular case studied. The benefit of this operation is derived from the way in which the relations within groups of otherwise seemingly idiosyncratic studies can be highlighted, making the 'conversation' between them more structured and explicit. It clarifies the relations between different mechanisms within the same 'family', the broader empirical domains where they have been studied, as well as between different concrete cases where they have been identified. The extent to which mechanisms are portable across different contexts, and the extent to which the findings of one case are actually applicable in another is then made more transparent.

As was brought out from the theoretical discussion in the previous chapter, crucial dividing lines were highlighted relating to different assumptions about agents and institutions. In the discussion of agents, the principal dividing line emerged between constructivist approaches where explanations start at the institutional level and played out at the level of agents and approaches where explanatory power is derived from the intentions of rational agents. Correspondingly, the discussion on institutions relied on a division between theories that treated them as primarily regulative or primarily constitutive. As was made clear, the emphasis on the constitutive aspects of institutions does not exclude their regulative effects. Similar to differences in the understandings of agents, these differences concern starting points and where the emphasis of analysis is placed. The dimensions implied by these dividing lines can be used to group different mechanisms that relate to the same kind of theoretical problems.

In sum, situating mechanisms derived from the analyses of particular processes in inductive typologies help make causal arguments explicit. It adds much needed transparency to interpretive accounts and allows others a clearer view of how the insights of particular studies relate to existing research in a broader research field. The problem of a never-ending list of new mechanisms derived from isolated process analyses might be partially addressed by highlighting how mechanisms differ or overlap with existing ones with respect to certain dimensions, such as these competing understandings of institutions and agents. The specific trade-off between generality and specificity, between contextually derived meanings and more general causal accounts implied by interpretive process tracing is but one of many possible ways to imagine such a trade-off. As this chapter has discussed, it provides a reasonable answer to the type of problems that this book addresses and corresponds to the aim of exploring the potential of constructivist perspectives to make sense of the dynamics of institutional conflict in the EU.

## Summary part I

This first part of the book has brought us from a first assessment of the two cases under study to a discussion of the particular difficulties faced by constructivist theories in theorizing the dynamics of institutional conflict, and more generally institutional change. To further explore the untapped potential of those theories to address such issues, the analytical framework brought out specific elements of three crucial concepts: agents, institutions and time. The notion of actorness as an emergent property of agents and the implications of emphasizing both the constitutive and the regulative aspects of institutions, it was argued, serve as a point of departure for better developing this potential. These concepts were then related to discussions, not least from historical institutionalist theorization, on ways to theorize institutional developments over time. The methodological implications of these discussions were subsequently examined in the present chapter. Interpretive process tracing and a focus on mechanisms was discussed as a tool to study institutional change in the EU; a way to capture crucial steps of the process that leads to the outbreak of institutional conflict, and which can help explain why they ended in favour of the Commission.

Part II addresses the first of these questions by turning to an analysis of how conflict broke out in the *environmental crimes case* and then the *small arms case*. This is followed by a third chapter in which the insights from these cases are used as a basis for theorizing the *rupture mechanism*. The discussion situates this mechanism in a broader typology of crisis mechanisms. The focus is then turned in Part III to the dynamics of these institutional conflicts once they had erupted and attends to the second question, concerning why the Commission emerged victorious in these highly controversial conflicts. Similar to Part II, this final section concludes by drawing out the central mechanism of *discursive lock-in* and situates it in a typology of lock-in mechanisms.

## Notes

1 For a more detailed presentation of data selection and processing, see Appendix.
2 A caveat is in order here: the argument for process tracing based on constructivist tenets should not be read as a totalizing move, implying that all interpretivist research should employ this method, or indeed necessarily be concerned with causality.
3 For recent discussions on process tracing emphasizing deductive and Bayesian procedures, see in particular Bennett (2014).
4 Elster (1989, 1999) and Hedström and Swedberg (1998) constitute seminal contributions in this context. See also Bennet and Checkel (2014) and Bennett and George (2004). For systematic overviews, see Gerring (2008) and Hedström and Yliksoski (2010).

# Part II

# 4 Institutional conflict in EU criminal law

Here we engage with the question of why institutional conflicts break out over decision-making competencies, and we do so through an in-depth analysis of the processes which led to the most controversial institutional conflicts in recent decades. The present chapter deals with this question in the field of EU cooperation in Justice and Home Affairs. The following chapter turns to the analysis of these dynamics in the field of the EU's external actions. In a subsequent chapter, the insights from these process analyses are brought together to formulate a general mechanism central to these cases.

A conflict arose in 2003 between the Commission and the Council in the policy field of criminal law. The Commission demanded that the European Court of Justice annul a JHA decision on the protection of the environment through criminal law (Council 2003a). The Council and the Member States, however, refused to acknowledge this more prominent role of the Commission in this policy field. When the Commission tabled a competing proposal for a Directive on the same issue, the reaction among the national representatives in the environmental working group of the Council was one of complete opposition (Commission 2001a).[1] After a lengthy period of discussions, the Council adopted the Framework Decision in 2003 (Council 2003a), whereupon the Commission took the issue to the European Court of Justice.[2]

On the face of it, the struggle over the division of decision-making competencies in environmental criminal law corresponds to rationalist assumptions of the Commission as a 'competence maximizer', with the Council and the Member States carefully guarding national sovereignty. Through an in-depth engagement with the process leading to these events, the chapter demonstrates, contrary to this image, that there had been several previous instances where we would expect institutional conflict to have arisen given these assumptions, but it did not. Previous legislation adopted in the fields of money laundering, fraud of Community funds, counterfeiting of the euro and immigration policy were all similar cases where the Commission would have had reasons to take the Council to Court; however, no institutional conflict broke out. The first section of this chapter thus discusses that little in this longer-term process lends support to explanatory models supplied by rationalist institutionalists. Another image emerges in the following sections as the analytical framework is applied. Keeping in mind the general mechanism model presented above, the analysis is structured in accordance with the macro-micro-macro links of this model. The presentation of the process-tracing evidence begins at the macro-level by identifying broad institutional developments. It then moves down to the micro-level, demonstrating how these broad pressures affected the actions and interactions of particular agents, which subsequently helps to explain the final outcome in terms of the outbreak of institutional conflict.

The process-tracing evidence demonstrates how the outbreak of conflict was conditioned by tensions between shared understandings in the field of EU criminal law and the formal institutional structures of the EU that developed incrementally during more than a decade. At the macro-level, a taken-for-granted link between effective implementation and criminal sanctions was gradually established. This was a result of the general transformation of the European project, from an international organization to a political order with important federal characteristics and in combination with the transfer of ideas from the Council of Europe. Increasing tensions arose between these shared understandings and the formal distribution of decision-making competencies in the JHA field. At the micro-level, these tensions became increasingly difficult to negotiate for officials in the Commission Legal Service. The shared understandings on the issue of criminal sanctions were translated into the notion that the Community had a legitimate role to play in the area of criminal law. This eventually activated the latent institutional role of the Commission Legal Service as 'guardian of the treaties'. Legal Service officials subsequently embarked on attempts to mobilize broader support within the Commission for challenging the Council in this area. Important micro-level conditions thus concerned the internal dynamics of the Commission. In the final stage, the Commission Legal Service eventually found support from officials in the Commission DG for the Environment, whose frustrations were tied to the substantive issue of environmental governance rather than the principal issue of Community competencies in criminal law. The combination of their institutionally defined self-understandings pushed the Commission to emerge as a unified organizational actor and sparked the conflict with the Council and the Member States.

## A 'competence maximizer' in European criminal law?

When widening the time frame of the analysis, several instances become visible in which the Commission, contrary to assumptions of its inherent pro-integration preferences, assumed a rather passive position in relation to criminal law. There seems to be little evidence of any longer-term strategies on the part of the Commission as a whole to push the issue of Community criminal law that would help us explain the outbreak of conflict in the *environmental crimes* case. Among the previous instances of policymaking in the field of criminal law, the 1991 Money Laundering Directive stands out as an instance where, given the assumptions of its pro-integration preferences, conflict would have been expected to happen, but it did not.

The Money Laundering Directive was adopted in 1991 (Council 1991a). If we rely on the assumption of the Commission as a 'competence maximizer' (Héritier and Moury 2012), the Money Laundering Directive would seem the ideal case for institutional litigation against the Council. In this instance, the Council kept the central element of the legislative measure out of the reach of the Community. It did so by placing the principally important criminal law aspect of the measure in a non-legally binding declaration attached to the Directive in which it was stated that the Member States agreed to 'enact criminal legislation' in relation to this measure (Council 1991a). The Member States thus seemingly exploited the legislative structure of the Community without taking on the consequences in terms of the move of criminal penalties to the supranational level.

The original proposal for this Directive as formulated by the Commission *did* include references to criminal law, more specifically stating in Article 2 of its proposal, 'Member States shall ensure that money laundering of proceeds from any serious crime is treated as a criminal offence according to their national legislation' (Commission 1990). The Council and the Member States obviously did not accept these formulations and they were consequently excluded from the final legal text. The Commission, however, did not contest the final decision, by neither any formal statements, declarations nor threats to take the issue to Court. This was in spite of the fact that the Council had clearly side-stepped the legislative and procedural rules of the Community. In short, no institutional conflict erupted. When compared with the strong reactions of the Commission on the Council's Framework Decision on environmental criminal law and its decision to escalate the conflict to a legal action before the ECJ, it is not obvious why this was not the case in the early 1990s. The cherry-picking strategy of the Member States, who used the Community structure for the adoption of the Directive but left the principally important issue of criminal law outside, would seemingly supply good reasons to challenge the Council. The Commission, however, showed no strong signs of seeking to expand its competencies into the field of criminal law. To the contrary, at this point there were explicit attempts within parts of the Commission, namely those dealing with agricultural policy, to *steer clear* of the field of criminal law.[3] This was in spite of the fact that the policy field of agriculture was acutely concerned with addressing the mismanagement of Community funds.[4] Thus, in this field the Commission not only was passive, but actually assumed a position in direct opposition to the notion that there was a Community competence in criminal law.

At this point, the DG for Financial Control constituted the exception to the rule. For this part of the Commission, the protection of the financial interests of the Community through criminal law was a central matter of concern. Already in 1989 a senior official in the DG organized a conference with legal experts with the express purpose of discussing the issue from this perspective (Commission 1989). However, rather than seeking broader support within the Commission, activities concentrated on cultivating these ideas among members of the European legal profession. In 1990, officials in the DG for Financial Control set up a Commission-funded study into the issue of the protection of the financial interests of the Community (Spencer 1998: 83). This project was followed by a slightly more ambitious one, called *Corpus Juris*, which eventually published a report that included a range of concrete proposals on the topic of the protection of Community financial interests through criminal law.[5] The report was widely discussed (cf. House of Lords 1999) but many of the proposals, most prominently the setting up of a European Public Prosecutor's Office (EPPO), were for a long time deemed unrealistic.[6] A notable characteristic of these activities was that they took place outside the policymaking machinery as such, in the form of seminars and efforts to initiate debate on the issue among European legal scholars. Thus, while certain parts of the Commission were early supporters of the notion of European criminal law, these activities instead indicated the limited resonance of this issue within the Commission more broadly. Even in the mid-1990s there were little signs of the Commission forging plans to expand its competencies in the area of criminal law.

Discussions on the protection of the financial interests of the Community through criminal law did eventually lead to a proposal in 1994 on a Convention regarding the protection of the Community's financial interests. However, this proposal again indicates that the notion of a Community role in the field of criminal law was at this point mainly limited to the DG for Financial Control. Officials from this DG sought internal Commission support for a proposal for a Directive on the issue, that is, a Community measure.[7] However, in this instance the Commission Legal Service argued instead in favour of a proposal for a convention in the third pillar (Commission 1994b). The weakness of this measure is demonstrated by the fact that it took more than a decade for the convention to even be ratified by all Member States (Council 1995b). Important to note is that in the case of this convention the Commission Legal Service held back. That is, it actually opposed a Community measure (the Directive) which would have brought this issue into a supranational framework if adopted. Instead, it supported a convention, an intergovernmental instrument, which effectively excluded the Commission as well as the European Court of Justice.

The Commission's lack of engagement in the field of criminal law during the 1990s also created the impression that there was very little in terms of formal rules in place to explain the Commission's ability to take the Council and the Member States to Court in the *environmental crimes* case. To recall, supranational institutions would be expected by rationalist institutionalists to be most influential in areas where there is well-established jurisprudence in their favour, or where their formal powers are the greatest (Farrell and Héritier 2007a; Jupille 2007; cf. Pollack 2003a). However, there was no immediate precedent in the then intergovernmental field of Justice and Home Affairs policy. In the first years of the new millennium, several legislative measures, similar to that proposed by the Danish government, had been enacted by the Council (Council 2000b, 2001c, 2001d, 2002c) without provoking legal actions by the Commission. Its formal role in this policy field, like that of the Court, was at this time marginal.

From a rationalist perspective, it could of course be argued that the Legal Service deemed that these prior measures did not present favourable opportunities to pursue the issue more aggressively. However, if this was the case, there is not much in the Framework Decision on environmental criminal law that separates it from these measures. It still remains unclear why the Commission would attack this particular measure. In the following account, it is demonstrated that to explain the outbreak of institutional conflict we need to turn to the specifics of the process through which the issue of EU criminal law became institutionalized, and seek to understand how these institutions affected agent-level dynamics that eventually led to conflict.

## Macro-level developments

Two macro-level institutional developments created the overarching conditions that led to institutional conflict in the *environmental crimes* case. The first was the restructuring of the EU's political system from an international organization to something resembling a federal polity. This brought the issue of implementation and sanctions to the centre of policy discussions in the EU. The second concerned the transfer of ideas and expertise from other organizational venues, not least the Council of Europe,[8] in the field of criminal law. These two factors served to create wide-ranging consensus on the need for criminal sanctions at the European level. This broad consensus would, however, eventually create unbridgeable tensions with the formal institutional structures of the EU. This produced the conditions eventually leading to institutional conflict.

### *Problems of compliance*

The transformation of the European project into a constitutionalized political order with important federal elements was an important macro-level factor for the eruption of institutional conflict in the *environmental crimes* case. This was a process that put the implementation of Community legislation at the very top of the EU's political agenda. It was also a process which increasingly brought with it the understanding that implementation problems would be most effectively addressed by equipping EC legislation with different forms of sanctions. This eventually reshaped self-understandings of certain Commission officials and their perceptions of the role of the EU in the field of criminal law.

The issue of criminal sanctions first entered the European Community very much as a result of the transition from an international organization to that of a 'denser' political system having more in common with a federal system. During the mid-1980s, the European Community in important respects had ceased to exist as an international organization due to the combined effects of two central shifts in the character of Community law (Weiler 1991: 2407; cf. Alter 2009; Weiler, 1999). The first shift was the establishment of the legal doctrine of direct effect, which meant that Community law did not have to be ratified in national parliaments to apply, but applied directly as soon as they had been adopted at the European level.[9] The second was the establishment of the legal doctrine of supremacy of EC law over national law, it had been established gradually from the mid-1960s and had become an institutionalized part of the EU political system by 1980 (Alter 2009).[10] As Weiler argues regarding the character of (what was then) Community law:

> Constitutionalism, more than anything else, is what differentiates the Community from other transnational systems. (. . .) Even the most superficial comparison between, say, a Council of Europe and European Community policy with similar objectives and even similar material content will illustrate the differences. The former will look very much like a traditional treaty; the latter will often be indistinguishable from national legislation in the same field in any federal state.
>
> (Weiler 1999: 221–2)

The issue of compliance had thus been moved to the very centre of the European project (Weiler 1991: 2464), further exacerbated by the creation of the Single Market. However, the issue of Community criminal law was raised as early as the 1970s when protocols to the treaties were discussed.[11] In this context, the Commission presented draft proposals on the protection of the Community's financial interests (Commission 1976a) and on the criminal liability of Community officials (Commission 1976b). These proposals, however, did not bear fruit in terms of legislation, mainly due to problems of determining the proper jurisdiction within which officials should be brought to justice.[12] After the establishment of the Single European Act in 1986, however, the issue of compliance was given new impetus. The goal of creating a new 'border-less' Community also seemed to logically necessitate a range of flanking measures which would compensate for the opportunities that the Single Market would provide for criminal elements.[13] The process through which the Community evolved from an international organization to a more integrated political order thus created a preoccupation with a new set of problems connected to the very functioning of the Community, resembling the spill-over dynamics described by neo-functionalist scholars.

More specifically, the fundamental justification for bringing discussions of criminal sanctions to the European level at this point was the protection of this political system in a dual sense. Firstly, criminal sanctions were regarded as an important element in the protection of its funds from fraud and mismanagement. In the late 1980s, officials in the Commission noted that fraud and mismanagement of structural funds was hardly dealt with at the national level, partly as a result of lack of interest but also because such cases were extremely complicated to deal with due to their cross-border implications.[14] Secondly, criminal sanctions were discussed in terms of the protection of the Community's administrative order in the sense of ensuring that the legislation adopted at the European level would be implemented and enforced effectively at the national level.[15] Two regulations that had been adopted in the policy field of the Community's fisheries policy would become important reference points in this context (Council 1987, 1993). These regulations, adopted in 1987 and 1993, in fact, included articles stipulating that Member States should impose sanctions in relation to breaches to the rules drawn up by them. More specifically, they stated that those sanctions could be either 'administrative or criminal' in character. While they did not impose one or the other, the fact that a reference to criminal sanctions was incorporated in a Community measure would become important in reinterpreting the scope of Community competencies in criminal law.

With the entry into force of the Maastricht Treaty in 1993, the pace of European integration accelerated. The inclusion of cooperation on Justice and Home Affairs also meant that the issue of criminal law became increasingly linked to the Community sphere. However, the specific problem of effective implementation of Community law had not been addressed by the Maastricht Treaty itself.[16] In response to this problem, around the time of the entry into force of the Maastricht Treaty, both the Commission and the Council issued several policy texts on the theme of implementation and enforcement (Commission 1992b, 1993b, 1994a, 1995; Council 1992, 1994, 1995a). The fact that these policy documents formulate the issue in very similar ways indicates that broad consensus on the issue existed across institutional boundaries.

### *The* Greek Maize *case*

The policy documents on implementation, enforcement and sanctions, in several instances, mobilized the ECJ ruling in the so-called *Greek Maize* case. The ruling had been issued in 1989 and had established the obligation of Member States to penalize non-compliance with Community law in ways analogous to those penalties that would arise for non-compliance with similar rules at the national level, and ensuring that such penalties were made 'effective, proportionate and dissuasive' (Court 1989: paragraphs 23–24). The ruling thus established what would become known as the principle of assimilation.

The court case essentially concerned two cases of fraud in which a Greek cereal company had imported maize from what was then Yugoslavia, and with the help of Greek civil servants had evaded the agricultural taxes to the Community by declaring that these maize shipments, which were later exported to Belgium, were in fact of Greek origin. The Court argued that

> [b]y failing to institute criminal or disciplinary proceeding against the persons who took part in and helped conceal the transactions which made it possible to evade the above mentioned agricultural levies the Hellenic Republic has failed to fulfil its obligations under Article 5 of the EEC Treaty.
>
> (Court 1989)

Based on this ruling, the Commission released a Communication in 1995 which further moved the focus towards the role of different types of penalties to ensure effective implementation of Community legislation. It also established two standard phrasings, in part brought from the ruling in the *Greek Maize* case, which henceforth would be included in the proposals for all EC Directives and Regulations.[17] Importantly, this Communication formalized a rather specific interpretation of the *Greek Maize* case.

The case and the subsequent Court ruling had primarily emphasized the need for loyal cooperation and, more specifically, the equality of infringements of EC law with those of national law, that is, the principle of assimilation. The ruling made clear that the enforcement of EC law at the national level should not be discriminated against in relation to equivalent national legislation. The 1995 Communication, however, invoked the ruling to argue not only for the necessity of credible sanctions to implement EC law, but also for disassociating the issue of penalties from an area which could be left solely to national legislators. In the communication, the Commission also referred to a 1994 Council Resolution on the same subject, as it stated:

> [T]he Council itself noted that it is essential for the proper functioning of the Community to increase mutual confidence and transparency between administrations and thereby ensure that Community legislation is enforced effectively, efficiently and uniformly in all Member States. The penalties issue is not, therefore, one which is purely national in scope and which can be viewed separately from the general problems associated with the operation of the internal market.
>
> (Commission 1995: 6)

This shift might not seem very drastic. However, it was an important step in the reinterpretation of the ruling in that it more clearly linked the issues of penalties to Community law. Importantly, however, this process of reinterpretation was not just the work of the Commission. The broad shared understandings around the issue of effective implementation were also manifested in the 1994 Council Resolution on administrative cooperation to facilitate implementation and enforcement of internal market legislation. Here the Council stated:

> [I]t is essential for the proper functioning of the Community to increase mutual confidence and transparency between administrations and thereby ensure that Community legislation is enforced effectively, efficiently and uniformly in all Member States.
>
> (Council 1994: 1)

Statements such as this are, it can be argued, of a rather general character but do indicate the continued preoccupation with efficient implementation also in the Council. In a subsequent Resolution of 1995 (Council 1995a), however, the Council dealt explicitly with the issue of penalties to ensure efficient implementation of Community law:

> [I]n particular, the absence of effective, proportionate and dissuasive penalties for breaches of Community law could undermine the very credibility of joint legislation and affect the situation of citizens of the Union, in certain cases possibly harming conditions of competition and the general interests referred to in the common rules.
>
> (Council 1995a: 1)

The Resolution also refers favourably to the Commission's 1995 Communication on penalties and refers explicitly to the *Greek Maize* ruling. It does this by reiterating the need to ensure that the penalties administered at the national level are 'effective proportionate and dissuasive' (Council 1995a: 2). Finally, the Council states that it

> [e]ncourages the Commission in its role as watchdog of the Treaties and in the framework of its powers to act to: (. . .) include, where necessary in future Community acts, provisions on penalties, taking into account the examples of forms of words suggested in its communication (. . .) of May 1995.
> (Council 1995a: 3)

Thus, while the Commission, as the institution charged with the implementation of the EC policy, necessarily played an important role in highlighting and furthering the issue of compliance, it remains clear that it did not necessarily push for more competencies in this area. The Member States and the Council, especially in the period after the entry into force of the Maastricht Treaty, seem to have been equally preoccupied with the problem of compliance, and increasingly so by means of the imposition of different forms of sanctions. Importantly, both the Commission and the Council took part in the process through which the 1989 *Greek Maize* ruling was reinterpreted and made part of the general understandings regarding the relation between Community legislation and the use of sanctions as an implementation tool.

### The transfer of ideas and the Council Secretariat

The second important element of the institutionalization of these shared understandings was the transfer of ideas and expertise from the Council of Europe. Thus, external pressures in the form of prevalent ideas regarding European criminal law shaped how the issue was conceived in the EU. Ideas that were formulated within this organization were later incorporated into legislative measures of the EU. It also became important because experts on European criminal law were recruited and thus transferred into the Community structure, notably to the Secretariat of the European Council. Consequently, the Secretariat became an important node in the evolution of EU criminal law.

The Council of Europe drew up conventions that served in more than one instance as blueprints for Community legislation.[18] The non-binding character of Council of Europe conventions served as a form of laboratory for new ideas and a sort of dry run for new legislative instruments. The work done in the framework of the Council of Europe became a central point of reference for the EU, especially in the field of criminal matters (Monar 2001: 749). It was only after the establishment of the Council of Europe convention on money laundering (Council of Europe 1990) that the EU adopted the Money Laundering Directive.[19] Further on, in 1998, the Council of Europe adopted the Convention on the Protection of the Environment through Criminal Law. The subsequent initiative of the Danish presidency in 2000 on the same issue was a nearly identical measure.

Both the Money Laundering Directive and the Danish initiative that would later be adopted as a Council Framework Decision can thus be regarded as instances of 'policy transfer' (Radaelli 1999). They were both measures that had largely been negotiated under different institutional conditions and then 'imported' to the EU. The fact that these measures were based on Council of Europe conventions on the same topic indicates the dependence of this institutionalization process on attempts to formalize European criminal law in other settings.[20]

As was brought out of its communications in the first half of the 1990s, the general issue of compliance remained central, not least for the Commission (Commission 1992b, 1994a, 1995a). However, in the post-Maastricht period, the Commission's organizational capabilities and its formal role in criminal law were clearly circumscribed. This was in particular the case before the entry into force of the Amsterdam Treaty and the subsequent Tampere Council in 1999.[21] There was thus not much activity in the Commission in the field of criminal law as such. There was little expertise, and at this point the Commission DG for Justice Liberty and Security (DG JLS) had not even come into existence.[22]

Instead, while the late 1980s and early 1990s witnessed a flow of ideas and impulses from the Council of Europe, the mid-1990s saw these ideas being followed into the Community structure by the professionals who had previously been highly involved in formulating them. This was a development which strengthened the Secretariat of the Council in the field of criminal law and made it an important actor in terms of diffusing new ideas within the EU structure. The first Director General of the Council Secretariat directorate for Justice and Home Affairs, Charles Elsen, was a former chairman of the European Committee of Crime Problems (CDPC) in the Council of Europe. Another senior official recruited in this period had been largely responsible for the drafting of the Convention for the Protection of the Environment through Criminal Law (Council of Europe 1998), which was later more or less copied into the Danish initiative[23] as well as for the previous Convention on money laundering.[24] The appointed head of the JHA unit of the Council Legal Service, who had also previously chaired CDPC in the Council of Europe, also assumed his position at this point. This development contributed to the rather unique position of the JHA directorate within the Council Secretariat. The secretariat of the Council is formally tasked with acting as the administrative support to the Member States in the Council and for giving legal advice.[25] However, as Nilsson (2004) states:

> In the JHA sector, the Council Secretariat has played a role which is markedly different from that of other areas of the secretariat. Apart from the normal role of note-taking and reporting, advising on procedures and being the 'honest broker' and 'institutional memory', the Council Secretariat has in this particular field played the role of motor, legal drafter and initiative-taker.
>
> (Nilsson 2004: 138)

The Council Secretariat's active role in JHA came to the fore when formulating the idea to set up EUROJUST,[26] a coordinating body for European prosecutors

(Mangenot 2006; Nilsson 2004). This was an idea largely originating in the Secretariat and which convinced the Presidency to include it in the Council conclusions of the Tampere Council of 1999.[27] Its commitment to criminal sanctions was also demonstrated by the support of its Legal Service for the Commission's competing Directive on environmental crimes (Council 2001a), and further on by the arguments of the director of its JHA DG, Gilles de Kerchove, in favour of the 'communitarization' of criminal law in the Constitutional Treaty (de Kerchove 2002).[28]

Thus, two partially intertwined institutional developments helped create widespread consensus on the need for different forms of sanctions to ensure the proper implementation of Community law. The primary one was the transformation of the European project, which served to put the spotlight on compliance and implementation and sanctions more generally. This was an issue of broad concern, transgressing institutional boundaries. Secondly, the ideas and expertise that flowed from other venues, not least the Council of Europe, reinforced the link between implementation and *criminal* sanctions. These macro-level institutional developments on the one hand produced widespread consensus on the need for criminal sanctions to ensure effective implementation of Community law. On the other hand, these developments created tensions with the formal institutional set-up of the EU that would eventually lead to open institutional conflict.

## Micro-level dynamics and the Commission

The macro-level developments played out on the level of agents by creating expectations among certain Commission officials that the Community had a legitimate role to play in the field of criminal law. These expectations manifested themselves first in the Commission Legal Service, which unsuccessfully sought to mobilize the Commission internally to challenge the Council in relation to the 2002 Framework Decision on Unauthorized, Entry, Transit and Residence (Council 2002c).

Prevailing notions of EU criminal law found a concrete expression in the Amsterdam Treaty, and especially in the so-called Tampere conclusions of 1999. These documents seemed to indicate that the Member States were ready to engage with issues pertaining to JHA in a more ambitious way (Council 1999c).[29] The extension of Qualified Majority Voting (QMV) in the Council to the field of JHA, while not realized, was also discussed at the 2000 intergovernmental conference (IGC) (Occhipinti 2002: 94). Thus, while the Maastricht Treaty had signalled the clear separation between the Community and the JHA, the Amsterdam Treaty indicated that this separation was no longer as rigid. This being said, even after Amsterdam the field of cooperation on criminal law formally remained outside the Community sphere. However, even if the formal rules in place were more or less the same in the field of criminal law since the Maastricht Treaty, important shifts in the shared understandings on the substance of this issue were occurring.

### Decision on unauthorized entry and the Commission Legal Service

In the period after the Amsterdam Treaty, several legislative measures were adopted that strengthened the already existing link between efficient implementation of Community legislation and criminal sanctions (Council 2000b, 2001c, 2001d). These measures were all Community acts accompanied by separate texts defining the criminal sanctions that would be imposed if breached. The consensus on the need to equip Community legislation with criminal sanctions was thus considerably reinforced in this period. As one Legal Service official stated, 'In early 2000–2001 there was an acceleration regarding these issues. . . . We had the feeling of being a bit ready. It [criminal law] was in the air'.[30] However, the legislative proposals put forward by the Commission as Community instruments in this period were later partially adopted under 'third-pillar' procedures.

> [I]n all of these previous cases proposed as such, as a Directive by the Commission, in the legislative process you would end up in the Council by the Council carving out anything which is criminal and split in two texts; the Directive and Framework Decision.[31]

According to this practice, the Council had adopted several Directives which contained the substantive policy and separate 'third-pillar' decisions which contained the sanctions that would be incurred by infringements to the legislation, thus circumventing the Community procedure. The Framework Decision on Unauthorized Entry, Transit and Residence constituted the last in a row of several of such measures. The tensions between the notion of criminal law as an implementation tool for Community legislation, and the formal institutional divisions were thus given a concrete expression.

There were clear parallels between these measures and the 1991 Money Laundering Directive. In 1991 the criminal law part of the Directive had also been cut out of the legislative act itself. However, in 2002, reactions from the Commission Legal Service were different. Not only did the officials feel that the Community was unjustly excluded, but it was in a manner that was increasingly perceived as breaking with common legislative practice. While the Commission legal service had previously taken a passive stance on the issue of European-level criminal penalties, officials in the service now felt there were few reasons for the Commission's exclusion from this field (Respondents 40, 49). The formal institutional divisions had been more or less the same for the last decade since Maastricht. However, the self-understandings in the Commission Legal Service had evolved in a different direction. In view of the continuity of the formal institutional arrangements, officials in the Council were surprised by what appeared to them as a seemingly sudden change of position by the Commission.

> [The Commission] had never raised [the issue] before. It had not raised it for years, and years, and years. And there had been a lot of other cases where the Commission could have made the same point. If it was possible to put

criminal sanctions to ensure the effectiveness of Community legal instruments, why was it that they had not asked for it in the money laundering directive? . . . Why is it that all of a sudden they had decided to change!? (Respondent 5).

Officials in the Legal Service were eager to challenge the Council in the case of the Framework Decision on Unauthorized Entry, Transit and Residence.[32] However, the actualization of their institutional role as 'guardians of the treaties', brought on by the previous decade of discussions on compliance, sanctions and effective implementation was not, as it would turn out, enough to unify the Commission as a whole and take legal action against the Council. The Legal Service was unable to mobilize enough support among the officials in the Commission service responsible for the substantive issue of migration, the DG JLS.[33]

The lack of internal Commission support for the Legal Service was partly a legacy of the dominance of the Council Secretariat in the criminal law field during the 1990s. While the JHA DG of the Council Secretariat possessed a considerable amount of authority in terms of its professional expertise, the Commission's DG JLS had a far less well established position.[34] DG JLS had only been set up in 1999, just a few years before. Its officials, along with the responsible Commissioner, were thus hesitant to pursue such a controversial legal action at that point.[35] A JLS official illustrated the initially marginal position of DG JLS:

[T]his DG is a very young one. . . . And at the very beginning we had nothing to say, we were nothing, when our Director General went to a meeting with Member States he did not have a microphone. . . . Just to give you an idea. Now, when he speaks he has a microphone, and he is listened to, and his thoughts and his position are respected.[36]

The Framework Decision on Unauthorized Entry was not as clearly associated with the general issue of proper enforcement of Community legislation. There were widespread concerns that the Commission would be regarded as the 'bad guy' if it stalled such a sensitive issue which had both security and human rights implications.[37] As one respondent, a former senior official of the Commission Legal Service, stated:

[W]ithin the Commission you always have the [substantial] services in the forefront that have negotiated the texts, that are very much convinced of the substance of the text, and which care much less if there is one text or two texts. . . . They are very much convinced that you need to have these measures, but whether they are in a Framework Decision or . . . [T]hey don't give a damn. They don't see the institutional interest underlying and they are always scared that it will annoy member states.[38]

As a general characterization of the differences between the Legal Service and the substantial services, the statement is obviously a bit simplified. Legal Service officials are not insensitive to the political aspects of specific measures, just as Commission officials in the substantive services at times have a very clear appreciation of the institutional implications of specific actions. In the case of the Framework Decision on Unauthorized Entry, Transit and Residence, however, this characterization seems to have had some leverage. It illustrates the different institutional roles dominating in different parts of the Commission. The procedural role of the Commission Legal Service, as guardian of the treaties, can be contrasted with the more substantive, portfolio role connected to the specific policy fields of specialized DGs.[39] The tensions between shared understandings on the need for criminal penalties to ensure effective implementation of Community legislation and the formal institutional set-up had reached their breaking point in the Commission Legal Service, actualizing its institutional role as guardian of the treaties. However, the service did not find a match for these frustrations in the newly established DG JLS.

As no unity could be found to pursue the case more aggressively, there was instead a compromise in the Commission to issue a declaration on the adoption of the Framework Decision where it expressed the opinion that the Community *did* have the right to impose criminal sanctions if it was necessary for the efficient implementation of community policy.

> The Commission is . . . of the opinion that the Framework Decision does not constitute the appropriate legal instrument to impose on Member States to put in place such sanctions and consider that its adoption should not create a precedence. According to the Commission, the Community is competent to impose on Member States to take sanctions, in the present case, criminal, at the national level when this proves necessary to attain a Community objective.
>
> (quoted in Commission 2003a: 12)[40]

The Legal Service had been able to push through a warning in terms of formulating this reservation in relation to the Framework Decision on Illegal Entry, Transit and Residence. Its position had thus changed markedly from the mid-90s. To recall, in relation to the 1995 convention on the protection of the Community's financial interests through criminal law, it had actively opposed a Community measure.[41] At that point the service sent a clear signal that the Community did not have a more prominent role to play in the field of criminal law. In spite of this change, explicit institutional conflict did not break out in the case of the Framework Decision on Unauthorized Transit. The failure to mobilize broader internal support stopped the Commission as a whole from emerging as a unitary actor ready to challenge the Council in Court.

### *The DG ENV and the eruption of institutional conflict*

In relation to the 2002 Framework Decision on Unauthorized Entry, the Legal Service emerged as a purposive organizational actor in the field of EU criminal law. However, this was not enough to unify the Commission as a whole. Thus, there was no institutional conflict. To the contrary, on the adoption of the 2003 Framework Decision on the Protection of the Environment through Criminal Law, the Commission coalesced around a common position. In this case the internal dynamics in the Commission were slightly different. The principled motivations of the Legal Service were now complemented by the substantive ones nurtured in the DG for the Environment (DG ENV) that had previously been absent in DG JLS.

For the Commission Legal Service, the reason for pushing for a legal action in Court was strictly related to the issue of criminal sanctions itself. The substance of the case from this perspective was immaterial.[42] As stated by the former Director-General of the Legal Service involved in the case,

> It was not viewed by us as an environmental case at all. It was viewed as an institutional debate on what was the limit of competence which could be given to a Directive or a Regulation in any of these policies under the treaty.[43]

While the Legal Service had failed to elicit support from DG JLS in relation to the Framework Decision on Unauthorized Entry, it now found a willing ally that could match its level of frustration, namely the DG ENV. The frustrations of the officials in DG ENV were intimately connected to the issue of effective implementation and had been generated by the glaring discrepancies in enforcement and penalties for derogations from environmental legislation. From their perspective, the proposal for a Framework Decision on environmental crimes protected the Member States from the oversight mechanisms of the Commission, thus compromising the possibilities to have an effective environmental policy.[44] It also in a very tangible way represented an intrusion into a long-standing and well-established policy area of the Community.[45] Its institutional role, brought to the fore by the environmental crimes decision, was thus clearly substantive, centred squarely on the policy issue as such.

The official who was in charge of the file in DG ENV at the time seemed, if anything, to be concerned about the ability of the Commission to perform the function of ensuring proper implementation of and compliance with the environmental legislation.[46]

> [I]f the Member States do not implement the Framework Decision, nothing happens. . . . [T]he first aim of all this . . . was to get a better implementation and enforcement of the environmental law. Necessary to get a better environment; more protection. If the law is not well enforced and well implemented, everything is useless. So let's use a useful instrument![47]

That is, the officials of DG ENV were less preoccupied with the delimitation of competencies in a general sense and more concerned with how the considerable body of environmental legislation that the Commission, and in particular DG ENV, had devised would actually be implemented.[48]

> [I]f you look into this issue of enforcement of EU legislation, in the environment field this is a mine field. You will find thousands of cases where

legislation is not complied with. The case is very often that Member States copy a Directive word by word and then forget about it.[49]

At its establishment in 1973, the DG ENV was initially envisaged as a horizontal organization akin to the Legal Service. Its task would have consisted of ensuring that the totality of the policies of the Community was in conformity with its environmental goals.[50] This, however, did not happen, although in parallel to the discussions on the protection of the financial interests of the Community, there had been growing frustration in the broader environmental field. In spite of an abundance of conventions, and also a growing body of EC legislation, little was being done at the national level.[51] It was also felt that in many parts of this policy area there existed considerable discrepancies between environmental protection legislation in different European countries.

> We didn't want forum shopping by European companies, to go to places where the punishment levels are more lenient. And, indeed we have compared the sanctions levels for a certain number of offences and in some cases it was absolutely outrageous! You have the same pollution offence where the punishment is ten years of imprisonment in one Member State and it's fines without any imprisonment in other Member States.[52]

Thus, the institutional role of DG ENV was primarily connected to the substance of the policy field rather than the procedural issue related to the delimitation of decision-making competencies.

In DG ENV, the scheduled adoption of a Framework Decision by the Council provoked intense activity. In the unit for Environmental Governance, a competing proposal for a Directive was prepared in just a few weeks. However, while the competing environmental crimes Directive was drafted in DG ENV, even in this very DG, challenging the Council and Member States in Court initially met with resistance.[53] Officials in the Legal Service, however, put a considerable amount of effort into pushing for this issue.[54] Michel Petite, the Director-General of the Legal Service at the time, was subsequently able to convince the then president of the Commission, Romano Prodi, to back the decision to go to Court.[55]

The 2003 Framework Decision had some specific elements that also fed into the task of convincing other parts of the Commission of the viability of taking legal action against the Council. This was an instrument connected to a long-standing policy of the EU and a rather technical one at that.[56] What made the *environmental crimes* case favourable in this respect was also partly the standing of the environmental policy in the EU, and by consequence of DG Environment itself within the Commission. As an official in the Legal Service stated regarding DG ENV:

> They know their stuff; they have made all these rules. They have been there for many years. It's like DG MARKT[57] or Competition. You don't just say, 'go home'. It's an intellectual power and also a power in terms of number of people.[58]

DG Environment is responsible for the implementation of more than 200 legislative acts in the field of the environment and can independently take legal action in cases where environmental law is infringed.[59] In its 2001 proposal for a Directive on environmental crimes, it listed no less than fifty-one Community instruments that had been enacted in the field of the Community environment policy, the infringements of which would be covered by the Directive (Commission 2001b: 240–43). This was not just a technical detail defining the scope of the Directive, but also served as a clear manifestation of bureaucratic authority in this particular policy field: a statement to the effect that the protection of the environment constituted a central Community issue. As one respondent put it, 'The environment is at its core a trans-border issue. Just look at the clouds!'[60] As such there was also a rather more obvious connection between environmental criminal law and earlier discussions on effective implementation in the 1980s and 1990s. This separated it from the Framework Decision on Unauthorized Entry, Transit and Residence, which pertained to the field of the rather newly established immigration policy.

From the tabling of competing legislative proposals on environmental crimes there ensued a rather lengthy period of discussions. Both proposals were sent to the European Parliament for it to deliver its opinion. The two proposals were also amended in various ways. Finally, however, the Parliament issued a Resolution in favour of the Commission proposal asking

> the Council to refrain from adopting this Framework Decision prior to the adoption of European Parliament and Council Directive . . . on the protection of the environment through criminal law, as proposed by the Commission.
>
> (European Parliament 2002)

In spite of this, the Council finally adopted its proposal for a Framework Decision. Following the adoption, the Commission sent its application for an annulment procedure to the European Court of Justice, thus initiating the formal institutional conflict. It was the alliance between the DG ENV and the Commission Legal Service that would enable the legal action against the Council, which it had not pursued on previous occasions. It combined the respective frustrations regarding the substantial issue of the environment and the constitutional issue on the delimitation of competencies. The tensions between shared understandings in the field of EU criminal law and the formal institutional structures of the EU finally erupted in an explicit institutional conflict.

## Summary: institutional conflict in EU criminal law

We began here by posing the general question of why institutional conflicts erupt, and why, specifically, they erupted in relation to the Framework Decision on environmental criminal law. The analysis demonstrated, contrary to the assumptions of rationalist approaches, that the pro-integration preferences of the Commission emerged in the field of criminal law only as a result of a long and messy process through which the widespread consensus on criminal sanctions as an implementation tool clashed with the formal institutional set-up of the EU. Macro-level pressures developing over several years as well as the internal dynamics of the Commission eventually prompted the emergence of a unified Commission position in relation to the Council in this case.

There were few indications of a unified Commission preference to further the issue more aggressively in previous cases. It was posited that the final decision to initiate institutional conflict had less to do with instrumental calculation and more to do with the emerging self-understandings in the Legal Service of its legitimate role, as the representative of the Community in this particular policy area. In view of these self-understandings, the exclusion of the Community was the object of increasing frustration among its officials, eventually bringing its institutional role of guardian of the treaties to the fore. This frustration, while not finding support in DG JLS in relation to the Framework Decision on Unauthorized Entry, finally found its match in the well-established DG ENV, where officials nurtured similar frustrations tied to the substantive issue of the environment. The analysis demonstrated how the development of shared understandings and consensus on a particular issue in this institutional setting can lead to unexpected outcomes. In the *environmental crimes* case, rather than leading to a gradually deeper integration, it sparked one of the most intense institutional conflicts of the 2000s in the EU.

The relations between institutional developments and agents as brought out by the analysis in this chapter are illustrated in Figure 4.1. On the macro-level we find the rising tensions between shared understandings on Community criminal law, which clashed with the formal institutional set-up of the EU. This tension reproduced itself at the agent level, eventually reaching the breaking point and

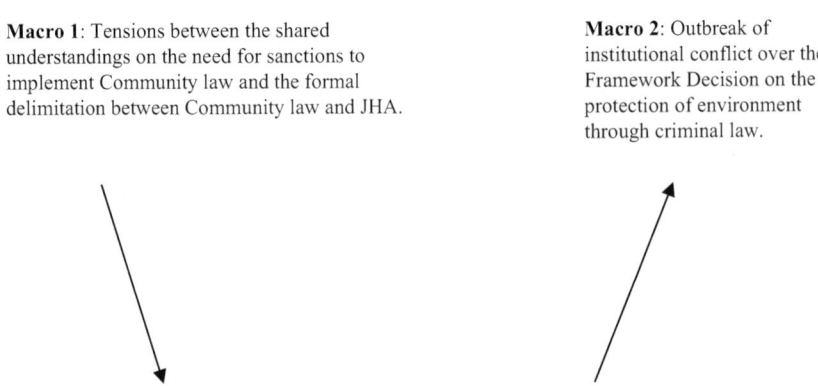

**Macro 1**: Tensions between the shared understandings on the need for sanctions to implement Community law and the formal delimitation between Community law and JHA.

**Macro 2**: Outbreak of institutional conflict over the Framework Decision on the protection of environment through criminal law.

**Micro 1:** Commission officials perceive themselves as unjustly excluded from the field of criminal law in relation to Council decisions in this field, activating its institutional role as 'guardian of the treaties'.

**Micro 2**: Internal mobilization driven by the Legal Service makes the Commission unite around a common 'pro-integration'-position.

*Figure 4.1* Outbreak of institutional conflict in the environmental crimes case

activating the pro-integration institutional role of the Commission Legal Service. This in turn explains the actions of legal service officials aimed at mobilizing internal support in the Commission. After finding support in DG ENV, the Commission eventually emerged as a unified actor initiating its legal action against the Council. The account of this process can now be summarized in its component parts in the macro-micro-macro model, taking us from the broad institutional developments evolving over a considerable period of time, and eventually producing the specific outcome, the institutional conflict, in the *environmental crimes case*.

## Notes

1 As one Commission official who presented the Commission proposal in the Council meeting recalls, all Member States said 'no' with the French representative adding: "*nous n'accepterons jamais une texte de cette nature! Jamais!*" [We will never accept a text of this kind! Never!]. Interview with Commission official, formerly DG ENV (Respondent 11).

2 The difference between a Directive and a Framework Decision is that Framework Decisions, based on the 'intergovernmental' EU Treaty, were part of the 'soft law' of the EU. Directives based on EC law, however, had direct legal effect and could, if breached, become the basis of legal actions before the ECJ (Wasmeier and Thwaites 2004: 615). Thus, while Framework Decisions left a considerable amount of autonomy for Member States in implementation, Directives restricted this autonomy to a greater degree.

3 Interview with Commission official, DG JLS (Respondent 42). Throughout the analysis, references to interviews are placed in footnotes.

4 The lion's share of the Community budget was, and remains, dedicated to the Common Agricultural Policy.

5 For the full report of the *Corpus Juris* project, see Delmas Marty (1997).

6 As late as 2010 for EU officials as well as national representatives, this remained an unrealistic project, even with the possibility of setting it up formally enshrined in the Lisbon Treaty. Interview with official of the Council Legal Service (Respondent 44); interview with official of the Council Secretariat (Respondent 36); interview with official of the Council Secretariat, former director of DG JHA (Respondent 14); interview with official of the Permanent Representation of Germany (Respondent 14); interview with official of Permanent Representation of Italy (Respondent 10). The Commission, nonetheless, put forward a proposal in July 2013 on the setting up of the EPPO, exclusively in the sphere of the protection of the financial interests of the Union (Commission 2013b).The particular form of this office is currently discussed in the Council.

7 Interview with former Commission official (Respondent 13).

8 The Council of Europe is not to be conflated with the European Council. Whereas the European Council is an EU body in which representatives of Member States meet, the Council of Europe is a purely international organization. The Council of Europe has 47 Member States including the EU 28; non-EU states such as the Russian Federation and Turkey are also here. References to 'the Council' in the text refer exclusively to the European Council.

9 The establishment of this doctrine is commonly accredited to the ECJ ruling in two cases in the mid-1960s, *Van Gend en Loos v. Nederlandse Administratie Belastingen* of 1962 (Court 1963) and *Costa v. ENEL* of 1964 (Court 1964). However, as Alter argues persuasively, the fact that these rulings subsequently had such far-reaching effects was due to a much broader process, not least in terms of professional and political follow-through at the national level (2009: 73; 202).

10 As one respondent suggested, the arguments of the Commission in the *environmental crimes* court case can indeed be read as a continuation of the doctrine of direct effect (interview with official of the Parliament Legal Service [Respondent 8]).

11 Interview with official of the Commission Legal Service (Respondent 49). Interview with official of the Council Legal Service (Respondent 44).

12 Interview with official of the Council Legal Service (Respondent 49).

13 As Fletcher et al. (2008) point out, the connection established between organized crime and a Europe without internal borders was not primarily based on analyses of rising crime levels and their relation to this new arrangement, but mainly argued out of logical necessity (Fletcher et al. 2008: 26; cf. Fijnaut 2001; Mitsilegas et al. 2003).

14 Interview with former Commission official (Respondent 13).

15 Interview with official of the Council Legal Service (Respondent 44). Discussions between Member States mainly took place within the so-called European Political Cooperation (EPC). This was mainly a forum for discussion on foreign policy issues and diplomatic coordination (Smith 2004). However, as a venue unconstrained by the procedural and legislative rules of the European Community, it was also used for discussing informally other matters that had not yet been made part of the Community structure, such as criminal law.

16 Interview with Commission official, Legal Service (Respondent 49). To recall, Justice and Home Affairs cooperation was placed in the intergovernmental 'third pillar'.

17 'Member States shall lay down the system of penalties for breaching this Regulation and shall take all the measures necessary to ensure that those penalties are applied. The penalties thus provided for shall be *effective, proportionate and dissuasive*' (Commission 1995: 9 italics added).

18 Interview with official of the Council Legal Service (Respondent 44). Interview with former Commission official, DG ENV (Respondent 31); interview with Commission official, Legal Service (Respondent 49); interview with official of the Council Secretariat, DG JHA (Respondent 36).

19 This was in turn preceded by the so-called UN Vienna convention focusing on money laundering in relation to drug trafficking (United Nations 1988).

20 This is largely in accordance with how many sociological institutionalists view institutional change. See, for instance, Benson and Jordan (2011); Haas (1992); Monar (2001); Radaelli (2000); Stone (2004).

21 In the conclusions of the Tampere Council of 1999a, the Member States outlined a more ambitious JHA policy, affirming the need to create an 'Area of Freedom, Security and Justice' which included the setting up of EUROJUST (Council 1999c).

22 DG JLS was set up in 1999 after the Amsterdam Treaty. Before that, the Commission had only a small task force connected to its general secretariat dealing with JHA issues (Mangenot 2006: 3).

23 It can also be noted in this context that the official who succeeded him and helped finalize the Convention later became head of the unit on justice cooperation in DG JLS of the Commission, a unit which is also responsible for the specific issue of environmental crime (interview with Commission official, DG JLS [Respondent 12]).

24 The official acted as the Secretary to the Council of Europe's expert committee that elaborated the money laundering convention (cf. Nilsson 1991).

25 Several recent studies have pointed out that the secretariat has, not least by force of its legal expertise, gained an increasingly important position in EU policymaking process. See Beach (2004); Christiansen (2002); Dijkstra (2010); and Stetter (2007) on the independent role of the Council Secretariat.

26 The European Union's Judicial Cooperation Unit.

27 Interview with official of the Council Secretariat, DG JHA (Respondent 36); interview with official of the Council Secretariat, former director of DG JHA (Respondent 14).

28 De Kerchove served as the Director of the JHA DG in the Council Secretariat in 1995–2007.

29 The conclusions from this Council had a particular focus on JHA issues and introduced the aim of creating an 'Area of Freedom, Security and Justice' in Europe. It also introduced judicial cooperation in the field of civil law as a Community competence.
30 Interview with Commission official, Legal Service (Respondent 49).
31 Interview with former Commission official, Legal Service (Respondent 40).
32 Interview with Commission official, Legal Service (Respondent 49).
33 DG JLS was split in two in 2010, bringing into existence two new DGs: DG HOME and DG JUSTICE.
34 Interview with Commission official, DG JLS (Respondent 35).
35 Interview with Commission official, Legal Service (Respondent 49).
36 Interview with Commission official DG JLS, formerly DG ENV (Respondent 11).
37 Interview with Commission official, Legal Service (Respondent 49).
38 Interview with former Commission official, Legal Service (Respondent 40).
39 For recent studies mapping the different roles of Commission officials, see Elinas and Suleiman (2011); Hooghe (2012); Schafer (2014).
40 *La Commission est . . . d'avis que la décision-cadre ne constitue pas l'instrument approprié pour imposer aux États membres de mettre en place de telles sanctions et considère que son adoption ne saurait créer un précédent. Selon elle, la Communauté est compétente pour imposer que les États membres prennent des sanctions, le cas échéant, pénales, au niveau national, lorsque celas'avère nécessaire pour atteindre un objectif communautaire*[.]
41 Interview with former Commission official (Respondent 13).
42 Interview with Commission official, Legal Service (Respondent 49).
43 Interview with former Commission official, Legal Service (Respondent 40).
44 Interview with Commission official, DG ENV (Respondent 1).
45 Interview with Commission official, DG ENV (Respondent 28); interview with former Commission official, DG ENV (Respondent 31).
46 Interview with Commission official DG ENV (Respondent 1); interview with Commission official DG ENV (Respondent 28).
47 Interview with Commission official, formerly DG ENV (Respondent 11).
48 Interview with Commission official, formerly DG ENV (Respondent 11); interview with former Commission official, DG ENV (Respondent 31); interview with Commission official, Legal Service (Respondent 49).
49 Interview with former Commission official, DG ENV (Respondent 31).
50 Ibid.
51 Interview with Commission official, DG JLS (Respondent 12); interview with Commission official, formerly DG ENV (Respondent 11).
52 Interview with Commission official, DG JLS (Respondent 12).
53 Interview with former Commission official, Legal Service (Respondent 40); interview with Commission official, formerly DG ENV (Respondent 11).
54 Interview with Commission official, formerly DG ENV (Respondent 11); interview with Commission official, Legal Service (Respondent 49).
55 Interview with former Commission official, Legal Service (Respondent 40).
56 Interview with Commission official, Legal Service (Respondent 49); interview with Commission official, DG JLS (Respondent 12).
57 DG Internal Market and Services.
58 Interview with Commission official, Legal Service (Respondent 49).
59 Such cases are initiated by the DG itself or as a result of complaints from external actors after a formal decision in the College of Commissioners. In 2011 the Commission had no less than 299 active infringement cases in the field of the environment (Commission 2012).
60 Interview with Commission official, DG JLS (Respondent 35).

# 5 Institutional conflict in the EU's external action

After a short period of contentious discussions within the Council, the Commission launched a legal action against the Council in 2005 to annul a CFSP instrument against the proliferation of small arms and light weapons in West Africa (Council 2004f). The Commission argued that the Council Decision should be replaced by a Community instrument in the framework of the Community's development cooperation policy. Member State representatives in the Council along with its Legal Service perceived it to be beyond discussion that this was a clear-cut CFSP measure.[1] In the words of one respondent in the Council Legal Service, 'if SALW isn't about security, what is?!'[2]

The analysis demonstrates that two broad institutional developments created the conditions for the outbreak of institutional conflict in the *small arms* case. Firstly, the historical connection between the Community's development cooperation policy and the specific region referred to as African, Caribbean and Pacific (ACP) countries played an important part in producing the conflict around the 2004 Council Decision. The contested decision had an explicit connection to the EU-ACP development cooperation agreement, the Cotonou Agreement. This cooperation agreement and its predecessors had for years become firmly institutionalized as the domain of the Commission.

The second interconnected macro-institutional factor concerned the paradigmatic changes in the parallel fields of security and development, beginning in the 1980s and becoming increasingly well established in the 1990s and 2000s. In the process leading up to the conflict in the *small arms* case, consensus emerged regarding the increasingly taken for granted notion that security and development could not be imagined without one another. These changes seeped into the EU as a result of internationally established professional practices. These practices emerged in contradiction to the formal legal-institutional set-up of the EU, and more specifically the strict formal separation between the CFSP and the development cooperation policy. These two macro developments created tensions at the agent level within the Commission.

In contrast to the *environmental crimes* case where the Commission Legal Service had ultimately been pushed to initiate conflict, the service had at the time of the *small arms* case already emerged as a unified actor. When the tensions in relation to the 2004 SALW decision arose, this part of the Commission was already on the look-out for possible cases which could help define the delimitation between the Community policies and the CFSP. The drive of the Legal Service to devise a mirror case to the *environmental case* court ruling thus fed into and exacerbated the tensions between professional practices and formal rules that eventually led to institutional conflict in this case.

## The Commission and turf maximization

After a 1998 CFSP Joint Action (Council 1999a) that drew out the EU's general approach to combating the proliferation of small arms and light weapons in third countries, the Council took a range of decisions under the CFSP that had as their aim to implement the Joint Action (Council 1999d, 2002b, 2003c, 2004b, 2004c, 2004d). These decisions, six in all, were in terms of their aim and scope very similar to the Council decision of 2004, which the Commission would later challenge before the Court. None of these cases, however, were challenged by the Commission.

The CFSP decisions concerned SALW action in geographical settings as disparate as Mozambique (Council 1999d), South East Europe (Council 2002b, 2004c), Latin America and the Caribbean (Council 2003b), Albania (Council 2004b) and Cambodia (Council 2004d). Apart from this, they were more or less identical. It should also be noted that the measure aimed at Mozambique actually included a state which forms part of the general Community development cooperation regime. Thus, the similarities between this measure and the one contested in 2004 are particularly strong. So, why were there no demands from the Commission to annul any of these measures?

As was argued in relation to the initial assessment of the case, it would be unreasonable to expect that the general pro-integration preferences posited by rationalist institutionalists would manifest themselves in a legal action against the Council as soon as there was a difference of opinion regarding the legal basis of a particular legislative act. From these perspectives there are several considerations on the part of the Commission that could feed into the decision to take the Council to court, or indeed to abstain from doing so, especially in a controversial policy area like the CFSP. However, these *six* previous acts were adopted during the course of five years. The Commission did not issue any form of protest in any of them, and it certainly did not instigate any legal actions. Thus, the generally defined motivations to expand institutional turf do not seem immediately helpful for the understanding of why the Commission instigated institutional conflict in this case.

Regarding the formal institutional environment, there were also no significant changes during the time period these measures were adopted. What appears as a sudden urge of the Commission to challenge the Council and the Member States in this field cannot be attributed to any obvious changes in the system of rules that would enable such actions.

To recall, as rationalist institutionalists have pointed out, the formal standing of the Commission in a particular area is important to understand when it enters into open conflict with the Council and the Member States. As indicated above, the Community did not have any particularly strong formal role in the field of SALW itself. There was thus little in terms of jurisprudence that would make the 2004 SALW measure particularly promising as a point of attack. It should also be noted that the formal position of the Commission in the field of the CFSP was, and remains, marginal. While cooperation on JHA had seen a gradual, albeit tentative, integration in the normal decision-making procedures of the Community, especially as a result of the Amsterdam Treaty, the CFSP remained a thoroughly intergovernmental sphere of EU policymaking.

## Macro-level developments

Two broad institutional developments emerged in conjunction and created the conditions for the institutional conflict regarding the 2004 Council decision for a contribution to the ECOWAS in the field of SALW. The first was the process through which the close link between the Community development cooperation policy and the ACP countries became institutionalized. The second was the emergence of a widespread consensus on the intrinsic connections between security and development, a process that particularly affected EU SALW policy.

### Community policy towards ACP countries

The long established connections between the Community's development cooperation policy and the so-called ACP countries would serve as an important condition for the outbreak of the conflict in the *small arms* case. The 2004 Council decision on SALW included support for the ECOWAS, forming part of this region. This particular aspect of the decision would contribute in part to the perception among Commission officials that it constituted an encroachment on the policy areas normally governed by the Community.

The links between Community development cooperation policy and the ACP states was based on the colonial legacy of the founding members of the Community. In its first decades, the Community's development cooperation policy was intimately connected to France and to some extent Belgium as colonial powers. In fact, the French government in 1957 made the linkages between its colonies and the European Economic Community (EEC), as well as the establishment of a European Development Fund (EDF) from which these states would be beneficiaries, a condition for signing the Treaty of Rome (Hewitt and Whiteman 2004: 134).[3] At the time of the installation of the first Commissioner responsible for development in 1958, France was still a major colonial power, with many of its dependencies not gaining formal independence until 1960 (Hewitt 1989: 286). The first years of EC development policy can thus be regarded more or less as a direct outgrowth of French policies towards its (soon to be former) colonies.[4]

With enlargement, most notably of the UK in 1975 and Spain and Portugal in 1986, French dominance declined. The geographical scope of development policy was renegotiated to accommodate these new Member States and their interests in retaining connections with their former colonies. While large Asian states, such as India and Bangladesh, were left out of the 1975 Lomé convention, English-speaking Africa and several Caribbean and Pacific island states were included. Yet, the UK government saw the slightly clientelistic and personalized relationship between the overwhelming French presence in the EC development machinery and France's ex-colonies as a hindrance to the incorporation of the Commonwealth states in the EC development regime.[5] Hence, it pushed for the introduction of new procedures for the allocation of development aid, which would be based to a certain extent on need and be more codified in development programmes. This would be instead of relying on *ad hoc* agreements between Commission officials and political elites in recipient countries (Dimier 2006 cf. Dimier and McGeever 2006).

The codification and bureaucratization of development aid in the Lomé Convention was thus the result of a compromise between the French with their colonial ties and the UK's insistence on the inclusion of Commonwealth States, or as Claye (2004) puts it, the French regionalist defence against globalism (Carbone 2007: 31; Claye 2004: 118). The gradual bureaucratization of the EU's development policy after the first enlargement of the EC was further strengthened by successive Community enlargements, not least Spain and Portugal in 1986, which, due to their connections with South America, broadened the scope of EC development action (Arts 2004). However, in spite of the enlargement and the broadening of the scope of the Community's development cooperation policy to accommodate new Member States, the policy remained intimately connected to the ACP countries. The financial instrument of the Community's development policy, the EDF, also remained tied to the agreements signed between the EU and this group of countries.

### Restructuring development aid and the emerging development security link

An equally important factor that would help create the conditions for institutional conflict in the *small arms* case was the broad institutional developments through which the respective fields of security and development practice were redefined. While for a long time widely considered wholly separate fields of political action, the post–Cold War era saw a paradigmatic shift through which these fields became increasingly regarded as being inseparable.

During the Cold War of locked geopolitical positions, the IMF and the World Bank, as Call (2008) points out, sought to refrain from engaging in actions that would be deemed 'political'. Indeed it was explicitly forbidden through its own constituent rules to take into account 'non-economic considerations' (Williams and Young 1994: 85; cf. Carbone 2010; Hettne 2010). With the end of the Cold War, this hindrance effectively disappeared, and the free trade development policy was accompanied by more assertive efforts aimed at building effective and stable institutions (Stillhof Sörensen and Söderbaum 2012: 13). For Community development policy, the fall of the Berlin Wall and the end of the Cold War also signalled a redirection of development field.

Already in 1989 the World Bank introduced the concept of 'good governance' in a much cited development report (World Bank 1989). Therefore, in a sense the neo-liberalization of development aid and the inclusion of 'political' elements were parallel movements.[6] However, in the post–Cold War era, they seemed to increasingly coalesce and mutually reinforce each other.

Just a few years on, in 1991, the concept of 'good governance' appeared for the first time in an official document of the European Community, a Council Resolution (Council 1991b). As Arts and Dickson (2004) point out, the period afterwards, in the early 1990s, saw a considerable degree of activity geared towards formulating human rights and governance conditions for development (2004: 9). Gibert states:

> From Lomé IV, the partnership agreement concluded in 1990, each new agreement signed with the ACP defined with greater precision and ultimately reinforced the political conditions to be met if EC aid and trade cooperation were to be maintained.
>
> (Gibert 2009: 622)

Conditionality and a preoccupation with internal factors of recipient states had not been wholly absent in previous decades. For instance, in 1987 within the framework of the EPC, the then twelve Member States set up the working party on human rights (COHOM) which had as its mandate to coordinate the positions of the Member States on human rights issues in its external relations. However, the range of issues which now entered the development policy agenda was unprecedented.

The perceived need to bring to the fore the political dimensions of development policy is not least witnessed by the considerable overlaps between the Council Resolution of 1991 and the previous Commission communication on the issue in March of the same year (Commission 1991) as well as the Commission Green Paper that was released in 1996 on EU-ACP relations (Commission 1996). Of particular importance is the redirection towards decentralized cooperation, the inclusion of new actors such as NGOs and the emphasis put on development cooperation that is 'based on the central place of the individual' (Council 1991b: 122).

This redirection departed from the state-centred approach to development cooperation. It opened up for a development policy that also took into account the situations of individuals and the factors that appeared as hindrances to their benefiting from and contributing to the economic development of a given society. In principle, the door opened for devising an endless range of measures that had development as their ultimate goal. Importantly, this redirection towards an 'individualized' development policy fit hand in glove with the parallel widening of the concept of security.

The concept and practice of security was at this point embroiled in a process of a wide-ranging redefinition, in foreign offices, defence ministries, NGOs and, not least, academia.[7] This redefinition challenged the dominant concept of security in terms of military security and the maintenance of territorial sovereignty of states. This traditional concept was gradually being complemented by a more multifaceted notion of security. This new conception of security could be applied to different levels, within and beyond the state, as well as in different sectors. It gave rise to such terms as food security, environmental security, economic security and, perhaps most important in this context, human security.

The 1994 *Human Development Report* of the United Nations Development Programme (UNDP) took further strides in this direction and signified an important move towards a 'transition from the narrow concept of national security to the all-encompassing concept of human security' (United Nations Development Programme 1994: 24). By refocusing the concept of security at the individual level, as well as fleshing out its different dimensions, such as economic, health, and political security, the report established a range of new linkages between the two fields of security and development. The interrelatedness of the concepts as formulated in the 1994 report was thus an early statement of the later widespread contention that security and development are intrinsically connected.

### The security–development link and EU SALW policy

By the end of the 1990s, the widened notion of security and its intimate link with development policies structured discussions on the issue of SALW in the EU. From this perspective, policies geared towards anti-proliferation of small arms and light weapons, while retaining an important security component, were often formulated as having sustainable development, rather than security itself, as their ultimate aim. Again, this was not a policy agenda driven exclusively or even mainly by the Commission. A clear indication of the extent to which these ideas were widely shared is a Council Resolution issued in May of 1999 by the development ministers of the EU meeting in the Council, which included explicit references to the connections between the EU's development policy and SALW (Council 1999b). The Resolution, under the headline of 'Conflict Prevention, Management and Resolution' stated in its very first paragraph that

> the excessive supply of small arms and a lack of controls [have] fuelled internal and interstate conflict and has been an obstacle to peaceful economic and social development.
>
> (Council 1999b: article 1)

The Resolution also referred to the 1998 Joint Action on SALW having entered into force earlier the same year and to other parts of the international community where similar resolutions had been made, such as a UNESCO conference in October of 1998 titled 'The Brussels Call for Action'. This conference had as its theme 'sustainable disarmament for sustainable development' (UNESCO 1998) as well as the so-called 'Oslo platform' which was a conference convened by the UNDP in Oslo in April of 1998 on the creation of a moratorium on SALW in West Africa in the framework of ECOWAS (UNDP 1998).[8] In this context, the Council pointed specifically to the 'humanitarian, developmental and security concerns provoked by small arms' (Council 1999a: article 3). It further stated that there was a need to address 'political, economic and social causes' and take account of security as a prerequisite for development (Council 1999a: article 4). The link between security and development was thus clearly articulated here, not just in a general sense, but explicitly in relation to the issue of SALW. The several references to other international initiatives in the area of SALW, not least by the UN, also indicate that the Resolution was shaped by broader debates on these issues, originating in other settings.

The Council Resolution drew out a number of recommendations regarding specific areas where the development policies of Member States and most importantly the Community should be directed. Among these it included development cooperation support to countries for anti-SALW measures and support for efforts in developing countries to demobilize, rehabilitate and reintegrate combatants into civil life (Council 1999a: article 5):

> The Council recommends that in the field of development cooperation, the Community and the Member States devote particular attention to the following measures: Inclusion of the small arms issue in the political dialogue with ACP and other development cooperation partner countries; development cooperation support for countries seeking assistance in the control or elimination of surplus small arms, as well as other incentives to encourage the voluntary surrender of small arms and their destruction.

It was also stated that the Council and the Commission would 'in accordance with their mandates, take care of the implementation of their respective activities' (Council 1999a: article 7). The Member States and the Council thus expressed the view that the Commission and the Community development cooperation policy had a clear role to play in the field of SALW. Furthermore, the Resolution defined more clearly the specific regional focus of these measures. In this context, ECOWAS was especially mentioned.

> The first interventions could be focused on Southern Africa (SADC) and on West Africa (ECOWAS), where significant progress has been made and frameworks for combating small arms proliferation have been developed and agreed.
> (Council 1999a article 5)

The 1998 Joint Action on SALW was also an indication of the fuzzy lines separating security and development, specifically in the area of SALW. The Joint Action clearly dealt with the implications of SALW proliferation for regional security. However, the connections to the Community's development policy runs through its preamble as well as the concrete actions it identifies. In the preamble it specifically states:

> The excessive and uncontrolled accumulation and spread of small arms and light weapons (. . .) has become a problem of great concern to the international

community and this phenomenon poses a threat to peace and security and reduces the prospects for sustainable development in many regions of the world.

(Council 1999a)

The preamble also mentions that

the European Community has supported actions of demobilisation and reintegration of former combatants and of weapons collection in the context of its humanitarian aid, reconstruction and development cooperation policy.

(Council 1999a)

The Joint Action can thus be read as an indication of the fact that the broader field in which security and development were inextricably linked had started to become taken for granted to the degree that the possible legal implications of including development objectives in a CFSP measure were not even considered. Not only were there several references to development objectives, the substance seemed also in many ways to point to the fact that the fight against the proliferation of small arms could be done through development cooperation instruments, as the Joint Action had stated:

The Council notes that the Commission intends to direct its actions towards achieving the objectives and priorities of the Joint Action, where appropriate by pertinent Community measures.

(Council 1999a: article 8)

The 2000 Cotonou Agreement reinforced the identity of the Community development policy as intimately linked to the ACP countries, as well as the links between the SALW and the Community development cooperation policy. Contrary to previous agreements,[9] the 2000 agreement contained explicit references to security, as well as, most importantly, references to landmines and SALW. The preamble to the Cotonou Agreement stated:

[A] political environment guaranteeing peace, security and stability, respect for human rights, democratic principles and the rule of law, and good governance is part and parcel of long term development.

This was an element which had not been covered by previous agreements. More specifically, under the heading of 'peace building policies, conflict prevention and resolution', it explained:

In this context particular emphasis shall be given to the fight against anti-personnel landmines as well as to addressing an excessive and uncontrollable spread, illegal trafficking and accumulation of small arms and light weapons.[10]

From a formal legal point of view, the inclusion of these articles in the Cotonou Agreement did not imply that there was a Community competence in the field of SALW. An important aspect of the agreement is that it was formally a *mix* between different competencies. While it contained important elements of traditional development aid, it also contained 'political' provisions enabling the Union to enter into consultations with governments of states where the political or human rights situation has deteriorated.[11] For instance, the agreement specified that the EU under the CFSP can take decisions to suspend aid if the political conditions in a recipient country deteriorate.[12] Thus, from a formal point of view it did not specify that SALW had become part of the EU's development cooperation policies. However, irrespective of the formal legal issue, the inclusion of SALW in what is broadly considered the primary development instrument of the EU was not insignificant. Its inclusion was a clear manifestation of the paradigmatic shift in prevalent conceptions of security, development and the relation between these respective fields.

The 2000 Cotonou Agreement marked the end of a long period during which the Community development cooperation policy had been radically redefined in terms of its focus on the internal conditions of recipient states. The parallel process of widening the concept and practice of security after the end of the Cold War fitted right into these developments. Security and development had gradually become perceived as being inextricably linked, as two sides of the same coin. Importantly, it was also a notion that seemed to transgress institutional borders, as it was reproduced by the Commission as well as the Council.

If taking into account the 1999 Council Resolution and the 1998 Joint Action, the inclusion of references to security and SALW in the 2000 Cotonou Agreement becomes more understandable. It would appear as if the Council had begun to recognize a *de facto* competence for the Community development policy in the field of SALW.

Accordingly, in 2001 the Commission was planning contributions to anti-SALW action in West Africa. It is notable that this appears not to have been very controversial at all. As an illustration of this, in 2001 the then Swedish Minister for Foreign Affairs, Anna Lindh, together with the Commissioner for external relations, Christopher Patten, contributed to a Commission report entitled *Small Arms and Light Weapons: The Response of the European Union*. While the report mainly reviewed a range of CFSP measures in the field of SALW, it also included a heading under which it was stated that the Commission already indirectly supported the ECOWAS moratorium on SALW as well as investigating the possibilities for direct support.[13]

From a legislative point of view, the intermingling between security and development also became explicit in the neighbouring field of policies concerning landmines. The process of negotiating what would ultimately be the twin Council Regulations concerning action against anti-personnel landmines constituted something of a landmark (Council 2001e, 2001f).[14] It was an instance through which the security–development link was formalized and given expression in a Community instrument.

The cumbersome policymaking process that resulted in these regulations involved long discussions between representatives of the Council and the Commission. The Council was reluctant to award competencies in this matter that was close to the traditional security politics.[15] There were also intense discussions *within* the Commission between DG RELEX and DG DEV regarding the scope and limitations of what constituted development policies. The officials of DG RELEX, who were preparing the legislative proposal, faced a difficult task in trying to convince officials at DG DEV:

> The negotiations on these regulations were much harder than I had expected. I had myself drafted the regulations and had therefore to go and defend them within the Commission services. And there were tough discussions between DG RELEX where I was at the time and DG DEV. There was a sort of blocking at the time of Commissioner Nielsen[16] about what development cooperation could do and not do.[17]

However, the fact that the de-mining regulations were adopted in the end also testifies to the degree to which the notion of the interconnectedness of security and development had actually become established. That is, in spite of the fact that the formal legislative process pushes actors to consider in detail issues of legislative competence and institutionally defined divisions, mutual agreement was found.

The inclusion of an explicit reference to SALW and landmines in the Cotonou Agreement, alongside the standard development articles, together with a range of other documents, demonstrates how far-reaching the consensus on the intrinsic relation between security and development had become. In the Cotonou Agreement, the evolution and redefinition of international development practice coalesced with the historically defined role of the Community to manage development cooperation with, in particular, West Africa. The 2004 CFSP Council Decision on SALW, however, highlighted the tensions between these two broad institutional processes and the formal distribution of competencies between the Community and the CFSP. That is, when the legal implications of the security–development linkages became explicit, they created tensions that would spur institutional conflict.

## Micro-level dynamics in SALW and tensions in the Commission

The process through which security and development had been redefined was important for the eruption of conflict. It produced a set of professional self-understandings among Commission officials which created the impetus to challenge the Council in the *small arms* case. The clash of these self-understandings with the formal legal institutional structure of the EU would further push the parties towards conflict. The redefinition of security and development would thus be combined with the pressures created by the history of the Community development policy field to trigger institutional conflict in the *small arms* case.

### Council decision of 2004 on SALW and tensions in development policy

In the fall of 2004, in the RELEX group of the Council, the Member State representatives agreed on a proposal for a CFSP decision for a contribution to ECO-WAS to support the creation of a moratorium against SALW (Council 2004). This was the point at which the tensions between the intersubjective institution in the form of consensus on the security–development link and the formal institutional setting of the EU became explicit.

Even if the Community development cooperation policy had successively broadened its geographical scope since its inception, the Lomé agreements and the successive Cotonou Agreement, with their focus on sub-Saharan Africa, the Caribbean and the Pacific island states. was and remains regarded as the principal development instrument of the EU. Indeed, the formal name of DG DEV was the 'Directorate General for Development Cooperation and Relations with African, Caribbean, and Pacific States'.[18] The management of the EDF, the financial instrument of the Cotonou Agreement, was at the time the very *raison d'être* of the DG DEV.[19] Thus, the Commission's reaction to the Council's decision can be understood by taking into account the highly institutionalized role of the Commission in managing the EU's relations and agreements with the ACP countries. The inclusion of SALW as a matter of concern in the Cotonou Agreement, while not formally regulating the division of competencies between the Community and the CFSP,[20] nevertheless contributed to the sense among Commission officials that SALW did indeed form part of the broadened development agenda, and consequently that the 2004 decision was a clear intrusion on already existing Community development cooperation instruments. On the adoption of the Council decision to contribute to ECOWAS in the field of SALW, the Commission issued a Declaration (Council 2004d: annex) in which it stated:

> In the view of the Commission this Joint Action should not have been adopted and the project ought to have been financed from the 9th EDF under the Cotonou Agreement. This is clearly borne out by Article 11(3) of the Cotonou Agreement which specifically mentions the fight against the accumulation of small arms and light weapons as a relevant activity.
>
> (Council 2004d: paragraph 2)

The inclusion of SALW in the Cotonou Agreement was of central importance for highlighting the tensions that brought the Council and the Commission to a state of conflict. The importance can be demonstrated by examining the other measures adopted in the field of SALW in this period. As was mentioned above, the CFSP decision on the contribution to ECOWAS was not the first to implement the 1998 Joint Action or its successor, the 2002 Joint Action on SALW. A closer look at these measures reveals something else which is perhaps more important still in terms of understanding the Commission's action in this case and highlights the importance of bringing the longer-term process into the analysis. What differentiates them from the 2004 decision to contribute to the SALW measures of ECOWAS (Council 2004e) was that they were not related to the Cotonou Agreement.[21] In aim and substance they were very much alike. However, they did not concern the geographical area that was covered by the EU-ACP agreement, but focused on South East Europe, Ukraine, Albania and Cambodia.

Mozambique, which is the country targeted in a 1999 CFSP decision (Council 1999d) on SALW, does indeed also form part of the ACP states. This decision, like the one in 2004, implements the 1998 Joint Action and characterizes SALW as a hindrance to sustainable development. So, from this perspective we would perhaps expect conflict to have broken out here as well, if the focus of the EU's development regime on ACP states is part of the explanation of the outbreak of institutional conflict around the decision in 2004. However, at the time when the Mozambique measure was adopted, the Cotonou Agreement had not come into being and SALW had not become an institutionalized part of EU-ACP relations, as it did through this agreement. Thus, from a legal point of view there was not much that differentiated the Mozambique decision on SALW from that contested in the *small arms* case. The difference was the explicit connection to the Community's primary development cooperation instrument, the Cotonou Agreement, and its financial mechanism, the EDF. The measures aimed at Mozambique and ECOWAS respectively were adopted before and after an important step in the institutionalization of the security–development link in the EC development regime, namely its inclusion in the Cotonou Agreement. The sequence in which these steps in the process unfolded was thus crucial.

The repeated references by the Council to the role of the Community development cooperation policy in SALW had contributed to the emerging self-understandings among Commission officials that they had indeed a legitimate right to act in this area. As the Commission representative in the RELEX group also stated, when the Member State representatives sent the proposal for adoption to the COREPER, the Commission was already under way in preparing a similar measure financed through the EDF (Council 2004c; annex). The decision of the RELEX group to ignore the doubts expressed by the Commission regarding the legal basis of the decision was thus perceived as an illegitimate exclusion of the Commission from a field where it had a given role to play. As one official of DG RELEX commented:

> [The] position of the Commission in lodging this court case really was the result of a tiredness of the Commission vis-à-vis the arrogance of the Council Secretariat and the Member States. (. . .) It led the Commission to say, listen, there are other aspects to our relations which are interrelated with CFSP (. . .) but we think that this can be safely done under Cotonou, under an EDF program, and we think that's a better method.[22]

The official who had been in charge of the file in DG RELEX at the time seemed to be concerned about how the lack of clarity regarding the distribution of competencies prevented the Commission from doing its job as efficiently as possible in the field of SALW. That is, she was less concerned with law and more concerned with how the programmes that the Commission devised would conform to stand-ard development practice as well as the environment on the ground where these programmes would actually be implemented.[23]

As other respondents have stated, there is little room to devise programmes that are tailor-made to fit the division of competencies that are specific to the EU.[24] External actors often have a limited understanding of the legal-institutional sensitivities expressed by EU representatives when negotiating concrete meas-ures or contributions to specific development programmes. Thus, rather than any concerns regarding the need to further European integration, the Commission officials involved perceived the 2004 Council decision on SALW as a break with established practices. This was both in the sense of a break with procedures, since the Commission was already preparing measures based on the EDF, and in the sense of a break with prevailing development practice.

The Commission was already engaged in several similar projects, in particu-lar the field of de-mining. In fact, the official responsible for SALW issues in DG RELEX at the time had been at the very centre of the drafting and negotiations on the previous de-mining measures.[25] It was also obvious from this point of view that the sort of action that was the object of the small arms Decision was clearly the type normally carried out by civilian personnel, NGOs and civil society and usually coordinated by the UNDP, as it mainly involved financial contributions and tech-nical assistance, but very rarely by military personnel. Thus, the definition of the development field to include these issues was connected to how the concrete profes-sional practice of administrating and carrying out development aid had evolved. The fact that there appeared to be a need to take this issue to Court came across as a nec-essary evil rather than an opportunity to expand the influence of the Commission.[26]

There were also indications that even those officials who supported the Com-mission's action in the *small arms* case also saw clear limits to what could be done on the basis of development cooperation policy. As several respondents indicated, when the centre of gravity of a particular measure was clearly on the side of secu-rity rather than development, it was clear that it pertained to the CFSP.[27] Their perspective was thus not an indiscriminate support for expansion in any field pos-sible, but a concern with the appropriateness of specific measures.

The motivation to push for legal action was from this point directly related to prevalent professional practice in the development field. Basically, it indicates the importance of the self-understandings of officials in the substantive directorates and how such self-understandings are connected to the professional fields they work in. That is, their assessments of why it was legitimate to challenge the Coun-cil and the Member States in this sensitive area was because they perceived it to be beyond discussion that the aims of the 2004 Council Decision on SALW was in fact development and not security.

## From micro-level dynamics to conflict over SALW

The *small arms* case had important similarities with the *environmental crimes* case in that it also concerned delimitation between the intergovernmental policies of the EU and those of the Community. Indeed, from the perspective of the Commission Legal Service, this case represented a test case regarding the delimitation of competencies between the first and the second pillar, and this was to mirror the *environmental crimes* case:

> When a situation came where . . . more or less the same [thinking] could be applied between the first and second pillar we decided to go for a sort of mirror case. . . . And we did it almost immediately because in the Legal Service I think the fight and gain in the penal environment case had made everybody in the Legal Service aware of the issue and also of the potential of a good case. So, the external affairs team in the Legal Service immediately woke up with this ECOWAS case when there was a debate on whether this could be [a] second pillar issue when it was in fact cooperation policy.[28]

The Legal Service had thus gained the impetus to test the constitutional issues raised in that case in relation to CFSP. However, the conviction of its Director that this was a good case was not as clear as it had been in the *environmental crimes* case.[29] The Commission's victory in the *environmental crimes* court case, which preceded the institutional conflict in the *small arms* case, was an important factor that contributed to push the case all the way up through the hierarchy of the Legal Service and onwards to the head of the Commission. This determination in the Legal Service was also important for shaping the Commission's position as a whole.[30] As a result of the previous process through which it had earlier emerged as a unified actor, the Commission Legal Service was now acting as a form of policy entrepreneur in this field, attempting to mobilize support for taking the Council to Court. Again, the sequence of these steps were important.

The fact that the Legal Service officials decided to pursue the case in Court was again because they deemed that there was a good chance for a judgment in favour of the Commission on the principal *legal* issue concerning the principles regarding interpretation of article 47 TEU, which regulated the relation between the first and the second pillar, but not necessarily on the substance of the Council Decision on SALW as such.[31] Thus, what was interesting for the Legal Service officials of the Commission was the general question of the delimitation of competencies between the Community and the CFSP and much less on the substance of anti-SALW policy, which was the principal issue for the officials in DG RELEX and DG DEV working on these issues.[32]

Several respondents referred to the considerable resistance in not least DG RELEX more generally to take an action of annulment to the Court.[33] As one Legal Service official stated: 'First of all the RELEX people are diplomats. They don't like court cases. Viscerally not.'[34] However, the Director General of DG DEV at the time[35] together with the Director General of the Commission Legal Service[36] were able to elicit support from the officials in DG RELEX to go ahead with the case.

Interestingly, the perceptions among officials in the Legal Service CFSP unit regarding the position of the officials of DG RELEX diverged radically from those of its then Director General. This senior official's view was instead that the DG RELEX officials were enthusiastically supporting the case, since, as he formulated it, this represented an opportunity to clarify the grey areas in which these officials worked on a daily basis.[37]

This discrepancy between the respondents' views of their colleagues in DG RELEX highlights the importance of not only taking into account the multifaceted character of these large organizations. They also point to the importance of differentiating between different points in the process through which interservice consultations take place before ultimately taking the final decision to instigate legal action. The officials that first launch discussions on such controversial cases are more likely to face a certain amount of resistance before consensus is reached.[38]

Similar to the *environmental crimes* case, there were at times fierce discussions within the Commission until the issue was finally settled, with some officials in the substantive services taking the position that such a controversial case, and the resistance it would incur from Member States, would actually make policymaking more difficult.[39] This is consonant also with rationalist explanations. That is, the long-term costs of engaging in an institutional conflict might outweigh the possible benefits that can potentially be secured by a win.

However, the fact that the Commission finally decided to initiate an institutional conflict only makes sense in light of an understanding of the process through which development cooperation had evolved with its specific focus on the ACP states, especially in light of the inclusion of SALW in the Cotonou Agreement. It was this development that had prompted the Commission to prepare an instrument in the field of SALW financed through the EDF. Furthermore, the motivations of the Commission officials to initiate the case makes far more sense if we take into account how their understandings of their roles in this context had been shaped by the recurrent indications emerging from the Council and elsewhere that development had become intrinsically connected to security and that there was a clear development component in the field of SALW. From this perspective, then, these broad institutional developments shaped the contextually defined self-understandings of these Commission officials and prompted them to challenge the 2004 Council Decision on SALW.

## Summary: institutional conflict in EU external actions

The conjunction of two broad macro-institutional developments in the setting of the EU created the tensions that led to institutional conflict in the *small arms* case. The first was the specific shape of the EU's development cooperation policy and its historical connections to the ACP region, of which the ECOWAS was a part. The other was the paradigmatic change through which the boundaries between security and development, conceptually and professionally, became blurred. These developments merged in the formal institutional setting of the EU and created self-understandings among Commission officials working on SALW and the legitimate right of the Community to act in this area. The 2004 Council Decision in the field of SALW tapped into both of these institutional developments. The self-understandings of Commission officials regarding their legitimate right to participate in this policy area were challenged by this decision in ways that the previous SALW decisions had not been. This created the impetus for initiating the institutional conflict.

The analysis traced the evolution of the EU's development cooperation policy and its relation to the EU's broader foreign and security policy. Thus the analysis focused on the parallel movements through which the state-centric concept of security was widened in parallel with the paradigmatic shift from narrow economic austerity programmes to an increasing concern with the internal social and political conditions of recipient states. These two broad movements, taking their own specific trajectories in the framework of the legal-institutional environment of the EU, conditioned the Commission's ability to challenge the Council and the Member States in this highly sensitive area of EU external action.

The impact of structural transformations in specific professional fields was more clearly pronounced in the process leading up to the *small arms* case, as compared with the *environmental crimes* case. While the process of the *environmental crimes* case was intimately connected to the evolution of the European project itself, the process leading up to the *small arms* case was to a higher degree shaped by the paradigmatic transformations in the respective political and professional fields of security and development.

What emerged from the analysis of the process was that with time, the concept of security and development could hardly be imagined without one another; this notion was habitually reproduced not only by the Commission but also by the Council in its different configurations. This notion, which seemed to have attained the status of being taken for granted, eventually clashed with the formal institutional set-up of the EU.

The Legal Service on its part was at this point already up and running after the *environmental crimes* case and was actively searching for a case through which the delimitation of competence that had been redrawn between the Community and JHA could be repeated with respect to the CFSP. In this sense, the actorness that it had established in the early 2000s in relation to criminal law was already in effect when tensions between the respective fields of security and development arose on the issue of SALW in West Africa, and as such facilitated the forging of an alliance with frustrated Development officials, which finally made possible the case against the Council.

In Figure 5.1, the results of the analysis are summarized by unpacking how the institution-agent relations produced institutional conflict in the *small arms* case. The first macro-micro link illustrates how the tension between the broad consensus on the security development link and the formal institutional set-up of the EU played out among Commission officials as a tension between their self-understandings as legitimate actors in SALW and intergovernmental CFSP legislation in this field. This enabled the Commission as a whole, and the instigation of institutional conflict.

**Macro 1**: Tensions between the shared understandings on security-development and the formal delimitation between the Community's development cooperation policy towards ACP states and the CFSP.

**Macro 2**: Outbreak of Institutional conflict in relation to the 2004 Council decision on SALW.

**Micro 1**: Self-understandings created by consensus lead Commission officials to perceive themselves as unjustly excluded from the field of SALW in relation to Council decision.

**Micro 2**: Emergence of institutionally defined actorness and preferences in the field of SALW. The Commission unites around a pro-integration position.

*Figure 5.1* Outbreak of institutional conflict in the small arms case

## Notes

1  Interview with Council Secretariat official, Legal Service (Respondent 23).
2  Interview with Council Secretariat official, Legal Service (Respondent 21).
3  The EDF remains even today an intergovernmental fund outside the EU budget, to which the Member States contribute to various degrees. France and Germany, for instance, are substantial contributors, while the UK and Italy contribute less in relation to their size. Newer Member States generally contribute very little. The Commission has argued in many instances that the EDF should be made part of the EU budget (Commission 2003c).
4  For accounts of the history of EC development policy, see Carbone (2007 ch. 2); Clayes (2004); Dimier (2006); Hewitt and Whiteman (2004). For a history of this policy field with a special focus on the emergence of the concept of 'good governance' in the EU, see Carbone (2010). For a discussion of European integration as intimately tied to its colonial roots, see Hansen and Jonsson (2014).
5  As Hewitt and Whiteman show, the first head of the EDF committee retained an exclusive focus on French-speaking Africa and set up a network of EDF delegates in the eighteen signatory countries of the development agreement accountable to him personally (Hewitt and Whiteman 2004: 136). Decisions on aid allocation were thus taken with a minimum of transparency and without any clearly stated criteria or programmes.
6  A foundational document for the neo-liberalization of development was the report released by the World Bank in 1981. This report on structural adjustment programmes, the so-called Berg report, would resonate in its policies throughout the 1980s and beyond (World Bank 1981).
7  A standard reference in this context is by Buzan (1983), who presaged the broader widening movement of the security concept. Work in the immediate post–Cold War era include Booth (1991), Crawford (1991) and Krause and Williams (1996). For an overview of several works in this period, see Baldwin (1995).

8  United Nations Development Programme (1998).
9  These previous agreements were the so-called Lomé Conventions, first signed in 1975. The last one, Lomé IV, ran from 1990 to 2000, when it was supplanted by the Cotonou Agreement.
10  Article 11, paragraph 3 of the Cotonou Agreement.
11  Cotonou Agreement, articles 96 and 97.
12  As many have pointed out, this agreement represents something of a watershed in EU-ACP relations. Firstly it reorganizes development aid from non-reciprocal trade preferences to the introduction of so-called Economic Partnership Agreements (EPAs), which are essentially free trade agreements between the EU and groups of ACP states (Forwood 2001). Secondly, it strengthens the emphasis on political conditionality: conditions which if not met can trigger mechanisms of political consultation with a recipient state, and eventually the suspension of aid (Gibert 2009: 622).
13  Commission (2001a: 17). In this context it is useful to bear in mind that Sweden was actually one of the Member States that intervened in support of the Council in the *small arms* case.
14  The fact that there were two almost identical instruments, one based on the development article 179 TEC and one on 308 TEC, was that it aimed to cover mine action not only in those countries considered to be developing countries but also in non-developing countries where landmines presented a problem.
15  As the analysis of the *small arms* court case will show, the fact that a Community act had been adopted in the field of landmines was later mobilized to support the argument of a Community competence in SALW.
16  Poul Nielsen, Commissioner for development and humanitarian aid 1999–2004.
17  Interview with Commission official, DG DEV, formerly DG RELEX (Respondent 17).
18  Since the establishment of the European External Action Service, many of its central tasks have moved into the new service, in particular the programming of aid. The DG has also changed its name to Directorate General for EuropeAid, Development and Cooperation (DG DEVCO).
19  Interview with Commission official, DG DEV (Respondent 6).
20  As the Council would later point out repeatedly in its defence before the Court in case C-91/05 (Council 2005b).
21  Or its predecessor, the Lomé Convention.
22  Interview with Commission official, DG RELEX (Respondent 7).
23  Interview with Commission official, DG DEV, formerly DG RELEX (Respondent 17).
24  Interview with Commission official DG RELEX (Respondent 53); interview with Council Secretariat official (Respondent 15); interview with Commission official, DG RELEX (Respondent 7); interview with Commission official, DG DEV (Respondent 41); interview with EEAS official (Respondent 48).
25  This official had also been chair of the Commission's Mine Action Coordination group (Commission 2006a: 5).
26  Interview with Commission official DG DEV (former DG RELEX) (Respondent 17).
27  Interview with Commission official, DG RELEX (Respondent 53); interview with Commission official, DG RELEX (Respondent 7); interview with Commission official, DG RELEX (Respondent 52).
28  Interview with former Commission official, Legal Service (Respondent 40).
29  Interview with former Commission official, Legal Service (Respondent 32); interview with former Commission official, Legal Service (Respondent 40).
30  Interview with Commission official, DG RELEX (Respondent 2).
31  Interview with former Commission official, Legal Service (Respondent 32).
32  Interview with Commission official, Legal Service (Respondent 19).
33  Interview with former Commission Official, Legal Service (Respondent 32); interview with Commission official, Legal Service (Respondent 19); interview with Commission

official, DG DEV (formerly RELEX) (Respondent 17); interview with Commission official, DG RELEX (Respondent 53).

34  Interview with former Commission official, Legal Service (Respondent 32).

35  Stefano Manservisi served in this position 2004–2010. It can also be noted that Manservisi previously served as the Head of Cabinet of Romano Prodi (2001–2004).

36  Michel Petite served as Director General in the Commission Legal Service, 2001–2007.

37  Interview with former Commission official, Legal Service (Respondent 40).

38  When an issue has reached the level of the Director General of the Legal Service, a large part of the intra-service consultations have already taken place. This does not mean that contentious discussions cannot occur at the higher level of the hierarchy. However, for a specific case to actually reach the higher levels of the Legal Service hierarchy, a considerable amount of the resistance from the substantial services would have had to be overcome, involving the Director General at a rather late stage of the process.

39  Interview with former Commission official, Legal Service (Respondent 32); interview with former Commission official, Legal Service (Respondent 40).

# 6 Explaining institutional conflict

The *rupture mechanism*

The results of the process analyses are reconceptualized here by defining the component parts of the *rupture mechanism* which explain the outbreak of institutional conflict. The mechanism is placed within a broader family of similar *crisis mechanisms* in IR and EU studies and in a discussion which re-engages with different theories on institutional conflict and change. This family of crisis mechanisms is ordered in a typology that helps define the different assumptions regarding the institutions and agents on which they rely.

The *rupture mechanism* is essentially an institutional mechanism where the emergence of specific intersubjective understandings and practices, including the associated self-understandings of particular agents, clash with a system of formal rules. Importantly, this shift in shared understandings helps explain how institutional roles, associated with the Council and the Commission respectively, were brought to the surface. It makes sense of the actions that led to the outbreak of institutional conflict in the *environmental crimes* case and the *small arms* case.

In the *environmental crimes* case, the widespread acceptance of the need for sanctions, and more specifically criminal sanctions, to ensure effective implementation of Community law emerged from the early 1990s onwards. In the *small arms* case, important macro-level developments consisted of the emergence of the widespread idea regarding the intrinsic link between security and development after the Cold War. These intersubjective shared understandings clashed with the formal institutional set-up of the EU, and more specifically the strict separation between the Community framework and the intergovernmental policies found in the JHA and the CFSP.

Changes in intersubjective institutions gradually created self-understandings among Commission officials on the legitimate role of the Community in the respective policy fields of criminal law and SALW. These self-understandings were, however, frustrated by the Council's repeated recourse to formal intergovernmental procedures that excluded the Commission. At a certain point, these tensions became difficult to manage, as officials, especially in the substantive services, realized that the current state of affairs actually impeded them from doing their jobs properly. In the *environmental crimes* case, the frustrations of the DG ENV officials were related specifically to their inability to secure efficient implementation of the policies they had devised. Criminal law was awarded specific

meanings in this context as it became increasingly associated with general functioning of the Community, and as such became connected to the very foundations of the European project. Officials in the Legal Service experienced these
frustrations on a more principled level. Rather than being tied to any particular
policy issue, these officials developed a concern with the general exclusion of
the Community from using criminal sanctions as an implementation tool. The
issue of SALW, on the other hand, became part of the more general redefinition
of the respective fields of security and development, a redefinition which made
the exclusion of the Community from this field increasingly untenable for certain
officials. The evolution of SALW towards a development issue in the international
sphere, which was also reproduced by the Council, highlighted discrepancies with
the EU system.

For officials in the Council, however, these tensions did not become acute.
There were indeed officials in the Council Secretariat that supported the Commission's standpoints, especially regarding criminal sanctions in Community law. It
is important to recall the Council Legal Service even issued an opinion arguing
for the existence of a Community competence in criminal law. However, the central mission of the Council bureaucracy is to support the Member States in their
actions. Thus, the tensions that became more and more palpable for Commission
officials were not felt by Council Secretariat officials to the same degree. This
highlights an important point regarding how widespread shared understandings
play out in different ways depending on how they interact with contextual factors
at the level of agents. One particularly important factor for these cases was the
position of particular agents in the organizational structure of the EU.

The *rupture mechanism* can be said to exhibit what Pierson (2004) characterizes as a threshold effect. This means that the mechanism is not triggered until a
certain threshold is reached. Thus, rather than thinking about causality in these
processes as linear, pressures are built up during a longer period of time before
finally having any manifest effect. As Pierson puts it:

> Incremental or cumulative forces may not generate incremental changes in
> outcomes of interest. Instead, these processes have a modest or negligible
> impact until they reach some critical level, which triggers major change.
>
> (Pierson 2004: 83)

Here, this means that a gradual process of informal and in some cases even formal
institutionalization can go on for a considerable amount of time before tensions
are felt so strongly as to push agents to perceive a given situation in terms of a
zero-sum game of, for instance, political influence. Once triggered, the mechanism can be said to have a 'radicalizing' effect on agents. Flexibility, pragmatic
problem solving and deliberation are supplanted by a situation structured by
binary choices.

Institutional tensions do not trigger the mechanism deterministically. There is
a variety of possible ways through which tensions could be handled. In particular, such tensions could be managed in ways that would not necessarily have an

unbridgeable conflict as their outcome. For instance, deliberative dynamics might enter the picture and supply a pressure valve by directing agents to a problem-solving mode and compromise. However, the latent tensions of the European project itself played an important role. The self-understandings of agents concerning substantial issues increasingly came to correspond to the institutionally predefined roles supplied by the organizational set-up of the EU, with the Commission as the 'Guardian of the Treaties' and the Council as protector of national sovereignty.

The adoption of the respective legislative measures by the Council triggered the mechanism. However, the run-up to the outbreak of conflict in the two cases did involve a great deal of discussion between Commission officials on one hand and Council and Member State officials on the other. The difference between discussions across the two cases illustrates how the *rupture mechanism* is triggered. In the *environmental crimes* case, discussions between the Commission and the Council persisted to varying degrees of intensity for two years. In this case there was a certain amount of openness on the part of the Council to at least contemplate concessions to the Commission in regard to the Framework Decision on environmental crimes. The Council proposal for a Framework Decision was sent to Parliament and was also slightly redrafted. Furthermore, the Council Legal Service produced an opinion that actually supported the Commission's proposal for a Directive (Council 2001a). Through the final adoption of the Framework Decision, however, the broader range of solutions that had been available were reduced to a zero-sum situation. In the *small arms* case, the Council gave no room for concessions of any kind. The dispute in the RELEX group was characterized by the respondents as rather intense and, most succinctly by the Advocate General in his opinion on the court case, bitter. The position of the CFSP unit of the Council Legal Service was also far more unyielding in relation to the issue of SALW. The time-span of the discussions that ended with the SALW decision and the outbreak of conflict was thus much shorter.

The two processes exhibit important similarities, not least in terms of their outcomes. However, the analyses also showed that the paths through which shared understandings formed were the result of somewhat different dynamics. In the *environmental crimes* case, the notion that the implementation of Community law needed to be backed up with different forms of sanctions, and in particular criminal sanctions on the EU level, came out of the transformation of the European project itself, especially widespread concerns regarding lack of compliance with EC law. This notion was further reinforced by policy discussions in other international venues. In particular, the Council of Europe served as a source of both policy output and expertise. A more proximate factor that triggered the conflict was identified in the fact that the contested issue arose in the field of the Community's environmental policy. This was a policy field in which concerns about enforcement and implementation were long-standing issues. It was also perceived as one of the core policies of the Community. From this point of view, it was the Danish presidency that ultimately introduced this largely contingent, but crucially important ingredient as it tabled its initiative in 2000 to incorporate the recently adopted Council of Europe Convention on the Protection of the Environment through Criminal Law in an EU Framework Decision. The status of Community environmental policy made it possible to mobilize broad support in the Commission that had not been possible in previous cases.

In the *small arms* case, shared understandings evolved around the taken-for-granted notion that security and development were inextricably linked and that security was a fundamental condition for sustainable development. These shared understandings were the result of the rise of new professional practices in the development field and a paradigmatic change in the conception of security after the Cold War. The standing of Community development policy and its relation to the ACP countries was important here as well. The dynamics of the *environmental crimes* case also had an impact on the process of the *small arms* case. The Commission Legal Service was, as a result of the victory in the *environmental crimes* case, already eager to find a mirror case that could be applied to the delimitation of the Community and the CFSP. In this regard, the win of the Commission in the *environmental crimes* case was a factor that contributed to the outbreak of conflict in the *small arms* case. The Commission Legal Service had already been 'radicalized' by the outbreak of conflict in this prior case and had thus emerged as a strategic actor in relation to the principal issue of the delimitation of intergovernmental and Community policies of the EU.

These differences in the respective processes highlight an important point. They reveal the proximate factors that might accelerate the process through which the mechanism is triggered. The role of the Legal Service in the *small arms* case acts as a case in point. Strictly speaking, these officials were not affected by the mechanism. Instead, the 'entrepreneurship' it exerted in relation to the general constitutional issue regarding delimitation between intergovernmental and Community policy fields made it act as a catalyst that triggered the mechanism and led to the outbreak of conflict.

## Theoretical underpinnings of the *rupture mechanism*

To recall, a fundamental assumption of the analytical framework is that agency is an emergent property of agents, and that intentionality has an important *situational* component. When agents are confronted with an environment of different and overlapping systems of practices, constraints will inevitably appear and make formerly implicit 'ways of doing things' explicit. Agency itself arises in the face of contradictions and ambiguities that habitual practices are increasingly unable to deal with. This also points to the need to take both constitutive and regulative aspects of institutions into account.

The mechanism is activated when the possibility for creative adaptation is no longer available and agents are effectively forced to act *in*appropriately in relation to one of the systems of norms and practices with which they are confronted (cf. Finnemore and Sikkink 1998: 897–8; Sending 2002: 460). Faced with a situation in which incoherencies arise between different systems of practices and appropriate action, actors are pushed to articulate certain preferences and come to perceive parts of the social world in terms of constraints, in relation to which there is a need to act strategically (cf. Müller 2004). In this context, the two cases signified for the Commission a need to challenge the formal institutional order, and for the Council to assume its institutionally defined role as guardian of national sovereignty. Thus, as the analyses demonstrated, actorness in relation to the specific policy issues developed in conjunction with the process itself. Gross (referring to Whitford 2002) elegantly captures the relations between process, self-understandings and preferences, as he argues:

> [M]eans and ends are not always given prior to action, as assumed in rational choice models, but are often emergent from action, as lines of activity are initiated that lead actors to see themselves in new ways, to value different kinds of goods, and to become attached to problem solutions they could not have imagined previously.
>
> (Gross 2009: 367)

The mechanism does not *primarily* rely on an analysis of the constraints and possibilities that actors are faced with. Contrary to rationalist institutionalists, agents are not assumed to nurture more or less stable preferences that they are enabled or constrained to pursue, depending on the current state of the system of rules that surround them. The perspective argued for here does take regulative aspects of institutions into account but assumes that such regulative effects can only be adequately understood if taking the constitutive aspects of institutions as the point of departure. The *rupture mechanism* explains how shifts in the self-understandings of agents prompt them to interpret their environments in new ways. To recall, the formal rules stayed more or less constant across different points in the processes analyzed. It was the intersubjective institutions, and thus the self-understandings of the agents involved, that changed.

As described in the analysis of the two cases, shared understandings on specific issues created self-understandings and habitual ways of approaching problems. It was only when these habits clashed with the formal institutional structure that agents came to perceive parts of the social environment in terms of constraints. The *rupture mechanism* explains the shift through which habitual or scripted action becomes reflected upon and a matter of contestation. Structure from this point of view moves from connoting shared understandings and taken-for-granted ways of acting to representing itself to specific actors in terms of opportunities and constraints. The constitutive effects of institutions recede into the background while their regulative effects become more prominent.

The mechanism can help explain sudden changes in the forms of social interaction. This theme, it was argued above, has received less attention in constructivist theorizing on international political orders than the self-reinforcing mechanisms associated with the emergence of deliberative practices and socialization. Interpretive process tracing highlights the importance of practices and habitual action but also includes the tools to understand how what is 'taken for granted' can change and how specific actions and events can alter the context in which they appear. In this sense, it helps to theorize the point at which what is unreflected

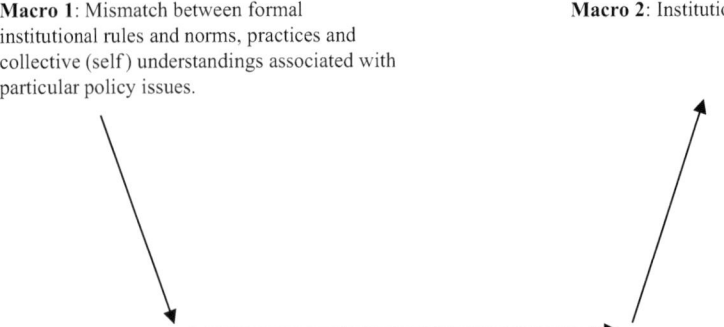

**Macro 1**: Mismatch between formal institutional rules and norms, practices and collective (self) understandings associated with particular policy issues.

**Macro 2**: Institutional conflict.

**Micro 1**: Clash between agents' norms and self-understandings and the system of formal rules in which agents activate institutional roles.

**Micro 2**: Emergence of explicit institutional preferences in relation to a particular issue.

*Figure 6.1* The *rupture mechanism*

actually becomes quite available for reflection or, in relation to the logic of argument (Risse 2000), when consensus or shared understandings give way to conflict.

To summarize, the *rupture mechanism* explains the outbreak of institutional conflict in these cases as a result of a clash between an intersubjective and a formal institution: a clash that played itself out at the agent level in the form of increasingly tangible tensions between professional self-understandings and the formal setting in which these agents found themselves (Figure 6.1). Formulated as such, this mechanism represents a way to address the limits of constructivist approaches in conceptualizing the turn from consensus to conflict. It also supplies an opening for a more comprehensive understanding of what prompts the emergence of strategic actorness in the specific institutional setting of the EU.

## The *rupture mechanism* in a typology of crisis mechanisms

The *rupture mechanism* as an institutional mechanism based on a constructivist theory of agents and institutions addresses the problem of institutional conflict and change. This ties into theorizing in IR and EU studies, from both rationalist and constructivist perspectives. It also forms part of a general family of *crisis mechanisms* ordered along the lines of their respective assumptions regarding agents and institutions.

The family of mechanisms captured by the typology share a common baseline as they all seek to account for the social dynamics which cause an agent to abandon or radically redefine the nature of its relations with certain counterparts. The mechanisms pertaining to this general category are, however, based on different conceptions of the underlying dynamics that explain seemingly sudden instances of institutional change, such as breakdowns in cooperative arrangements and the departure from institutionalized norms, rules and habits. The typology is ordered along the analytical division between mechanisms that take their point of departure from the structural level and those that place primary explanatory power on the level of agents, whether in terms of their interests and intentions or cognitive processes. The other axis makes the distinction between mechanisms that emphasize and give primary value to the regulatory aspects of social institutions and those that emphasize their constitutive aspects. Based on these two dimensions, the typology highlights four categories, each identifying a distinct type of crisis mechanism. It is worth emphasizing that the categories in this typology define *starting points* in terms of the primary locus of causal power rather than static types, the latter relying exclusively on one conception of institutions and one logic of social action.

## Regulative institutions and agent-level explanations

While the typology relies on dynamic categories however, this first category of crisis mechanisms is perhaps the one most intimately associated with a singular and static view of institutions and social interaction. This type combines a conception of institutions as primarily (or even exclusively) regulative and places explanatory power firmly among particular agents. The crisis mechanism enters the picture when actors find themselves in situations where the trade-off between long-term and short-term gains becomes unbalanced. Institutional change is driven by changes in exogenously defined interests of agents. From this point of view, crisis occurs as agents discover that the long-term gains associated with a particular institutional arrangement will not cover short-term losses or the opposite: that short-term gains will not make up for the long-term negative effect of cooperating (Keohane 1984; Stein 2008). This creates tensions that ultimately will push a particular agent such as a state to abandon or radically renegotiate a given cooperative arrangement. This functional view of institutions is at the bottom of much research in the field of liberal institutionalism in IR. In EU studies, it is perhaps most clearly represented by Moravcsik's (1998) intergovernmentalist perspective on European integration. This approach awards a rather limited role to institutions themselves in favour of an emphasis on exogenously defined interests. The extent to which particular cooperative arrangements allow agents to further their interests will shape the likelihood of a crisis.

## Regulative institutions and structural explanations

In a second category we find crisis mechanisms that remain with the regulative conception of institutions but where the explanatory power of crisis is primarily located at the level of institutional structures. The mechanisms in this category rely on a more or less rationalist view of social action, but it is combined with an endogenous view of institutional change. Similar to rationalist institutionalist accounts, changes in the institutional setting in which agents find themselves is the starting point for understanding these crisis mechanisms. While rationalist approaches are commonly associated with methodological individualism, the mechanisms in this category in fact supply explanations that emphasize institutional structures. A case in point is Rittberger and Schimmelfennig's (2006) explanation of the empowerment of the European Parliament. They introduce a crisis mechanism of institutional change arising due to increasing discrepancies between 'is and ought', meaning a discrepancy between widespread and publicly voiced commitments to normative standards and the actual institutional arrangements in place. (2006: 1160). This mechanism, they argue, is important for understanding the process through which increasing decision-making powers have been awarded to the European Parliament. They state:

> The more a proposed or implemented step of EU integration is perceived to curb the competencies of national parliaments (. . .) the more salient the 'democratic deficit' of European integration becomes and the stronger the normative pressure on EU actors to redress the situations through strengthening constitutional rights at the EU level.
>
> (Rittberger and Schimmelfennig 2006)

Agents are not absent in this account. This type of normative pressure can be deployed strategically to put social and political pressure on actors to change their behaviour (Rittberger and Schimmelfennig 2006: 1159). However, the source of explanatory power is primarily located on the structural level of institutions, and in the sense that it is changes in institutional structures that, along with regulative normative rules, create tensions.

In this category we also find the type of crisis mechanisms implied by the power distributional approach to institutional change, as introduced by Mahoney and Thelen (2010). Institutions from this point are always associated with distributional effects and it is also these effects that generate crisis in institutional arrangements. This perspective accounts for institutional change by pointing to how such arrangements regulate the distribution of resources. If such arrangements systematically disadvantage a particular group, this will create resistance to these institutions that can ultimately lead to change. While agents play a crucial role for this mechanism, the explanatory power again originates from the structural level of institutions. From this perspective, it is the distributional effects that are also an intrinsic part of the institutional set-up itself and that ultimately create tensions that push particular agents or groups of agents to take actions to change those institutions. The crisis mechanism, similar to that discussed by Rittberger and Schimmelfennig, is one of endogenous institutional change. However, in their emphasis on the regulative aspects of institutions, these mechanisms leave aside constitutive relations between institutions and self-understandings which is crucial for understanding the dynamics of institutional conflict in the EU.

## Constitutive institutions and agent-level explanations

A third type of crisis mechanism places the explanatory power of crisis mechanisms at the agent level while at the same time relying on a notion of social institutions as constitutive. Here, focus is placed on how ideas shape agents' actions as well as on how the cognitive processes of individual agents interact with external environments. Crisis mechanisms from this perspective focus on the conditions under which cognitive scripts and internalized beliefs are altered.

Jacobs (2009) argues that agents rely heavily on ideologies, beliefs and world-views in judging specific situations and making choices. Furthermore, and similar to many constructivist arguments, these mental models have an important self-reinforcing aspect that tends to lead to ideational stability. Thus, the constitutive side of institutions is clearly factored in, as mental models are associated with a degree of 'stickiness'. The models that individual agents use as shorthand to deal with a complex reality are not updated automatically when agents are exposed to new information. As Béland and Cox (2010) argue, 'institutions (. . .) nurture peoples' identities, helping them to construct their fundamental values which, in turn, shape their beliefs and interests' (2010: 11) At the same time this is also a perspective that places considerable weight of explanations on the level of agents, especially concerning how such ideas change. Agents interpret particular situations on the basis of established beliefs and cognitive scripts. However, this 'confirmation bias' is not absolute. As Jacobs states, "multiple large and clear divergences from a pre-existing [mental] model will draw extra attention and provoke data-driven processing" (Jacobs 2009: 259). The crisis mechanism here is thus conceptualized as a discrepancy between prior beliefs and data. If such discrepancies are too large or if agents are exposed to them on repeated occasions, they are likely to update those beliefs to better fit with the data. In contrast to the *rupture mechanism*, this mechanism does not rely on changes in the social system in which agents find themselves, but on repeated exposure to information in the objective environment. Alternatively, as Béland and Cox (2010) argue, along with Schmidt (2008) and Parsons (2016), agents are to some extent able to place themselves outside of social institutions, 'to re-examine their surroundings, reconsider their positions, and develop fresh new approaches' (Béland and Cox 2010: 11). This means that while the constitutive side of institutions is emphasized, agents are the drivers of the type of crisis mechanism discussed here. A more comprehensive discussion of what I would take to be some obvious meta-theoretical tensions of this position is beyond the scope of this chapter. Suffice to say that, compared with the cognitive mechanism suggested by Jacobs, Schmidt's perspective seems to leave aside central questions regarding when and why agents can be expected to step 'outside' institutions that are also assumed to constitute their identities, fundamental values and interests.

## Constitutive institutions and structural explanations

The *rupture mechanism* belongs in the final category of ther crisis mechanism typology. In the broadly defined constructivist field, scholars have formulated similar crisis mechanisms while not connecting them to discussions on institutional conflict and change. Here the constitutive aspects of social institutions are emphasized. Their regulative aspects only become understandable by understanding how institutions such as norms, habits and taken-for-granted ways of doing things shape the way in which agents perceive particular aspects of the social world in terms of their enabling and constraining elements. The analytical primacy of structure and constitutive effects of institutions make the theorization of rapidly unfolding crises particularly challenging. Guzzini (2012) places such a mechanism at the centre of the varied emergence of geopolitical discourses in a number of European countries after the Cold War. This 'crisis management' mechanism derives its power from changes that, according to Guzzini and colleagues, set off existential anxieties. In the particular cases examined, these anxieties resulted from the way in which highly ingrained identities connected to the Cold War suddenly had no bearing, leaving a considerable gap to be filled in foreign policy identities. This void was filled through either the resurgence of geopolitical discourse or depending on certain process factors, other identities. This take on the crisis mechanism is related to the concept of ontological security where the actions of agents are fundamentally governed by the need to establish and maintain stable identities, and where this sense of ontological security is regarded as a fundamental condition of agency itself.[1] From this perspective, crisis mechanisms have an existential aspect which is far more pronounced than that of the *rupture mechanism*.

While professional identities and institutional roles are certainly important in shaping interactions between the Council and the Commission, conceptualizing institutional conflicts in terms of existential crises is not necessarily helpful and does not find support in the processes analyzed here. Somewhat more closely related to the *rupture mechanism*, Neumann and Pouliot (2011) draw on the Bourdieusian concept of hysteresis and argue for how a 'mismatch between the dispositions agents embody and the positions they occupy in a given social configuration . . . is often at the root of symbolic struggles in social political life' (Neumann and Pouliot 2011: 109). The formulation of this general mechanism is thus closely related to the *rupture mechanism*, and also analogous to the notion of the mismatch between 'is and ought', as formulated by Rittberger and Schimmelfennig. The 'trigger' of hysteresis is, however, slightly different than the one associated with the *rupture mechanism*. For Neumann and Pouliot, self-understandings, or agents' dispositions, change less rapidly than their position in a particular social system.[2] As was demonstrated above, this is not necessarily the case for the *rupture mechanism*. It is, in fact, quite the opposite: self-understandings among officials in the Commission seemed to evolve from the 1990s and further on in the 2000s as a result of reconfigurations of dominant professional fields, which then created tensions with the formal rules in place, making institutional roles more salient. The formal rules, which also assigned specific positions to the respective organizational actors, stayed more or less constant during the period studied. From this perspective, the notions of hysteresis and rupture might complement each other, hysteresis capturing an increasing mismatch between highly ingrained identities and more volatile social systems, and rupture connoting evolving self-understandings faced with inflexible rules. Relatedly, Michalski and Norman (2015), taking their cue from the general notion of multiple-embeddedness (cf. Beyer 2005), have sought to show how political elites, being embedded in multiple and sometimes competing international political orders, are in certain

*Table 6.1* A typology of crisis mechanisms

|  | Institutions as Primarily Regulative | Institutions as Primarily Constitutive |
|---|---|---|
| Explanatory power at the agent level | Cost benefit analysis causes agents to reevaluate (change/exit) institutionalized arrangements | Discrepancy between mental models and objective reality leads to crisis of existing models and updating in line with data |
| Explanatory power at the structural level | 1) Increasing discrepancy between 'is' and 'ought'. 2) Distributional effects of institutionalized orders push disadvantaged agents to strive for change | Increasing discrepancy between self-understandings and institutionalized orders push agents to strive for institutional change (*rupture mechanism*) |

situations pushed to abandon one order in favour of another. It might be argued that this version of a crisis mechanism follows the same type of logic, also pointing to the breaking points at which conflicting identities and social and political orders force agents to engage in particular actions to mitigate or overcome tensions.

Based on these discussions we can now visualize the full typology of crisis mechanisms (Table 6.1). A thorough discussion of each type is not necessary here, as each of these various types of crisis mechanisms opens the door to entire theoretical fields. What the discussion has sought to achieve, however, is the formulation of a template for thinking about this family of mechanisms that will help discriminate between different arguments for explaining the mounting of seemingly irreconcilable differences, breakdown of cooperation and the outbreak of conflict.

## Notes

1 For discussions on the concept of ontological security in IR, see Mitzen (2006); Steele (2008); Zarakol (forthcoming).

2 It might be argued that the Bourdieusian conceptual apparatus of habitus and field, and indeed the related concept of hysteresis itself, is not translatable to the present framework. For instance, treating dispositions as contextually defined self-understandings does a certain degree of violence to this conceptual apparatus. However, I would argue that the value of engaging with these discussions outweighs the risk of conceptual stretching.

# Part III

# 7    The *environmental crimes* case

In this third part of the book the dynamics of the actual institutional conflicts before the Court are considered starting with the field of criminal law. In spite of highly pitched protests from the Council and the Member States, in September 2005 the European Court of Justice ruled in favour of the Commission in the *environmental crimes* court case. Criminal sanctions were effectively included as an implementation tool of Community legislation with this decision. This chapter analyzes the institutional conflict leading up to the ruling of the Court in favour of the Commission, which formally moved the issue of criminal sanctions into the supranational framework of the Community. It does so by investigating the way in which the frames of the parties involved derived their force from the dynamics of the process that preceded the outbreak of conflict. The chapter also highlights that in relation to the formal rules in place and the jurisprudence of the Court in the field of JHA and criminal law, it becomes difficult to understand why the Court would rule in favour of the Commission. Given the sensitivity of the issue at stake, and the intensity of the conflict and commonly held expectations regarding the need for the Court to safeguard its image as an impartial actor, the final decision of the Court remains perplexing.

The chapter demonstrates how the intersubjective aspects of institutions that had been prevalent in previous stages, before the institutional conflict broke out, shaped the actions of agents in the context of the conflict. More specifically, it is shown that the fact that there had been a consensus on fundamental issues within the field of criminal law was in itself a factor that awarded legitimacy to the arguments of the Commission. To recall, this consensus had formed around the notion that criminal sanctions were the most efficient way to ensure implementation of certain policies. That is, the taken-for-granted foundation of these discussions had been that criminal law offered a more effective way in which compliance could be assured, especially in relation to other forms of sanctions, such as administrative sanctions.[1]

Thus, rather than a pure struggle over treaty texts, existing legislation and jurisprudence, the analysis demonstrates that the *environmental crimes* court case was in equal measure a conceptual struggle that went far beyond the confines of the institutional rules in place. The way in which the agents involved had previously formulated the issue in policy statements and Resolutions now made some interpretations of the issue of criminal law more plausible and convincing. Importantly, this constrained the ability of the Council to mobilize an effective defence. The Council was locked in by how it had previously acted in this field.

## The *environmental crimes* court case and the ECJ

As mentioned earlier, the intensity of the conflict and the lack of formal precedents make it difficult to understand the ruling of the Court in favour of the Commission. Furthermore, the rules in place in terms of the texts of the Treaties supplied only a marginal role for the Commission and the Court.

The use of criminal sanctions, as the Commission argued in front of the Court, should be available for the Community legislator as a way to ensure effective implementation of Community law. The Council and the Member States on the other side reacted strongly.[2] The court case, not to mention the final judgment in favour of the Commission's position, was extremely controversial and sent shockwaves through the European legal community.[3] In the conflict in front of the Court it was clear that most Member State governments were in intense opposition, if not outright hostile, to the idea that it could be *imposed* on them to criminalize certain behaviours.[4]

As many have argued, the ECJ is most accurately understood as generally pro-integrationist, or even activist. However, it is important to recall that scholars from both camps have also emphasized the limits of the Court's activism. An important condition for the ability to side with the Commission against the Council and the Member States is that there exist precedents in the jurisprudence of the Court. However, the observable implications of these approaches were not consistent with the dynamics of the case.

As for the formal rules in place, the Commission had very limited competencies to act in the field of JHA under the Treaties in force during this period. Thus, the central conditions posited by rational institutionalist explanations for when the Commission and Court are likely to be able to challenge the Member States were seemingly absent. Indeed, the Commission itself even pointed out that there was no precedent in this matter (Commission 2003a: 11). Furthermore, it maintained (in concert with the Council) that the Community did not have an autonomous or general competence in criminal law, but that this was only a tool in the service of Community policy (Commission 2003a: 7; 2004: 5).

Already in 1996 the Commission asked the Court to annul a JHA Joint Action, with the argument that this measure should have been based on Community law.[5] However, this time the Court instead ruled in favour of the Council and the Member States. This is especially significant since only three out of fifteen Member States[6] intervened in support of the Council as compared with eleven out of fifteen in the *environmental crimes* court case.[7] If we take the pro-integration leanings of the Court seriously, this previous case would seemingly have provided a far better opportunity to expand the competencies of the Community in the JHA field. The preferences of the collective of Member States were much less clearly expressed at that time, and the general attention attracted by the case was marginal in relation to the *environmental crimes* court case.

In fact, the intensity of the conflict in the *environmental crimes* case and the sensitivity of the issue involved would lead rationalist perspectives to expect that the Court would be unable to pursue its pro-integration preferences. It is not argued here that this case necessarily repudiates the whole idea of the Court (or the Commission) as a pro-integrationist actor in a more general sense. However, it does show that this is not enough to explain its actions, especially not in this particular instance. The intensity of the conflict also has implications for constructivist approaches that rely on the Commission's ability to mobilize bureaucratic authority. The element of social recognition that is an intrinsic part of this form of authority seemed to be questioned at its very core by more than two thirds of Member States in this case.

It is important to point out here that the Commission's arguments in front of the Court in the *environmental crimes* case were based on two central tenets. The first was that that criminal sanctions constituted a necessary element for the proper implementation of Community legislation. The second tenet was that the Council, through its statements and actions, had previously supported this position. Rather than strict invocations of formal treaty texts, legislation or the case law of the Court, the Commission's arguments relied on the largely informal consensus on EU criminal law that had emerged prior to the outbreak of conflict.

## The link between effective implementation and criminal sanctions

In its application to the ECJ (Commission 2003a),[8] the main thrust of the Commission's argument relied on an interpretation of a range of measures through which the European Community had previously sought to ensure efficient implementation through the imposition of different forms of sanctions. Thus, a central tenet of the Commission's argument revolved around sanctions as a necessary tool for the functioning of EC law.

> To guarantee the efficiency and effectiveness of Community law, infringements of Community legislation must be susceptible to being sanctioned, including through criminal law. It is that which justifies that the Community is competent to oblige the Member States to establish penal sanctions, when it concerns guaranteeing that Community law is efficiently applied.
>
> (Commission 2003a: 7)[9]

By making the efficiency argument the main pillar of its approach, the Commission established a position that was closely related to how the problems and solutions of the issue of compliance had been discussed in the EU since the 1980s, and more explicitly from the middle of the 1990s. This was not a general argument for criminal law, but the establishment of a link to the rather specific way in which the issue of criminal sanctions was introduced at the European level: efficient implementation through criminalization. It was this specificity that supplied clues as to why this argument was mobilized in the context of this institutional conflict. It was not primarily by invoking formal rules that the Commission levelled its arguments, but by supplying a very specific conceptualization of criminal law that was consonant with how the issue had been formulated previously in several instances by the Commission itself, and even more importantly, by the Council and the Member States. Thus, its position was supported by the long process in which a general consensus on this issue was established at the supranational level.

The institutional conflict in front of the Court was obviously also a legal conflict,[10] and the Commission naturally sought support in the jurisprudence of the Court. Among the cases discussed, emphasis was put on the *Greek Maize* ruling (Court 1989), especially for the way that it introduced the principle of loyal cooperation and the principle of assimilation (Commission 2003a: 8). However, the Commission's discussion of the *Greek Maize* ruling illustrates how the process of interpretation of this ruling, rather than the ruling itself, allowed for the Commission's argument. As the previous chapter on the process that led up to the outbreak of conflict in the *environmental crimes* case sought to show, the *Greek Maize* ruling became involved in a process where the gist of its fundamental argument became gradually reinterpreted through various policy statements that were formulated by both the Commission and the Council (Commission 1994a; 1995; Council 1994; 1995a).

In this context it is important to point out that the *Greek Maize* ruling did not concern the delimitation of competencies in the field of criminal law. The principle of assimilation as defined in the court ruling entailed that if a certain violation of a law was the subject of criminal penalties at the national level, violations of corresponding Community acts, adopted on the supranational level, should be punished in the same way. Consequently, in some instances, depending on the specific legal system, Community legislation would in practice have to be enforced by the use of criminal penalties.

> [W]hilst the choice of penalties remains within their (the Member States) discretion, they must ensure in particular that infringements of Community law are penalized under conditions, both procedural and substantive, which are analogous to those applicable to infringements of national law of a similar nature and importance and which in any event make the penalty effective, proportionate and dissuasive. Moreover, the national authorities must proceed, with respect to infringements of Community law, with the same diligence as that which they bring to bear in implementing corresponding laws.
>
> (Court 1989: paragraphs 24–25, quoted in Commission 2003a: 8)

Whether those sanctions would be applied through administrative or criminal law thus would depend on how the specific legal system dealt with similar offences. The fact that the Commission deduced from this that there existed a *de facto* Community competence to oblige *all* Member States to establish criminal sanctions in certain cases, irrespective of how they normally treat certain offences, would seem to stretch the argument of the ruling to its breaking point.

The Commission argued that the main result of the *Greek Maize* case was that Member States must in some cases punish a breach of Community legislation with criminal sanctions.[11] It continued to highlight other parts of the jurisprudence where the Court has elaborated on the principle of loyal cooperation and assimilation,[12] making essentially the same point: that these principles demonstrated how the enforcement of Community legislation, in some cases, requires the imposition of criminal sanctions.

A treatment of these rulings in exclusively formal terms would not tell us much about why they were mobilized or why they were later recognized by the Court as supporting the position of the Commission. However, if we instead read the *Greek Maize* ruling while taking into account the broader development through which criminal sanctions became regarded as the primary way to ensure efficient implementation, the ruling is seen in a new light. What started out as a concern with the need to ensure 'equal treatment' of Community and national legislation turned into a concern regarding the most efficient ways to ensure implementation. The most efficient way to ensure efficient implementation, identified in unison by the Council and the Commission in the previous process, was through criminal sanctions.

This means that the process of reinterpretation of the *Greek Maize* ruling resulted in a narrowing down of the choice regarding the instruments that could ensure efficient implementation. While the measures that were discussed in the late 1980s and the early 1990s referred to the imposition of either criminal *or* administrative penalties,[13] administrative penalties had seemingly lost their currency in the early 2000s. This was specifically brought out by the Commission's treatment of two fishing regulations from 1987 and 1993, which both foresaw 'administrative or penal' procedures against those committing breaches of fishing rules (Council 1987, 1993).[14] These measures treated in isolation cannot, similar to the *Greek Maize* ruling, be said to award much support to the position of a Community competence to attach criminal sanctions to Community legislation. Again, a more plausible interpretation of the original intentions behind these measures would perhaps be that *if* breaches of fishing rules were normally dealt with through criminal law in an individual Member State, then that Member State would be obliged to treat breaches to this regulation in a similar way also. Such a reading is also supported by the observation that the Commission around this time, in particular in the field of agriculture, had sought to avoid involving itself in criminal law.[15] However, read in light of the mounting preoccupation with the benefits of criminal sanctions to ensure implementation that characterized the evolution of this issue from the mid-1990s, the Commission's argument becomes more comprehensible.

### Mobilizing consensus on criminal sanctions

The Commission sought to firmly establish that the Council had long agreed, if sometimes implicitly, on the central point that the imposition of criminal sanctions represented the most effective way to ensure implementation. In doing so, the Commission mobilized a range of measures actually adopted by the Council and the Member States that pointed in this direction.

To prove its point that the Council had in fact often supported the use of criminal sanctions to implement Community legislation, the Commission examined more closely the 1991 Money Laundering Directive (Council 1991a) and the 2002 Framework Decision on Unauthorized Entry, Transit and Residence (Council 2002c). In relation to these measures, the Commission stated:

> Indeed, certain community acts foresee the obligation of Member States to establish sanctions that cannot be anything than criminal in nature, without however specifying that it is about criminal sanctions.
>
> (Commission 2003a: 11)[16]

The Commission pointed specifically to the declaration accompanying the Money Laundering Directive in which the Member States agreed to enact criminal legislation in relation to this measure (Council 1991a). It was argued, quite logically, that the whole rationale behind the Money Laundering Directive was the establishment of a common legislative framework for dealing with money laundering, and more particularly, that this would be done by imposing criminal sanctions on offenders. To support this argument, the Commission also referred to United Nations and Council of Europe conventions (Council of Europe 1990; United Nations 1988) on which the Directive was modelled, which both emphasized the need for criminal penalties.

Interestingly, the Commission also refers in this context to its own proposal for the Money Laundering Directive (Commission 1990). To recall, this proposal did contain explicit references to criminal sanctions in the actual legislative measure, which the Member States subsequently removed and placed in a separate declaration. At the time this did not lead to any overt institutional conflict, nor did it provoke any official statements on the part of the Commission. Furthermore, this proposal did not represent legislation in force, and as such lacked formal standing. However, the core of the Commission's argument here was not to prove to the Court that there was a formal competence in criminal law already established through these measures. The core of its argument was to demonstrate that the Council, like the Commission, had agreed with the fundamental assertion that criminal penalties, as opposed to the range of other types of sanctions that could be conceived of, were indeed the most effective ones. This moved the argument of the Commission outside the realm of strict legal analysis. Thus, the potential effectiveness of this argument was similar to the mobilization of the fishing instruments and the *Greek Maize* ruling dependent on the idea that the fundamental objective of these measures was to equip a certain policy field with criminal sanctions. The Money Laundering Directive and the twin measures on Unauthorized Entry served the role of demonstrating that the Council had recurrently affirmed the need for criminal sanctions to implement acts adopted within the supranational framework of the EU.

The Commission finally emphasized the central position of the protection of the environment for the Community and highlighted several of the measures that were listed in the annex to its proposal for a Directive on environmental crimes (Commission 2003a: 5). Thus, it emphasized not only the importance of the policy itself but also the long history of Community action in this area and its endemic implementation problems. In this sense, and similar to how the competing Directive on environmental crimes was framed, it seems clear that this policy area was a well-established part of Community policymaking, and lends weight to the Commission's position, as the protection of the environment is formulated as forming part of the very 'norms of the community'(Commission 2003a: 5, 10). This part of the Commission's argument also turns towards a somewhat more conventional conception of criminal law. Rather than being exclusively about efficient implementation, the fundamental norms of the Community are invoked.

To summarize then, the attack of the Commission was based on two central tenets: the importance of criminal sanctions for effective implementation of Community law, and the Council's previous agreement on this point. The Commission's position was supported only partially by jurisprudence and the legislation in force. The most important element that enabled the Commission to argue for a *de facto* competence in criminal law was the process through which certain pieces of jurisprudence, notably the *Greek Maize* ruling, had been gradually reinterpreted. The *Greek Maize* ruling was crucial for moving discussions on sanctions and later criminal law to the supranational level. The ruling had been an important point from which widespread consensus on the importance of criminal sanctions had been developed. It was in light of this previous consensus that the arguments of the Commission became more comprehensible. In terms of the formal rules in place, it was the constitutive, rather than exclusively regulative, aspects that explain the mobilization of these arguments by the Commission.

## The arguments of the Council: an uphill struggle

It was within the arguments of the Council that the constraints produced by the previous process of institutionalization emerged more clearly.[17] While this process seemed to have produced an abundance of material to support the Commission's position, the Council was pushed into a position that it had trouble getting out of and which appeared difficult to defend. This made possible the ruling of the Court in favour of the Commission, which moved the issue of criminal sanctions within the supranational framework of the EU.

The Council had in many previous instances supported the notion that criminal sanctions represented the most efficient way to ensure proper implementation. However, before the Court, the Council was pushed to defend the position that the general requirement to guarantee efficient implementation does not in itself necessitate the imposition of criminal sanctions, as opposed to other forms of sanctions. This argument came across as contradictory in light of its previous actions in this area.

> [T]he Council emphasizes that, due to the different legal traditions, the choice to resort to one or the other type of sanctions (administrative or penal) does not say anything by itself, about its character as efficient, proportionate and dissuasive which depends in fact on the context of the legal system in which it intervenes.
>
> (Council 2003a: 12)[18]

The Council supplied an argument that was based on what can be referred to as a more literal reading of the *Greek Maize* ruling. Its argument relied on a reading of the ruling itself rather than a reading that also included how it was subsequently reinterpreted through the institutionalization process of EU criminal law. It thus sought to contest the Commission's argument that effectively used the ruling to bring in criminal sanctions by the back door.

> The fact that, for one or several Member State(s), the application of the principle of assimilation can translate itself into a de facto necessity, to foresee criminal sanctions, does not legally prove, according to the Council, that the Community is competent to oblige (all) the Member States to foresee criminal sanctions, and criminal sanctions only, to sanction certain behaviours.
>
> (Council 2003a : 14)[19]

According to the Council, both the Community legislation in force as well as the jurisprudence of the Court showed that the choice of penalties rested with the Member States (Council 2003a: 8).[20] It agreed that the principle of assimilation and loyal cooperation, as defined in the *Greek Maize* ruling, might limit that choice, since in view of these principles infringements to Community legislation must be sanctioned in a similar way as equivalent national legislation. However, it maintained that

> this jurisprudence confirms that in the current state of the Treaty, the Community is not competent to meddle in the choice between criminal sanctions and administrative sanctions, a choice that can only be made at the national level, by the national legislator, taking into account all relevant elements of the national legal system, elements that determine the possibility of one rather than the other.
>
> (Council 2003a: 11)[21]

But in relation to the Commission's argument, the Council struggled against the wind to supply a convincing argument to the effect that criminal sanctions are not a necessary or important element of efficient implementation. The rationale of the contested Framework Decision on the Protection of the Environment through Criminal Law was indisputably that there *was* a need to deal with infringements of the rules protecting the environment through *criminal*, and not administrative, sanctions. At its foundation this decision aimed at reinforcing a legislative act that had been adopted within the supranational framework of the EU through the imposition of criminal sanctions. The argument of the Council, as the Commission also pointed out in its response (Commission 2003b: 3), seems slightly contradictory to the logic behind enacting this type of legislation in the first place.

Furthermore, the character of the Framework Decision in compelling Member States to enact *criminal* legislation to protect the environment also had its base in the Council of Europe Convention, which, in its aim and content, is more or less identical with that of the Framework Decision. The Convention relied on the fundamental notion that civil and administrative sanctions were not enough and that there was a need to agree on criminalizing certain breaches of environmental legislation. The Council thus struggled to supply a convincing argument in this context that *administrative* sanctions are equally efficient as criminal sanctions, while at the same time defending a measure that identified criminal sanctions as the most efficient when enacting legislation for environmental protection.

The Council's support for the general notion that criminal sanctions were indeed necessary in many cases to ensure proper enforcement of EC legislation was also demonstrated by the Commission. The Commission pointed to the several issues that had preceded the Framework Decision on the Protection of the Environment through Criminal Law, and in particular to the Framework Decision on Unauthorized Entry (Commission 2003a). The general aim of these measures was arguably to equip Community acts with criminal sanctions.

As a response to the Commission's arguments regarding the Council's support for the use of criminal sanctions, the Council attempted to demonstrate that the Commission had also at times argued for the efficiency of *administrative* penalties. However, its evidence for this claim did not seem to match that which was brought on by the Commission. To support its position, the Council cited a Commission working document from 1993, where it was stated that in some cases administrative penalties can be as efficient as penal sanctions (Commission 1993a cited in Council 2003a: 12). The Council continued by pointing out:

> The variations in the nature of sanctions (administrative or criminal) or their gravity (fines, imprisonment) can continue to exist in the different Member States, as long as they are sufficiently effective, proportionate and dissuasive.
> (Council 2003a: 12)[22]

The very essence of the process of institutionalization that led up to the conflict in the *environmental crimes* case was the gradual consolidation of the link between criminal sanctions and efficiency. It was on this point that a consensus which transgressed institutional boundaries had emerged. In its defence before the Court, the Council tried to disentangle this link. It thus levelled an argument against the taken-for-granted point around which much of the discussions on European criminal law had revolved for more than a decade: the notion that sanctions enacted through criminal law was per definition more likely to ensure efficient implementation than other forms of sanctions.

The Council and the Member States seemed trapped by the fact that they had in so many instances appeared in support of the general idea of reinforcing the supranational policies of the EU through criminal law. Even its own Legal Service, which was tasked with arguing for the position of the Council, had explicitly supported this idea. In a 2001 opinion the Council Legal Service largely supported the position, argued for by the Commission, that it was indeed possible for the Community legislator to impose on Member States the use of criminal sanctions to assure the effective implementation of Community law:

> The line taken by the Council Legal Service on this point has always been that, if the Community legislator considers that the only way of ensuring compliance with Community rules is to impose criminal penalties, it has the legal capacity to require Member States to impose such penalties.
>
> (Council 2001f: 2)[23]

The discrepancies between the Council's arguments before the Court and its actions in other settings was also demonstrated by the outcomes of the negotiations on the Constitutional Treaty that emerged in parallel to the conflict before the Court. The division of competencies that was so hotly debated in relation to the Framework Decision on the protection of the environment through criminal law had already been settled and included in the foreseen Article III-172.2 of the Constitutional Treaty. Most importantly, the Treaty was signed by *all* fifteen Member States in June of 2004.[24] This was something that the Commission pointed out in its observations on the arguments of the intervening Member States in the *environmental crimes* case:

> [A]rticle III-172.2 concerns the minimal rules for the definition of criminal infringements and sanctions in the areas that have been the object of harmonisation measures. These minimal rules are formulated as instrumental and incidental in relation to Union policy, and in that sense, the Commission reads article III-172.2 as a declaratory disposition which confirms the present Community competence.
>
> (Commission 2004: 7)[25]

This served as a clear demonstration that not only had the idea of the relation between implementation and the imposition of sanctions become part of the common sense of policy debates, but also the associated idea of the need for criminal law as part of this enterprise. Thus, while the Council was busy arguing in front of the Court that the Community had no business in the field of criminal law, the Member States had included those competencies in the future Treaty. The Council stated that in view of the specificity and importance of criminal law in the legal systems of the Member States, it was of little importance what the Commission assumed was implied by existing measures. Instead, it argued, any competence would have had to be attributed *explicitly* to the Community (Council 2003a: 15). However, as the ruling of the Court would demonstrate, this implied competence, as brought about by the development of the consensus on criminal sanctions, would prevail.

In sum, the Council faced considerable difficulties in levelling an effective defence against the Commission. Essentially it was forced to present an argument that ran contrary to how it had approached the issue of criminal sanctions in the past. The fundamental justification for bringing criminal sanctions to the supranational level had most often been for its purported efficiency as an implementation tool. In the face of the arguments of the Commission that seemed to flow naturally from the process of institutionalization, the Council was pushed into a position that came across as self-contradictory.

## The judgment of the Court: supranationalization of criminal sanctions

The ruling of the Court formally moved criminal sanctions out of the hands of the Member States and into the supranational framework of the EU. The ruling thus affirmed the Commission's arguments which were based on the notion of the intrinsic link between criminal sanctions and effective implementation. The Council's attempt to deny this link based on a more literal reading of the formal rules in place found little resonance in the Court. While the Court did affirm the position of the Commission, it also put particular emphasis on the importance of the policy field of the environment.[26] It thus emphasized a part of the Commission's argument that was concerned with a more conventional justification for the use of criminal law, namely the invocation of fundamental norms of a given community that are in need of special protection.[27] This element of the ruling indicates that the particular policy area where the institutional conflict arose also shaped the possibility of the Court in terms of the formal rules in place, to rule in favour of the Commission. In paragraph 41 of the judgment, the Court cites several rulings from the 1980s and states that it is common ground that the protection of the environment 'constitutes an essential objective of the Community'. In paragraph 42 it states again along the same lines, citing the TEU, that

> [e]nvironmental protection requirements must be integrated into the definition and implementation of the Community policies and activities, a provision which emphasises the fundamental nature of that objective and its extension across the range of those policies and activities.
>
> (Court 2005a)

The other element of the Court's argument was more closely tied to the main arguments of the Commission, and more specifically to the reinterpretation of the *Greek Maize* ruling. The Court argued, perfectly in line with the reinterpretation in the mid-1990s of the principle of assimilation brought from the *Greek Maize* ruling, that while criminal law as a policy area in its own right does not fall within the sphere of the Community, the use of sanctions and criminal sanctions in particular is sometimes necessary to ensure the effective implementation of Community policy. Thus, in paragraph 47 the Court argues that 'neither criminal law nor the rules of criminal procedure fall within the Community's competence' but adding in the very next paragraph:

> However, the last-mentioned finding does not prevent the Community legislature, when the application of effective, proportionate and dissuasive criminal penalties by the competent national authorities is an essential measure for combating serious environmental offences, from taking measures which relate to the criminal law of the Member States which it considers necessary in order to ensure that the rules which it lays down on environmental protection are fully effective.
>
> (Court 2005a)

In paragraph 52 of its judgment, the Court once more reiterated that harmonisation of criminal law cannot be ruled out 'where it is necessary in order to ensure the effectiveness of Community law'. The wide variety of factors that made up the messy process through which criminal sanctions were established as a commonsense part of efficient implementation of EC law had created the conditions for the Court to take this decision in the particular case.

The ruling thus validated not only the Commission's position, but represented a defining point in an incremental process that had gone on since the mid-1970s; a process in which the Council had at times played a crucial role. What is striking is the seemingly marginal importance of case law and legislation in force. Rather, as was argued above, the important aspects of the Commission's argument were indeed based on the process through which the *Greek Maize* case and the Money Laundering Directive had been reinterpreted over time, as opposed to a literal reading of those texts. The reinterpreted version of the ruling and the two fishing instruments of 1987 and 1993 were also what the Court leaned on and consequently enabled it to rule the way it did. That is, both the Commission's and the Court's arguments went beyond a narrow definition of institutions as mainly institutional rules; or a strict legal analysis. Without a grasp of the gradual process of reinterpretation that had taken place in relation to these acts, it would have been difficult to make sense of the ruling of the Court.

## Chapter summary

With the move of the conflict to the European Court of Justice, the Commission on the one hand and the Council and the Member States on the other emerged as clearly unified actors pursuing their explicitly defined preferences. However, as the analysis demonstrated, the longer process of institutionalization which had preceded the conflict made itself felt. In spite of the fact that the Commission and the Council had coalesced around their institutionally defined roles, the previous instances, wherein these roles had been far more ambiguous, shaped the conflict in important ways. The constitutive elements of the previous institutionalization process provided important clues not only regarding how the respective agents mobilized particular arguments in support of their positions, but also regarding the extent to which those arguments were effective.

The Commission could point to a range of instances where the Council had actually agreed on the conceptual issue of the need for criminal sanctions as an implementation tool for Community legislation. This included the Money Laundering Directive of 1991 as well as the several acts adopted after the Amsterdam Treaty, of which the Framework Decision on environmental crimes had been the last. This of course strengthened the Commission's position in front of the Court. More importantly, it also radically limited the options of the Council to defend itself. The Council's attempt to mobilize a literal and formal legal reading of these measures and the *Greek Maize* ruling had little traction.

The conflict was tilted in favour of the Commission in ways that would not have been clear at all if we had maintained the notion of the Court as a pro-integration actor in general and the notion of institutions as primarily regulative. It was before the Court that the process through which the issue of criminal sanctions had been reinterpreted at the EU level became important. Not only did this significantly shape how the Commission argued its case, but it also in a very tangible sense shaped how the Council and the Member States formulated their respective defences.

**Macro 1**: Inter-institutional consensus on the need for criminal sanctions for efficient implementation of Community legislation.

**Macro 2**: The move of criminal sanctions within the supranational framework of the EU.

**Micro 1**: The prior consensus on criminal sanctions makes the Council's argument to the contrary unconvincing. The Commission can mobilize its arguments in consonance with how the issue of criminal law has been institutionalized.

**Micro 2**: The prior consensus enables the Court to recognize the position of the Commission.

*Figure 7.1* Summary of the *environmental crimes* court case

In short, the previous process through which criminal sanctions had become institutionalized at the European level now shaped the actions of the agents involved in particular ways. The consensus on the efficiency of criminal sanctions enabled certain interpretations of existing legislation and jurisprudence that seemed more convincing than others. The Council was pushed into a corner by the Commission's argument and was effectively forced to supply interpretations of the existing rules that seemed to contradict its own past actions and statements in this field. The different aspects of this argument are summarized in Figure 7.1, in an effort to disentangle more specifically how macro-level developments, in this case the incremental process of institutionalization, created specific dispositions that shaped the dynamics on the level of agents. By relating the arguments underlying the positions of the Commission and Council as well as the final Court decision to what we know about the process that brought the agents to this institutional conflict, we have a sense of why the Commission mobilized its specific arguments. It also clarifies why the Council had problems of levelling a proper defence, and consequently, what allowed the Court to rule in favour of the Commission.

## Notes

1 Administrative sanctions in this context generally concern fines or the revocation of licenses, and are primarily directed at companies. The imposition of criminal sanctions is generally surrounded by stricter procedural rules, and also includes, besides the imposition of fines, incarceration. Furthermore, criminal sanctions within environmental law are able to target specific individuals, such as the presidents of firms.

2 No less than eleven Member States of the then fifteen intervened in support of the Council. Italy, Luxembourg, Belgium and Austria did not intervene.

3 See Apps (2006), Dawes and Lynskey (2008), Herlin-Kernell (2007), Ryland (2009) and Wasmeier and Thwaites (2004) for legal analyses of the case. It should be noted that a considerable amount of attention from the legal Community was given to the struggle over what was then known as article 47 TEU. The article was designed to protect the Community from encroachments by intergovernmental policies. While this article was indeed central to the case, the present analysis focuses on the conflict over the interpretation of criminal law that underlies this conflict.

4 This hostility became perhaps even more visible in the subsequent *ship-source pollution* case (Case C-440/05 *Commission v Council*) in which the Commission challenged a 2005 Council Framework Decision to strengthen the criminal-law framework for the enforcement of laws against ship-source pollution (Council 2005d).

5 The so-called *Airport transit visa* case (Court 1998).

6 The intervening Member States were Denmark, France and the United Kingdom.

7 It should be noted that the Netherlands, while supporting the Council in the *environmental crimes* court case, did argue that in instances where it can positively be demonstrated that the criminal sanctions are intrinsically linked to reaching the objectives of a Community act, the Community is indeed competent to prescribe such penalties (Kingdom of Netherlands 2003: 4). However, it continued to argue that this was not the case in the contested Framework Decision.

8 The Commission initiated its legal action against the Council on April 14, 2003.

9 '*Pour garantir l'effectivité et l'efficacité du droit communautaire, il faut que les infractions à la législation communautaire soient susceptibles d'être sanctionnées, y compris de manière pénale. C'est ce qui justifie que les communautés soient compétentes pour*

*obliger les Etats membres à instaurer des sanctions pénales, quand il s'agit de gar-antir que le droit communautaire est appliqué efficacement'.*

10  Indeed, from a strictly juridical point of view the *environmental crimes* court case revolved around the interpretation of what was then article 47 TEU (article 40 TEU under the current treaty).

11  Commission (2003a: 8).

12  More specifically, the Court's rulings in the so-called *Zwartveld* case (Court 1990: paragraph 17) and *Nunes and Matos* (Court 1999: paragraphs 9–11).

13  Again, the ultimate choice of penalties would depend on how the legal systems of Member States treated similar offences.

14  The Commission also refers to a range of measures in agriculture and transport, where sanctions have more commonly included the withdrawal of licenses.

15  Interview Commission official, DG JLS (Respondent 42).

16  '*En effet, certains actes communautaires prévoient l'obligation pour les Etats mem-bres d'instaurer des sanctions qui ne peuvent être que de nature pénale, sans toutefois qu'il soit précisé qu'il s'agit de sanctions pénale'.*

17  On July 1, 2003 the Council submitted its defence in the *environmental crimes* court case to the ECJ (Council 2003b).

18  '*[L]e Conseil souligne que, compte tenu de ces différentes traditions juridiques, le choix du recours à l'un ou l'autre type de sanction (administrative ou pénal) ne dit rien, de par lui-même, sur le caractère effectif, proportionne et dissuasif des sanctions qui dépend en fait du contexte du système juridique dans lequel il intervient'.*

19  '*Le fait qu'une application du principe d'assimilation puisse se traduire en un néces-sité de fait, pour un ou plusieurs État Membre(s), de prévoir des sanctions pénales, ne prouve pas, selon le Conseil, sur le plan juridique que la Communauté soit compétente pour obliger (tous) États Membres à prévoir des sanctions pénales et seulement sanc-tions pénales, pour sanctionner certains comportements'.*

20  Very similar variations of this theme were reiterated in the interventions of the Member States.

21  '*Le Conseil constate que cette jurisprudence confirme que la Communauté n'est pas, en l'état actuel du traité, compétente pour s'immiscer dans le choix entre des sanctions pénale et des sanctions administratives, choix qui n'est peut qu'être fait qu'au niveau national, par le législateur national, en prenant compte tous les éléments du système juridique national applicable, éléments qui notamment déterminent l'opportunité de l'une plutôt que de l'autre voie'.*

22  '*les sanctions variables quant à leur nature (administrative, pénales) ou leur gravité (amende, emprisonnement) peuvent continuer à exister dans les diverse États mem-bres, pourvu qu'elles aient une caractère suffisamment effective, proportionné et dissuasif'.*

23  Its opinion differed only with that expressed by the Commission in its proposal for a Directive on the same issue, on the point of determining the level of penalties.

24  That is, a full year before the Court issued its ruling in the environmental crimes case.

25  '*[L]'article III-172.2 porte sur les règles minimales relatives à la définition des infractions pénales et des sanctions dans des domaines ayant fait l'objet de mesures d'harmonisation. Ces règles minimales sont présentées comme instrumentales et accessoires par rapport aux politiques de l'Union et, en ce sens, la Commission lit l'article III-172.2 comme une disposition déclaratoire, qui consacre l'actuelle com-pétence communautaire'.* The provisions on criminal law that today are inscribed in articles 82 and 83 of the TFEU were originally drafted in working group ten of the Convention on the future of Europe in 2002 and are almost identical to the correspond-ing articles in the Draft Constitutional Treaty.

26  In this case (in contrast to the *small arms* court case) the Court argued largely in con-sonance with the opinion of the Advocate-General (AG) (Court 2005a). AG Colomer

put considerable weight on the centrality of environmental protection for the Community. However, he also reiterated the central notion in the Commission's argument that criminal penalties were the most effective in this case and would thus represent the *only* option for effectively enforcing environmental legislation (Court 2005: paragraph 84).

27  The ruling in the *environmental crimes* court case would become the object of an interpretive battle between the Commission and the Council where the Commission interpreted the ruling as a general competence to issue criminal sanctions (Commission 2005c) and the Council and the Member States sought to restrict it to the field of environment policy. This eventually led the Commission to initiate a follow-up case, the so-called *ship-source pollution* case (Court 2007b).

# 8 The *small arms* case

In 2008 the European Court of Justice decided, in favour of the Commission, that there was a Community competence in the field of anti-proliferation of small arms and light weapons in third countries, a field that the Council and many Member States argued was quintessentially part of the CFSP.

Similar to the institutional conflict in the *environmental crimes* case, it is not entirely easy to square this outcome with the assumptions of rationalist institutionalist approaches. It remains unclear how the Court would be able to contradict the Member States and side with the Commission in this extremely sensitive field, especially in light of the fact that the preferences of the Council and the Member States were so clearly defined and diverged radically from those of the Commission. Instead, the analysis in this chapter demonstrates that the conflict in the *small arms* case was fundamentally shaped by the specific ways in which the issue of SALW had become implicated in the consensus on the intrinsic link between security and development. These connections explain why specific arguments were mobilized by the Commission and why they were ultimately successful.

In contrast to the conflict in the *environmental crimes* case, which was very much shaped by the process through which the European project had been transformed, the arguments in the *small arms* court case were more intimately connected with 'external' factors. Both the Commission's arguments and the final ruling of the Court were fundamentally shaped by considerations of professional practices emanating from the international development sphere. This recourse to informal professional practices rather than law was made possible by the way in which both the Commission and the Council had previously engaged in characterizations of the fundamental goals of anti-SALW policies as intrinsically connected to development cooperation.

## Beyond formal rules and a pro-integration Court

Because of the intensity of the conflict, it is not only rationalist approaches that have difficulties in explaining the decision of the Court. Constructivist approaches, relying on framing and persuasion and the effects of bureaucratic authority, seem ill-equipped to explain how the Court could take such a controversial decision in favour of the Commission in the context of a sharply defined institutional conflict. Reactions to the case being brought to the Court were in some instances rather strong, particularly from the UK, which sought to convince the President of the Commission to discontinue the case.[1] As one Commission official at the time of the case put it, 'Some Member States really took this as a declaration of war!'[2] The Opinion delivered by Advocate General Mengozzi in the *small arms* case captured these tensions, stating:

> The bitter dispute between, in particular, the Commission and the United Kingdom Government concerning the interpretation of Article 47 TEU appears to be only the visible part of a more fundamental difference regarding the structure of the European Union.
>
> (Court 2007a: paragraph 84)

It is obvious that some Member States and in particular the UK were extremely provoked by the legal action taken by the Commission. As one respondent who represented Parliament and, regarding the pleadings of the UK, was present at the pleadings before the Court stated:[3]

> Pleadings were sometimes going beyond strict legal arguments; . . . saying [instead] that if the Court was to agree with the Commission and the Parliament, this would have dramatic consequences on the future of the external action policy of the Union because the Member States would be very reluctant to use the CFSP measures.[4]

Arguments, framing and persuasion, as conceptualized by constructivists, only become comprehensible if they are tied to wider structures of meaningful behaviour and if they enjoy a certain amount of social legitimacy. In this case, it seems as if social legitimacy was fundamentally questioned by the intensity with which arguments were levelled, especially on the part of the Council and the Member States. From this point of view it is far from evident that the Court would be comfortable with supporting the Commission.

The notion of the Court as an inherent pro-integration actor also seems rather unhelpful. The Court had not long before explicitly stating it had no competencies in the CFSP (European Court of the First Instance 2004: paragraph 35–40). The prior case concerned the much referred to 'terrorist-lists' where persons and organizations suspected of terrorism had their financial assets frozen as a result of Common Positions taken by the Council under the CFSP. Thus, these cases were not completely comparable to the *small arms* case. However, the fact remains that the Court argued it had no jurisdiction to review the applicants' claims for damages for being erroneously placed on the list as the result of the Council's Common Position (Court 2007: paragraphs 61–62). In this context it is important to note that with the Common Position there was a Council declaration annexed, and this specifically indicated the affected parties' right to judicial remedies in cases where they had been wrongfully included on the list (Council 2001f: 3). In spite of this declaration, a pointer from the Council that could indeed have been interpreted as an opening for the Court to enter into this field, the Court explicitly argued that a declaration of the Council 'could not suffice to confer jurisdiction on the Court to hear and determine an action for damages under Title VI of the EU Treaty' (Court 2007: paragraph 61). Arguably, if the Court had nurtured a stable pro-integration drive, it seems plausible to argue that it could have created an important precedent in the field of the CFSP through this ruling.[5]

As regards the formal rules in place at the time of the *small arms* case, there was not much that would explain the decision of the Court from the perspective of rationalist approaches. There were no clear precedents in the jurisprudence of the Court nor was there anything in the treaties which would allow the Court to affirm the position of the Commission. On the contrary, the separation between the Community structure and the CFSP was even more pronounced than that between the Community and the JHA. This being said, an important part of the institutional conflict revolved around competing interpretations of article 47 TEU.[6] This article was designed to 'protect' the *acquis communautaire* from encroachments from the intergovernmental policy fields. Basically, it was formulated so as to prevent Member States from legislating in areas which had already been made part of the Community structure. From this perspective, then, this article created the conditions for struggles over decision-making competencies. However, on the basis of the existence of this article, we cannot say anything in particular regarding what conditioned the Commission to mobilize certain arguments in the context of the *small arms* court case. Nor does it say much regarding what made it possible for the Court to rule in favour of the Commission in this case.

## The *small arms* court case and the impact of the security–development link

The *small arms* court case came to revolve more around how to define the issue of SALW in relation to the security–development link rather than in relation to the formal rules in place. The arguments of the Commission which shaped the conflict reveal a rather weak connection to formal legislation and treaty texts. Rather, these arguments were made possible by the process through which the largely informal consensus on the security–development link in the EU had been established. It is in light of this process that the Commission's arguments before the Court become understandable.

### *Evolution of development practice and reformulation of weapons proliferation*

The Commission's arguments in the *small arms* case relied heavily on informal professional practices rather than strictly legal reasoning.[7] The Commission argued that the boundaries of what constituted a security issue and an issue of development cooperation respectively were fluid and could ultimately be ascertained by

understanding the impact of a specific phenomenon on the prospects for sustainable development.

From the perspective of the Commission, any policy issue, no matter how
ingrained in the sphere of traditional security policy, could potentially be considered a development issue as long as it negatively affected the possibilities for
sustainable development. The Commission stated in its application to the Court
(Commission 2005a: footnote 35) and then later in its reply (Commission 2005b:
17) that, for instance, policies of anti-proliferation of weapons of mass destruction (WMDs) are not to be considered as falling under EC development, mainly
because the spread of WMDs is fundamentally different from the spread of SALW
in terms of its societal effects. The latter constitutes a 'grass roots problem', which
is the reason why 'many actions against the spread of SALW become an integral
part of development cooperation' (Commission 2006a: 5).

On the basis of this practice-based argument, the Commission attempted to 'de-
securitize' the issue of non-proliferation of small arms and light weapons.[8] From
this perspective, the notion that anti-SALW measures might be connected to the
objective of creating the conditions for sustainable development was mobilized to
support the argument that this policy field had become part of the Community's
development cooperation policy.

It is important to note that the Commission did not claim that the Community
had the right to act in the field of security. The crucial point of its argument was
not that there was a Community competence in the field of security, but that the
policy on non-proliferation of small arms and light weapons did not, in fact, have
security as its main objective, but sustainable development. Thus, it stated:

> It is clear . . . that EC development policy is not <u>pursuing</u> the objective of
> small arms non-proliferation as such, but is *using* small arms non-proliferation
> and disarmament to reach the . . . objectives of EC development policy, such
> as sustainable economic and social development.
>
> (Commission 2005b: 7, underlining in original)

The Commission elaborated its argument on the basis of institutionalized professional practices and common perceptions of the issue of SALW in the field of
development cooperation to demonstrate a legal development. Thus, the Commission established rather clearly the position that this was not just a struggle
between competing claims regarding the limits of a specific policy field, but also
a struggle over the legitimate basis of interpretation for making such claims. The
underlying principle for this line of argumentation is exemplified by the following statement in the Commission's application. It refers to how the 2000 Cotonou Agreement addressed small arms proliferation as a hindrance to development
objectives:

> Such developments in Community policy in respect of Development Coop-
> eration should not be cause of surprise; they are a natural adaptation to the
> changed circumstances with which development policy is confronted. ( . . .)

Community policy with respect to Development Cooperation must be able to follow the general development of that policy and make use of new instruments that the Member States also use; otherwise it will be doomed to atrophy.

(Commission 2005a: 18)

In this context, the Commission also drew on the case law of the Court, and more specifically the opinion of the ECJ in the so-called *natural rubber* case of 1979. This case involved addressing the Common Commercial Policy in which the Court stated:

[It] would no longer be possible to carry on any worthwhile common commercial policy if the Community were not in a position to avail itself also of more elaborate means devised with a view to furthering the development of international trade.

(Court 1979: paragraph 44)

Thus, the Commission highlighted that there was indeed a principle of *implied* powers that had a legal precedence in the jurisprudence of the Court. Examined more closely, this argument is based on a curious mix of formal rules and informal practices. The Commission essentially mobilized a legal precedent of the Court to argue for the redundancy of legal precedents in determining the scope of Community policies. This was thus part of the broader strategy of the Commission to demonstrate that the evolution of development practice was a more important reference point than the explicit powers conferred on the Community by the Member States. In particular, it pointed to instances where this was clearly manifested, not least in the Cotonou Agreement. The Commission relied heavily on a paragraph in the Cotonou Agreement which read:

[P]articular emphasis shall be given to the fight against anti-personnel landmines as well as to addressing an excessive and uncontrolled spread, illegal trafficking and accumulation of small arms and light weapons.

(Cotonou Agreement, article 11)

In the Commission's view, the Cotonou Agreement was a pure development agreement.[9] The inclusion of these articles in SALW was thus taken by the Commission to support the argument that the issue of SALW had been incorporated in the Community's development cooperation policy. The Commission thus argued in its application for a more organic view of how policy fields, and by implication the delimitation of competencies, evolve. To further support this position it cited documents that had been produced by various bodies of the UN as well as the OECD, and which pointed to the widespread idea that security and development are intimately connected (Commission 2005b: 11; United Nations 2002, 2003).

It also mobilized the recurrent references to the link between security and development that can be found since the late 1990s in a range of different documents and legislative acts produced within the EU, and by the Council in particular. One of the most important ones was the preamble to the contested Council decision of 2004, which stated:

> The excessive and uncontrolled accumulation and spread of small arms and light weapons poses a threat to peace and security and reduces the prospects for *sustainable development*; this is particularly the case in West Africa.
>
> (Council 2004e, italics added)

However, there was also a range of other documents of a more general character that seemed to support the notion of the intimate links between security and development. Those documents included the 2003 European Security Strategy (Council 2003d), the 2005 European Consensus on Development (Council 2005a) and the 2006 EU SALW strategy (Council 2006a). In response to the UK's rather fiercely argued intervention in support of the Council, the Commission argued that the use of the 'reality on the ground in developing countries' as a basis for determining the scope of development policies, while 'abhorrent' to the UK,

> would seem to the Commission an entirely legitimate and realistic approach, especially in an eminently practical subject-matter as development cooperation. If one cannot base oneself on such elements, where *can* the basis for interpretation be found?
>
> (Commission 2006b: 10)

Throughout its argument, the Commission consistently downplayed the security aspects of SALW action. Instead, it referred to the problem of the spread of SALW in developing countries as a 'grass roots problem' (Commission 2006b: 5). It also emphasized the need to take into account the reality 'on the ground' in the interpretation of what constitutes a security and a development issue respectively (Commission 2006b: 10). The Commission thus established clear links to the process through which a broad consensus had emerged on the intrinsic link between security and development. More particularly, it did so by pointing to the instances where the Council had actively participated in spreading this notion, especially in the field of SALW. The implication for the Commission was that the issue of SALW could be partially addressed within the EU's supranational framework.

## The triumph of professional practice over law

In contrast to the Commission, the Council levelled a set of arguments that was, as a general characterization, sternly legalistic. Its position was prompted by the Commission's broad definitional discussion on how to conceptualize SALW policies.[10] In an attempt to shield itself from the rather obvious discrepancies between its previous and current position on this issue, the Council narrowed the basis of interpretation for the definition of the development policy field, excluding everything but legally binding acts. Furthermore, in sharp contrast to how the issue of

SALW had been generally conceptualized ever since its introduction at the EU level, it insisted on the inherent 'securityness' of anti-SALW measures. These contradictions made it possible for the Court to take its decision in favour of the Commission, thus acknowledging a supranational competence in the field of SALW.

### The legalism of the Council: a last line of defence

The Commission's case depended crucially on its ability to show that there was a well-recognized link between security and development in general and more specifically between development policy and the field of SALW. The Council was more or less forced to take on the rather difficult task of denying this link. Instead, it reiterated repeatedly that anti-proliferation measures were exclusively about security, even to the point of mischaracterizing the Commission's argument, which rather more subtly held that the Commission did not claim a competence to pursue security objectives, only development ones. Nonetheless the Council argued:

> [F]or the Council it is simply not the case that the fight against small arms and light weapons representing a threat to peace and international security constitutes an area of Community competence, potential or otherwise.
>
> (Council 2005c: 4)

In a similar vein, this slight mischaracterization appears in relation to the Council's arguments regarding the *natural rubber* case; an ECJ ruling which the Commission mobilized to support its argument that concrete professional practices can help determine the scope of a particular policy field. The Council disputed that this case could be applied to broaden the scope of the Community's development cooperation policy. In doing so, however, it departed from how the Commission actually conceptualizes the issue of SALW.

> The Council does not accept that the same reasoning can be applied to the attempted broadening of the development cooperation policy by the Commission to include disarmament and non-proliferation *objectives* within its scope.
>
> (Council 2005c: 8, italics added)

The Council refused to acknowledge that the *small arms* case was actually and to a significant degree a definitional struggle where the scope of the *competing* concepts of security and development were to be fleshed out. Perhaps more precisely, it did not allow itself to recognize that such a struggle over concepts could not be confined exclusively to legal analysis. Instead, it held tightly to the idea that SALW was *by definition* an issue pertaining to the security field. This position was of course extremely difficult to maintain given the Council's own participation to the contrary on numerous occasions.

Already in the preamble of the 1998 Joint Action on small arms and light weapons (Council 1999a), which was the basis of the Council decisions in the field of SALW, the relation between measures against small arms and light weapons and the possibilities for sustainable development was explicitly mentioned. It stated that this phenomenon 'poses a threat to peace and security and reduces the prospects of sustainable development in many regions of the world' (Council 1999a). The preamble also spoke of the need for an 'integrated approach to security and development'. In the Joint Action it was also stated that the Council and the Commission would be responsible for the consistency of the actions in the field of small arms, especially in 'regard to its development policies' (Council 1999a: article 9).

Other than that, the measure mainly foresaw financial and technical assistance to programmes carried out by the Red Cross, and by the UN (Council 1999a: article 6). It was also stated that the Council noted that the Commission would work towards achieving the objectives of the action 'where appropriate' by Community measures (Council 1999a: article 8). As the Commission had argued, the Joint Action, while of course being adopted under the CFSP, clearly did not rely on any strict delimitation between the security aspects on the one hand and the development aspects on the other. Not only did the formulations of the preamble indicate this, but there were also several references to the Commission's role in using community instruments to implement the Joint Action.

The Council, however, sought to circumvent the arguments of the Commission that were based on the preamble of the 1998 Joint Action. To do this, it referred to a 2002 Joint Action (Council 2002a), which repealed the Joint Action of 1998. The reason for the adoption of the 2002 Joint Action had been the rather technical issue of the need to also include ammunition in the anti-SALW efforts, which was not covered by the 1998 Joint Action. Aside from the inclusion of ammunitions, the 2002 Joint Action was more or less identical to its predecessor, except for that one important feature. The preamble was minimal in size and did not draw out the overarching goals or reiterate the rather elaborate arguments of the 1998 Joint Action. According to the Council, the 1998 Joint Action did not have any relevance to the case. It argued that since this legislative act had been repealed by the 2002 Joint Action, it could not as such be consulted for guidance in the matter.[11]

This legalistic interpretation was, however, gainsaid by the emergence in the 2000s of several high profile documents that pointed to the widespread perception of the intimate connections between security and development. One example is the *European Security Strategy* (ESS) of 2003, largely authored by the office of the High Representative for the CFSP, the former NATO Secretary General Javier Solana.[12] Another was a document produced in 2005 by the Member States as well as the Commission and the European Parliament, called the *European Consensus on Development* (Council 2005a). In both these documents it was made clear that development and security were intimately interlinked and development was far more than just the alleviation of poverty. While the causal relationship in the ESS was formulated as unidirectional (no development without security) (Council 2003a: 2) in the 'Consensus' this was formulated explicitly as bi-directional, claiming:

> Without peace and security, development and poverty eradication are not possible, and without development and poverty eradication, no sustainable peace will occur.
>
> (Council 2005a: 8)

The ESS was published in 2003, two years before the legal action of the Commission against the Council. The Consensus on Development, however, was adopted jointly by the three EU bodies when the case had already been initiated. Thus, in spite of explicit institutional conflict, wide-ranging agreement on this text could be found, drawing out the general contours of EU development policy. An even clearer testimony of the taken-for-granted status of the security–development link could be found in the 2006 EU strategy on small arms (Council 2006a). The strategy was presented as a draft in the Political and Security Committee (PSC) of the Council in October and was later adopted by the Council in December 2005. Quite strikingly the strategy states (in capitals) that 'THE DESTABILISING ACCUMULATION AND SPREAD OF SALW CONSTITUTES A THREAT TO PEACE, SECURITY AND DEVELOPMENT' (Council 2006a: 3). Further on in the Strategy it is explicitly stated that its aims can also be achieved through

> Development and assistance programmes financed by the EDF (European Development Fund), in the framework of EC-ACP cooperation and through programmes which include a chapter on SALW and their ammunition.
>
> (Council 2006a: 9)

During the course of that very same year that the strategy was adopted, the Commission and Council were battling it out in Court, with the Council explicitly arguing against the role of development instruments to address the problem of SALW.[13] The inclusion of these statements in the strategy indicates the degree to which this way of thinking about development and its relation to security had become ensconced in the thinking of the EU policy community, even including national representatives in the PSC and the Council. Indeed, the adoption of the strategy provided ammunition for the Commission's argument during the actual course of the legal proceedings.[14] Furthermore, and rather remarkably, the Strategy was an initiative by the French government.[15] The latter was simultaneously intervening in support of the Council, stating:

> [I]f the non-proliferation of small arms and light weapons undoubtedly constitutes a precondition to development, it does not however form part of the Community's development cooperation policy. In fact, this non-proliferation does not contribute as such to the economic and social development of these countries.
>
> (Republic of France 2005: paragraph 35)[16]

The Council had played and continued to play a crucial role in establishing the security–development link. In front of the Court, however, this more pragmatic stance seemed to have become impossible. The Council was pushed into a corner where it argued that any anti-SALW measure had by definition as their objectives to achieve security, and by consequence, that the EC had no competence to act in that field.

In response to the Commission's attempts to demonstrate, through reference documents emanating from the UN, that SALW could indeed be conceptualized as a development issue, the Council argued:

> Concerning the so-called evolving nature of development cooperation policy, the Council does not accept that the Resolutions of the UN General Assembly ... can assist in determining whether or not the fight against the proliferation of small arms and light weapons is a matter of Community competence or not. Such issues can only be determined in relation to the legal bases to be found (or not) in the treaties themselves.
>
> (Council 2005c: 9)

In conjunction, the Council also argued for the simple fact that actions against small arms were included in the Cotonou Agreement, and did not in any way have relevance in determining the question of competencies (Council 2005c: 14). It argued in this context that the Cotonou Agreement was an agreement of *mixed* competencies, and that as such it contained aspects, like political dialogue, that would not fall under development cooperation policy. Furthermore, the legal basis of the Cotonou Agreement was article 310 TEC[17] on the conclusion of association agreements. From the point of view of the Council Legal Service, this meant that, legally speaking, it could not be characterized as a development agreement.[18] This position, however, seemed to create little resonance in the face of the thoroughly practice-based arguments of the Commission.

The anti-mining regulations to which the Council had obviously agreed now also seemed to play into the hands of the Commission. In its statement of defence, the Council argued somewhat bitterly that had it known the Commission would use the regulation of de-mining as a way to argue for the connection between security and development, the regulations would never have been adopted. It stated that

> [i]ndeed, the Council would suggest that adoption of the two Regulations could never have been envisaged if it had been thought then that the Commission would subsequently argue that the simple fact that the Community had taken some (carefully circumscribed) action in the field of development and economic cooperation would constitute the exercise of a supposed EC competence in the fight against landmines which would preclude future EU action against landmines in support of TEU objectives.
>
> (Council 2005b: 6)

The anti-mining regulations paved the way for the Commission's actions in the *small arms* case in two ways. Firstly, it was a concrete manifestation of the security–development link, and secondly, that institutionalized professional practice 'on the ground' had been allowed to enter into considerations regarding what the proper legal basis would be for these kinds of measures. Furthermore, de-mining was explicitly mentioned in direct conjunction with SALW in article 11 of the Cotonou Agreement.

Officials in the Council Legal Service who were involved in the *small arms* case would later refer to the inclusion of development in various policy statements, and more specifically in the preamble and the actual text of the 2004 Council Decision on SALW as 'sloppy drafting'.[19] In hindsight and with the Court's ruling in the *small arms* case in mind, this interpretation is understandable. However, I would argue that it was rather an expression of how this issue was actually conceptualized in consonance with dominant development practice. From such a perspective, this way of formulating the issue of small arms proliferation could only be justified in terms of the ultimate development goal.

The strictly legalistic position of the Council can be regarded as a last line of defence. The Council took a legal formalistic position because it was cornered by how it previously had characterized the issue of SALW and the broadening of the development agenda. It was clear that a broad range of organizations, such as the UN and the OECD as well as the policies of Member States, acknowledged the link between security, and more specifically SALW action and development. It was also clear that the Council itself had produced such statements in a range of different settings, most notably in the preamble of the 1998 Joint Action on SALW and through its 1999 Resolution on SALW, the ESS and the Consensus on Development. The most glaring example of this was perhaps the 2006 SALW strategy adopted during the course of the actual institutional conflict before the Court.

What remained for the Council was thus the insistence that none of these instances had any bearing whatsoever for determining the boundaries between security and development because of the fact that for the most part they did not constitute legally binding acts. As the decision of the Court in favour of the Commission would demonstrate, however, this would prove to be a less than convincing strategy.

## The Advocate General's dismissal of the Commission: a 'counter-factual' outcome

In contrast to the Court, the opinion of Advocate General (AG) Mengozzi in this case dismissed the legal action of the Commission.[20] However, at the same time, it maintained the principle of basing the arguments regarding the delimitation between security and development on institutionalized development practice rather than on exclusively legal arguments. This contrasting outcome of the case is enlightening because it is an indication of the extent to which conceptions of the security–development link were embraced. It demonstrates that even if there were other plausible interpretations available that would actually deny the claims of the Commission in relation to the specific Council decision, the fundamental notion of a development aspect of SALW more generally could hardly be denied.

The AG, while naturally focusing a great deal on the legal issue of how to interpret article 47 TEU, also referred to the practice of Community development cooperation.[21] Equally important, its argument resembled that of the Commission as it relied on the broad range of policy documents that had been produced, not least by the Council. These were documents that established the link between development and security and, more concretely, the link between sustainable development and combating of the spread of SALW. In this context, the AG stated:

> [I]n light of those documents drawn up by the Council, it seems inconsistent to argue, like the Council and the governments intervening before the Court (. . .) that combating the proliferation of small arms and light weapons under no circumstances falls within the scope of the Community policy on development cooperation.
>
> (Court 2007a: paragraph 186)

The AG's conclusion was not, however, in favour of the Commission position. Instead, the AG argued that due to the fact that the moratorium on SALW adopted by ECOWAS mainly had regional peace and security as its goal, peace and security consequently was also the main aim of the Council decision (Court 2007a: paragraph 186). Regarding the principal question of whether or not it was possible for the Community to act on the issue of SALW in the framework of its development cooperation policy, the AG argued in favour of the Commission. On the substance of the specific measure contested before the Court, the AG took the position of the Council.

Thus, the AG's opinion confirmed the position of the Commission in the sense of acknowledging that on the level of principle, there was indeed a development component, and thus a *potential* Community competence in the field of SALW.[22] Thus, while the AG argued for dismissing the legal action of the Commission, its opinion lent considerable credence to two important tenets of the Commission's argument. Firstly, it conceded that there was indeed a development component in SALW. Secondly, and equally important, it argued that the basis for interpreting the character and scope of the Community development cooperation policy could be based on an assessment of prevalent development practice as manifested by various policy statements of the Commission and Council.

## The ruling of the Court: moving SALW into the supranational framework

The Court ruling would go one step further. It clearly overruled the legalistic approach of the Council and instead affirmed the practice-based interpretations of the Commission. The widespread consensus on the inherent link between security and development, as manifested in the field of SALW, made it possible for the Court to affirm the position of the Commission. In article 66 of its judgment, the Court cited the European Consensus on Development directly, stating

> that there can be no sustainable development and eradication of poverty without peace and security and that the pursuit of the objectives of the Community's new development policy necessarily proceed via the promotion of democracy and respect for human rights.
>
> (Court 2008: paragraph 66)

It also argued further, referring to the Consensus paragraph 37, that insecurity and violent conflict are amongst the greatest obstacles to achieving the Millennium Development Goals 'while mentioning, in that context, the fight against the uncontrolled proliferation of small arms and light weapons' (Court 2008: paragraph 70). The Court further argued that development policy therefore need not be limited to measures focusing *directly* on the eradication of poverty, but can also include measures that have as their aim the elimination of obstacles to economic and social development. The Court declared:

> In that regard it is apparent from a number of documents emanating from the Union institutions and from the European Council that certain measures aiming to prevent fragility in developing countries, including those adopted in order to combat the proliferation of small arms and light weapons, can contribute to the elimination or reduction of obstacles to the economic and social development of those countries.
>
> (Court 2008: paragraph 68)

In its ruling, the Court referred to the 1999 Resolution of the Development Council (Council 1999b cited Court 2008: paragraph 69) as well as the 2006 'EU Strategy to Combat Illicit Accumulation and Trafficking of SALW and their Ammunition' (Council 2006a cited in Court 2008: paragraph 69). Even more crucially, the Court referred to the preamble of the 1998 Joint Action on small arms, where it was stated that the proliferation of small arms and light weapons act as impediments to both security and the prospects of sustainable development. The ruling of the Court thus affirmed the practice-based interpretation of this policy field, paying little heed to the legalistic position of the Council. To recall, the Council had argued that this preamble would be inadmissible as evidence, as it no longer constituted a legally binding act. Instead, largely informal and intersubjective conceptions of what constituted security, development, and SALW had been allowed to shape the Court's decision.

Similar to the *environmental crimes* court case, the *small arms* court case was fundamentally shaped by the broader processes through which the overarching policy issue had been institutionalized, to some extent in formal rules but more importantly through intersubjective shared understandings. In this case, the process through which the linkages with security had attained something resembling common sense conditioned the arguments mobilized by the Commission and perhaps more clearly contributed to their effectiveness before the Court. As was mentioned above, the jurisprudence in relation to this issue was far from well established, and legislative precedents were more or less nonexistent. Thus, a strict legal analysis or an analysis that would emphasize the formal aspects of institutions would not necessarily be able to shed much light on the outcome of the case.

## Chapter summary

The multiple references to the emergent development practice and its connection with security issues, which in many cases were formulated by the Council itself, illustrate well the point that I have sought to make: namely that the Council to a significant degree participated in the process through which the security–development link was established. The consensus on the fundamental aspects of the *small arms* court case shaped the possibility of the respective parties to formulate credible interpretations. The Council had locked itself in by its previous actions and statements. In this sense, it was forced to establish a position that was neither easy to defend nor convincing. The process that brought about the institutional conflict also conditioned the mobilization of specific interpretations, and to a certain extent, their effectiveness.

This lock-in effect becomes even more explicit in light of the Council's sternly legalistic approach. The case, aside from involving a conflict on the interpretation of the former article 47, was above all a conceptual struggle. That is, it was a struggle regarding the contents of the two concepts 'security' and 'development' in the EU context as chiselled out in practice by the respective institutions, and the broad range of actors with which it worked. In the face of this broad array of documents, often produced by itself, the Council's arguments came across as highly inconsistent with its past actions in the field of SALW.

The relations between the previous process which produced an inter-institutional consensus on security–development and SALW and the actions of the agents in front of the Court are summarized in Figure 8.1. The figure illustrates how broad developments on the level of institutions, in this case the emergence of shared understandings on security–development and SALW, conditioned the mobilization of specific arguments by the Commission and the Council. The arguments of the Commission seemed largely to be supported by the previous process, while those of the Council came across as contradictory. This made it easier for the Court to recognize the position of the Commission. The final outcome was the formal move of parts of the EU's SALW policies to the supranational framework.

**Macro 1**: Consensus on the inseparable relation between security and development and the consonant notion of SALW as a development issue.

**Macro 2**: The issue of SALW is moved from the intergovernmental field of the CFSP in to Community development policy.

**Micro 1**: The consensus on the security-development link constrains the Council's attempts to argue that SALW is exclusively a security issue. This strengthens the Commission's argument for the development aspects in SALW.

**Micro 2**: The prior consensus enables the Court to recognize the position of the Commission.

*Figure 8.1* Summary of the *small arms* court case

## Notes

1 Interview with former Commission official, Legal Service (Respondent 32).
2 Interview with Commission official, DG DEV (Respondent 17).
3 Represented before the Court by EU law professor Alan Dashwood.
4 Interview with official of the European Parliament, Legal Service (Respondent 38).
5 It could also be pointed out that this case had clear human rights connotations and that consequently, in terms of legitimacy, the case represented an opportunity for the Court to actually increase its standing. The Council was only supported by two Member States in these proceedings, Spain and the UK. Incidentally, the two European governments were most actively in support of the US administration's newly launched 'war on terror'.
6 Article 40 TEU in the current Lisbon Treaty.
7 After the Council's adoption of the decision on the EU contribution to the ECOWAS' SALW moratorium in December 2004, the Commission on 14 February 2005 lodged its application to the Court (Commission 2005a).
8 For the most widespread definition of (de)securitization, see Buzan et al. (1998) and Waever (1995). For applications in EU studies, see Balzacq (2008) and Huysmans (2000).
9 Indeed, as was also described above, the Lomé Conventions and the subsequent Cotonou Agreement remain the main instruments of the EU development cooperation policy, in particular in relation to ACP countries.
10 A sign of the distance between the position of the Council and the Member States in regard to the Commission was that even the jurisdiction of the Court to rule on the delimitation of the Common Foreign and Security Policy (CFSP) where it has normally no jurisdiction was contested. This was a point argued forcefully by the intervening

Member States in the *small arms* case (Kingdom of the Netherlands 2005; Kingdom of Spain 2005) and in particular by the United Kingdom (United Kingdom 2005).

11  Rejoinder of the Council (Council 2005c: 11). As one official of the Council Legal Service stated as a justification for this position: 'The Commission are *possibilists*. We on the other hand are surveyed by 27 legal services. We can't afford to be political. We must always be boring lawyers.' Interview with Council Secretariat official, Legal Service (Respondent 23).

12  The post of the High Representative was created, along with the European Security and Defence Policy (ESDP), with the Amsterdam Treaty (cf. Gosalbo Bono 2006). Solana held the post until the entry into force of the Lisbon Treaty in 2009.

13  The Commission sent its initial application to the Court in mid-February 2005, and the Council answered with its defence in May; the Commission wrote again in July, with a final rejoinder from the Council in September. By the time of the adoption of the EU strategy on small arms in December, the intervening Member States were filing their written arguments to the Court.

14  The Court also referred to the SALW strategy in its ruling as something that pointed to the legitimacy of the assertions made by the Commission regarding the development aspects of SALW (Court 2008: paragraph 90).

15  Interview with Commission official, DG DEV, formerly DG RELEX (Respondent 17).

16  '*[S]i la non-prolifération des armes légères et de petit calibre constitue sans conteste un préalable au développement, elle ne fait cependant pas partie de la politique de coopération au développement de la Communauté. En effet, cette non-prolifération ne contribue pas en tant que telle au développement économique et social de ces pays.*'

17  217 TFEU in the current treaty.

18  Interview with official of the Council Secretariat, Legal Service (Respondent 18).

19  Interview with official of the Council Secretariat, Legal Service (Respondent 23); interview with official of the Council Secretariat, Legal Service (Respondent 21); interview with French RELEX Counsellor (Respondent 37).

20  The role of the Court's Advocates General is to issue more comprehensive but non-binding opinions on the cases that appear before the Court.

21  A noticeable feature of the AG's opinion is that it focuses a great deal on the submission of the UK, even to the degree that the Council's argument is left almost completely in the background. The UK's nearly 40-page intervention in support of the Council indeed stands out, not only in volume, but also for its detailed elaboration of its argument, and its stern delivery.

22  Interview with official of the European Court of Justice, Cabinet of AG Mengozzi (Respondent 30).

# 9 Conflict dynamics

The *discursive lock-in mechanism*

In both cases before the Court, the Council seemed to have been pushed into a corner where it had great difficulties mounting a defence against the Commission. The analysis of the dynamics of these institutional conflicts sought to make sense of the actions of the respective agents as well as of the Court's decisions. The *discursive lock-in mechanism* discussed in this chapter explains the outcome of the institutional conflicts presented earlier by highlighting how the dynamics of these conflicts were conditioned by the emergence of shared understandings prior to their outbreak. It supplies a theoretical grounding for understanding a particular way in which discourses building up during longer periods of time can shape agents' actions. The mechanism identifies how the process through which specific institutional practices emerge can shape the arguments mobilized in institutional conflicts and produce particular institutional effects.

The *lock-in mechanism* in these cases is intimately connected to the *rupture mechanism*. In the processes analyzed here, the *rupture mechanism*, or rather its outcome, institutional conflict, can be identified as the trigger for the *lock-in mechanism*. To recall, the *rupture mechanism* creates a situation which pushes agents into their institutionally defined roles. In this context it thus forced them to mobilize interpretations that would support their respective positions in the conflict. The *discursive lock-in mechanism* brings the dispositional power of the previous process into a concrete setting. That is, it concretizes the 'bias' that is mobilized in the previous process and which favours specific ways of representing particular phenomena.[1] In the context of the institutional conflict, it translates itself into a bias that favours specific ways of formulating the concrete issues, and by consequence the mandates of the respective actors for dealing with them.

Given the outbreak of conflict, the *lock-in mechanism* can help us explain two things. Firstly, it theorizes where arguments come from and provides an understanding of why they are mobilized in a specific setting. In other words, there is a more concrete sense of how processes of institutionalization shape the mobilization of particular arguments. It also serves as a corrective to recent and influential accounts that have sought to 'bring agency back in' to analyses of institutional continuity and change (Schmidt 2008). The *rupture mechanism* relies on the notion that agency and intentionality need to be explained rather than being something we can simply assume. The *discursive lock-in mechanism* supplies the context that makes sense of the abilities of particular agents to draw on particular arguments and make those arguments convincing and persuasive. Secondly, the mechanism can help us understand the contextually defined effects of the active mobilization of such arguments in specific settings. The setting in the cases analyzed were the proceedings in the European Court of Justice. It is in this specific context that the actual lock-in effect becomes explicit and as such moves us closer to answering the question of the formal move of the contested issues into the supranational framework. The mechanism can also be regarded as a response to the unnecessarily narrow definition of institutions as favoured by rationalist institutionalists. As the analysis of the two cases sought to show, it was broader patterns of institutionalization that conditioned the dynamics of the conflict. Thus, the identification of the discursive lock-in mechanism is dependent on the analysis of the longer-term processes leading up to the conflict.

To simplify, the Council was handed a position which it could neither deny, given its institutional role and the arguments of the Commission, nor effectively defend, given its past actions. In the *environmental crimes* case, this resulted in the efforts of the Council to deny that the notion of the effectiveness and necessity of EU criminal sanctions was the underlying motivation for the contested Framework Decision on environmental criminal law, as well as a host of other legislative acts. In the *small arms* case this resulted in the untenable position that the broad range of policy statements emanating from the Council itself did not have any bearing on defining the relationship between development and security in regard to the SALW issue. The previous accumulation of a considerable body of reference material, such as policy statements and the 1999 Resolution of the Council, made these assertions unconvincing.

As was demonstrated in both cases, the formal properties of this reference material in the sense of being legally binding or not had less of a bearing in the actual court cases. Indeed, especially in the *small arms* case, the reliance on the legal standing of past acts, while forming the fundamental pillar of the Council's defence, had very little impact on the reasoning of both the Advocate General and the Court.[2] This was indicated specifically by the fact that the 1998 Joint Action which had been formally replaced by another legal act was still referred to by the Court as strengthening the arguments of the Commission.

The relation between broader systems of meaning and specific instances of argumentation is often thought of as constitutive. A social system makes certain ways of talking and acting possible, and explanations are thus thought of in constitutive terms, that is, without any temporal separation between the *explanans* and the *explanandum*. In contrast, the mechanism discussed here explains the relation between two broadly defined *events* in causal terms so that a change in institutional setting explains the particular outcome in the two cases via the *discursive lock-in mechanism*. More particularly, it concerned the relation between a change in the wider institutional setting in which the agents found themselves and the reconfiguration of decision-making competencies in the respective fields of SALW and criminal law.

As the analysis showed, the legal implications of certain acts did not arise automatically but were dependent on particular agents to supply such interpretations. For instance, in the *environmental crimes* case, references to the so-called *Greek Maize* ruling came to play an important role. The existence of this case and the references made to it within the argument of the Commission strengthened its position in the *environmental crimes* proceedings. However, the meaning of the *Greek Maize* ruling was not established in any final sense as soon as the ECJ came down with its judgment in 1989. Its importance in the emergence of the consensus on criminal sanctions and later in the *environmental crimes* court case was far from self-evident. It gained importance as it became involved in the wide-ranging discussions on effective implementation and the imposition of sanctions in which both the Commission and the Council participated. In this process it was also reinterpreted in specific ways and awarded with meanings which cannot be said to have been established with the ruling itself. A more literal reading of the ruling appeared, as was argued above, on the contrary to give limited support for the Commission's position. However, in the final stages of the process it was effectively mobilized to support the position that there was already a *de facto* Community competence in the field of criminal law.

The point is that the agents who included these original formulations had little ability to control the subsequent processes of reinterpretation that such formulations would open up for. Furthermore, they had little ability to control important changes in the context that would enable new interpretations of the references to sustainable development in the Joint Action. As the analysis demonstrated, the subsequent inclusion of references to SALW in the primary development cooperation instrument of the Community, the 2000 Cotonou Agreement, would open up for interpretations of the Joint Action that would reinforce the Commission's position in the *small arms* court case.

The *lock-in* took place in the way that the Council had to take recourse to a position in these two cases, and which came across as generally rather unconvincing. Why did it resort to this position anyway? Given its institutional role and the specific shape of the Commission's argument, it had very few options. The rather encompassing arguments of the UK in the *small arms* case indicated that there was perhaps room for more creativity than what was exhibited in the Council's defence. However, given the fact that the Commission built its arguments on the many instances where the Council had actually supported the connection between SALW policy and development, the available ways in which to refute the Commission's argument were few. What was left for the Council was to resort to the legal formalistic position from which it sought to disqualify any statements that did not represent legislation in force. As the institutional conflict took place in the setting of the Court, the dispositional bias of the previous process in favour of the Commission's position could be formalized through the Court's decision. A substantial body of 'reference material' had been produced in the processes that eventually led to the outbreak of institutional conflict. This *enabled* the Commission to mobilize specific policy formulations before the Court and *constrained* the ability of the Council to offer convincing competing formulations.

# Theoretical underpinnings of the
## *discursive lock-in mechanism*

In comparison with lock-in mechanisms based on assumptions of bounded rationality and material constraints, *discursive lock-in* directs the analytical gaze towards process through which widespread shared understandings are established, and posits that the effects of such processes of institutionalization are also best understood as unfolding over longer stretches of time. The *discursive lock-in mechanism* highlights the 'stickiness' of intersubjective institutions. While the *rupture mechanism* can be said to capture the process through which agency arises and conflicting preferences are formed, the *discursive lock-in* mechanism explains the outcome of such conflict with reference to the previous dynamics of the process.

The type of causal relationship that the mechanism seeks to capture, between the previous process and the lock-in effect, is characterized by its considerable time lag. That is, the effect of a certain event, in terms of the adoption of a piece of legislation, a general policy document or a ruling of the Court, does not become important until it is actualized at a later date, and in a different social context. It seems uncontroversial to state that the more institutionalized a particular policy becomes, the more it is embedded in professional practices and formalized procedures which carry with them their own 'stickiness'. However, the form of path dependency that is implied here is more open-ended in the sense that it crucially depends on the continuous interpretation of the participating agents. For instance, slight reformulations of concepts might open the door to make new associations and establish conceptual links which previously had not been possible. New ways of formulating policy issues or implementation practices suddenly appear natural and self-evident, while others seem obsolete or are simply not thought of. In that sense, however, there are no unequivocal 'increasing returns' which push the development onwards. Rather, the increasing institutionalization of a specific path of political development creates increasingly favourable conditions for formulating issues in specific ways while effectively excluding others.

To revisit Pierson's typology of causal arguments, this type of mechanism exhibits a combination of a long-term cause with a long-term outcome. Changes in the social system in which agents find themselves accumulate through long-term processes (Pierson 2004: 81). Once in place, these changes affect agents in various ways for longer periods of time. The analogy made by Pierson is that of global warming. Its causes, building over a long period of time, will continue to exert their effects even if emissions stopped today. Similarly, the *discursive lock-in mechanism* produces effects even after the accumulation of reference material has ceased. As was demonstrated in the analysis of the two court cases, the reference material produced by the Council's previous actions served as a resource on which the Commission could draw in arguing for its position while it worked as a serious constraint on the Council's ability to defend itself.

Interrogation into the broader processes of institutional development reveals the structural dispositions that make specific interpretations more legitimate and convincing. As such, the *discursive lock-in mechanism* serves as an analytical tool contributing to a nuanced understanding of the actions of the ECJ (cf. Alter 2009; Schmidt 2012). Thus, rather than assuming that the Court finds it easier to support the Commission's supranational position in general, we instead have a clearer sense of the process-specific factors that shaped the decision of the Court.

Previous actions are always open to a wide range of subsequent interpretations. The point is that the way in which agents engage in particular practices at a given time always carries with it an 'overflow' of meanings. Thus, strategic statements always carry with them meanings which go beyond the more narrow purposes for which they were intended. Particular actions, even if conceived of as part of a very precise strategy, can contribute to establish conditions for and award legitimacy to new ways of interpreting past and present situations, which actors will have difficulties in foreseeing or controlling. This is especially so as changes in the context will make new interpretations of past actions possible.

The *lock-in mechanism* thus represents a way to capture how agents, even when they have emerged in their 'utility maximizing' guise, are not unencumbered but partially shaped by both the institutions in which they act and how they have acted in various settings in the past. This mechanism can also be posited to be particularly effective in a structured environment, such as that of the EU policymaking machinery, where resolutions and statements as well as legal texts are readily available for anyone (in the cases analyzed here, the Commission Legal Service) who would seek to demonstrate discrepancies between past and present behaviour of specific actors. Central to the lock-in effect here is thus the actor's own previous participation in the construction of the path that constrains it at a later point in time. The component parts of the mechanism are specified in stylized form in Figure 9.1.

**Macro 1**: Accumulated body of 'reference material' produced in previous process of institutionalization makes certain interpretations less/more credible.

**Macro 2**: Institutional change.

**Micro 1**: The institutionalized 'biases' act as possibilities and constraints on institutionally situated agents. Disposes the mobilization of specific arguments.

**Micro 2**: Disposes authoritative agent/s to recognize certain interpretations.

*Figure 9.1* The *discursive lock-in mechanism*

## Situating *discursive lock-in* in a typology of lock-in mechanisms

The *discursive lock-in mechanism* can be related to a general typology of lock-in mechanisms (Table 9.1). On a general level, this group of mechanisms are clustered together because they each offer explanations of how agents contribute to establishing the institutions that constrain them at a later point in time. However, mechanisms differ in how institutions are conceptualized and how agents are seen to relate to such institutions. Similar to the discussion on the typology of crisis mechanisms in Chapter 6, the typology of lock-in mechanisms discussed here is also ordered around the categories of institutions as primarily regulative or primarily constitutive. A second dividing line places explanatory power primarily on the structural level or on the level of agents. To recall, the categories making up the typology define *starting points* rather than static categories.

### Regulative institutions and agent-level explanations

While this combination allows for some institutional effects, lock-in mechanisms do not figure prominently in this category. In fact, it is debatable to what extent assumptions regarding the institutions and agents that constitute this category can actually accommodate the notion of lock-in mechanisms at all. In IR and EU studies, the perspectives that rely on these assumptions typically are committed to what March and Olsen (1998) termed assumptions of *efficient histories*, meaning that institutional rules are expected to change in response to changes in the exogenous environment. This functional view of institutions, also found in liberal institutionalist and principal-agent perspectives in EU studies and IR, also means that individual agents will abandon any institutional arrangement that does not work to further their interests (cf. Garrett 1992). While agents might make sub-optimal decisions, for instance based on incomplete information, they are generally expected to design and alter institutional arrangements in line with their interests. Agents will not stay committed to institutional arrangements once constraints to their interests are encountered. Certainly, due to asymmetrical power relations, weaker agents may become 'locked in', as they might have few other options to choose from or because they are coerced to do so. However, such a situation does not tell us anything about the institutional arrangements but relies solely on the relative power relations between the actors to which the institutional arrangement applies. Drawn to its extreme, this perspective regards institutions, especially in the international sphere, as epiphenomenal to the balance of power (Cf. Mearsheimer 1995). There are thus no independent effects in the institutional arrangements themselves that could explain why agents would remain with them if those institutions are not conducive to their interests.

### Regulative institutions and structural-level explanations

This category of lock-in mechanisms includes perhaps the most well-known versions of this argument in political science more broadly. Here we find the path dependency arguments that are at the centre of large parts of historical institutionalism as well as the mechanism of rhetorical entrapment to which the *discursive lock-in mechanism* has a strong resemblance. From this point of view, agents are often constrained by their previous actions in ways that they did not necessarily reflect on at the time (Arthur 1989; North 1990; Pierson 2004). These accounts generally impute a considerable degree of contingency at the beginning of a process of path dependency. For instance, when focusing on markets, this notion has been used to explain why certain product standards, such as the QWERTY keyboard for typewriters and computers (Davids 1985), became pervasive in spite of the existence of competing standards that performed equally well or even better in initial tests. After a certain point, self-reinforcing processes of increasing returns kick in, making a switch to alternative paths increasingly costly and therefore less likely. Others have used similar arguments to explain why institutions with clear distributional aspects, such as social security systems (Hacker 1998; Mahoney and Thelen 2010) or subvention schemes like the EU's Common Agricultural Policy (CAP) have been so difficult to replace or reform (Daugbjerg and Swinbank 2004). Institutions, through their distributive effects, create groups and actors that have stakes in the status quo and will resist change even if the overall effects of institutional arrangements are clearly suboptimal. These mechanisms are intimately tied up to how institutional arrangements regulate the distribution of resources.

There are, however, variants of the lock-in mechanism in this category that open up for normative rather than exclusively distributive institutional structures, while remaining with the idea of institutional effects as primarily regulative. Schimmelfennig (2001) analyzes what compelled the governments that actually opposed Eastern enlargement of the EU in the late 1990s to finally support it nonetheless. In the end, this analysis is based on the notion that these actors nurtured stable preferences all along. However, tactical concessions to pro-enlargement actors, in terms of giving verbal public support to enlargement while seeking to obstruct the process in less visible ways, eventually locked them in. But why were they locked in? Because, as Schimmelfennig explains, 'with each small or general public commitment, the credibility costs of non-enlargement rose' (Schimmelfennig 2001: 74). It was because of the costs to their reputation and credibility as supporters of European values if their hypocrisy was unveiled that the oppositional actors were forced to finally accept enlargement. The preferences of these actors, whether pro or anti enlargement, did not change through the processes. Norms or values, in this account, are only allowed to play the role of a system of informal rules that, if broken, give rise to certain penalties and are thus largely devoid of their constitutive aspects. It is the 'or else' function of these norms (Ostrom 1986) that makes actors abide by them. In the context of Schimmelfennig's analysis, this meant supporting the Eastern enlargement of the EU to avoid costs in terms of loss of credibility, which would have had potentially adverse effects in future negotiations. At the same time, the explanation starts at the structural level, where tensions between different systems of norms to which agents are publicly committed clash with actual institutional structures. These tensions are then played out among particular agents who use these tensions strategically to push decision makers to act contrary to their interests.

## Constitutive institutions and agent-level explanations

The approaches that fit within this category are, like the first category discussed, not easily squared with the notion of lock-in mechanisms. Cognitive approaches which posit that agents' mental models, while associated with a certain stickiness, will be updated as agents are exposed to divergent data, do not make much room for lock-in mechanisms (Jacobs 2009). Similarly, approaches such as Schmidt's discursive institutionalism with its insistence on how agents use ideas to persuade other agents do not speak to these issues. To the contrary, the emphasis on agency in Discursive Institutionalism and approaches that emphasize the 'causal power of ideas' (Cox and Béland 2010; Parsons 2016) are often formulated as correctives to precisely the idea that discourses and intersubjective institutions such as widespread shared understandings and collective norms act as constraints and have self-reinforcing effects (Schmidt 2008: 316). Rather, the insistence on the need to bring 'agency back in' to institutional analysis is precisely informed by the notion, contrary to that of lock-in mechanisms, that agents can break with the constitutive effects of institutions. The process of institutionalization from this perspective, similar to how the mechanism of discursive lock-in is formulated, may come to make certain ideas dominant and might facilitate the efforts to persuade and reshape institutions (Schmidt and Carstensen 2016) but this does not imply the notion of constraints that are at the heart of the generally defined lock-in mechanism.

This being said, Risse et al.'s (1999) discussions on how norm entrepreneurs in the international sphere use 'shaming' as a strategy to convince states that derogate from human rights to abide by such norms might be one way of thinking about lock-in mechanisms from the perspective of constitutive institutions and agent-level explanations. They argue that 'shaming . . . convinces leaders that their behaviours are inconsistent with an identity to which they aspire' (Risse et al. 1999: 15). While some agents might be impervious to such strategies, others can be deeply offended by being cast as not belonging to the group of civilized states (Risse et al. 1999). The strategic mobilization of norms is important here, indicating that the starting point of particular explanations is at the agent level. At the same time, in cases of shaming, the lock-in effect does not occur due to the 'locked-in' agent's expected losses in instrumental terms. Rather, it is the constitutive side of norms that is emphasized as the agents that are shamed experience the loss of identity and social recognition that are intimately connected with certain norms. So while an important part of the explanatory power is placed on the actions of norm entrepreneurs, i.e. on the agent level, the constitutive, rather than the primarily regulative side of institutions, is emphasized.

## Constitutive institutions and structural-level explanations

The *discursive lock-in mechanism* found in the final category of the typology of lock-in mechanisms, instead combines emphasis on the constitutive aspect of institutions with explanations that originate at the structural level of social institutions. It uses these components to offer an explanation as to why actors mobilize specific arguments in struggles over policy issues, and what makes such arguments efficient. The ubiquitous references in EU studies to policy entrepreneurs and experts who are able to persuade others by mobilizing particular frames sometimes stop short by attributing such frames exclusively to the policy entrepreneurs who formulate them. References to broader ideational contexts, in terms of broader systems of ideas or worldviews and how such broader intersubjective institutions shape particular policy struggles are seldom engaged with explicitly in the way implied by the mechanism in this category.

Here it is worth recalling the process-oriented basis of the typology. The starting point for the *discursive lock-in mechanism* is the constitutive aspect of institutions. It is by emphasizing this aspect that we understand the emergence of institutions as specific ways of doing things tied up with particular rules, norms and identities. It is the constitutive aspects of institutions that drive the accumulation of reference material and later become important for the actual lock-in. So, while these constitutive aspects serve as the starting point of this mechanism, the lock-in itself highlights how the process through which the regulative aspect of these institutions becomes dominant. It enables and constrains in situations where, for one reason or another, agents have come to question previously taken-for-granted institutions.[3] The *discursive lock-in mechanism* has several commonalities with Schimmelfennig's (2001) rhetorical entrapment mechanism (cf. Morin and Gold 2010; Rittberger and Schimmelfennig 2006). However, it is based on a set of assumptions which differentiates it in important ways from rhetorical entrapment, as well as from how path dependency arguments relying on a general assumption of rationality formulate lock-in. It was precisely the fact that the actors' institutional roles had not been activated previously, and consequently that they had not formulated clear preferences, that enabled the final outcomes. Shared understandings regarding conceptualizations of the policy issues at stake transgressed institutional boundaries in ways that supplied a glaring contrast to the very notion of EU bodies as instrumental 'competence maximizers' (Héritier and Moury 2012) and carriers of stable preferences.

*Table 9.1* A typology of lock-in mechanisms

|  | Institutions as Primarily Regulative | Institutions as Primarily Constitutive |
|---|---|---|
| Explanatory power at the agent level | Lock-in through asymmetric power relations and coercion | Shaming mechanisms |
| Explanatory power at the structural level | Increasing returns mechanism; rhetorical entrapment mechanism | Discursive lock-in |

If applied to the case, the mechanism of rhetorical entrapment would hypothesize that the Commission and the Council nurtured opposing preferences all along but that due to careless public statements by the Council along the way, to secure short-term gains, it could at a later point in time be shamed into conceding to the position of the Commission. This was simply not the case. Quite on the contrary, the Council and the Member States argued for the Council's position rather ferociously before the Court. Thus, the process-tracing evidence did not correspond to the case-specific observable implications of the mechanism of rhetorical entrapment, and this would perhaps be the most obvious competing explanatory mechanism supplied by rationalist approaches.

By taking the gradual development of a broader issue area into account, a detailed understanding could be reached regarding why a certain way of drawing lines of decision-making competence between the Commission and the Council became more convincing and persuasive. While the controversial rulings of the Court in *the environmental crimes* and *small arms* cases at first seemed difficult to grasp, an analysis of the process that produced the conflicts made the outcomes more comprehensible. Importantly, such detailed analyses are able to provide insights that strike a balance between institutional context, meaningful action, and the development of local strategies of agents.

## Notes

1   As Bachrach and Baratz argue through quoting Schattschneider (1960), political 'organization is the mobilization of bias' (Bachrach and Baratz 1962: 949). For a similar argument from a constructivist standpoint regarding how a longer-term process produces a bias which can work to shape which perspectives are deemed plausible and persuasive in a particular setting, see Guzzini (1993: 471–2).
2   To recall, the fact that the Advocate General actually delivered an opinion in favour of the Council and the Member States had little to do with the Council's legalistic approach. Indeed, the AG based much of its principal reasoning on how the *practice* of development cooperation had evolved. However, while it to a large extent went along with the Commission on the principal issue, it came to a different conclusion regarding the specific Council decision.
3   To recall, the *rupture mechanism* aimed towards explaining precisely such instances where habitual patterns are broken.

# 10 Concluding remarks

In recent years the tensions between national and supranational decision making in the EU have become ever more pronounced as they have also become associated with a higher degree of complexity. The political dividing lines informing such tensions concern a wide range of issues dealt with at the European level. At the same time, EU Member States are a highly heterogeneous group of polities, with their own political cultures and sensitivities, including governments with sometimes significantly different interpretations of what the European project is and what it can be.

In the wake of the financial and economic crisis unfolding since 2008, unprecedented supranational competencies were established in the field of economic governance through the European Semester and led to stricter procedures of budget coordination. More broadly, the EU thus reached a level of political integration that would have been difficult to imagine thirty years ago. At the same time the shadow of disintegration has at times loomed large. Most recently observed in the form of the UK's possible exit from the Union, there is also the precarious status of Greece in the eurozone, along with the ascendance of national governments which are openly skeptical about further supranational integration in Europe.

If the field of EU studies has taught any lesson at all, it is that the *when* and *where* of European integration and disintegration is notoriously unpredictable. The intricacy of the social interactions occurring in the EU institutional setting calls for a fair degree of caution regarding the scope and application of theoretical frameworks. This book has been an attempt to take these seemingly contradictory tendencies seriously, and it was done by applying an approach that accommodates complexity and makes sense of how the tensions play out in two particular fields of EU policymaking, Justice Cooperation and EU External Actions. The cases captured the dynamics of instances where cooperation breaks down and conflicts emerge over the control of political decision making. It answered a need to depart from the tendency in constructivist perspectives on international political orders to emphasize successful cooperation and the establishment of common norms and identities. In EU studies, a significant amount of energy has been spent on establishing the link between the emergence of such social institutions and one particular outcome, namely that of deeper European integration. On the contrary, however, the emergence of such social institutions at the EU level seems to have produced a range of different effects associated with both integration and disintegration.

The questions addressed here relate precisely to these types of mixed and seemingly unpredictable patterns. Classical theoretical paradigms seeking to make sense of European integration often relied on aggregated understandings of the motivations of particular organizations, or Member States' governments. This has gradually had to give way to accounts that are more attuned to the layered and multifaceted processes that yield particular institutional outcomes. The discussions herein have built on such approaches with the aim of further developing their theoretical and methodological tools. The ambition has been one of seeking to make sense of the ostensibly incoherent character of some of the EU's institutional dynamics.

While the EU indeed features some aspects that are clearly *sui generis*, it is useful to think more broadly about the social dynamics that structure interaction in this setting in relation to international political orders. Professional identities, competing and conflicting systems of norms, rules and social practices interact in various ways to shape actions and produce particular outcomes. The mechanisms of institutional conflict identified in the two selected cases should be understood as efforts to make sense of the ways in which sometimes conflicting aspects of international political orders can shape the actions of the agents inhabiting them. They answer questions regarding what happens when latent tensions of international political orders become explicit and how the social institutions in which agents are embedded can condition various actions to deal with those tensions.

By using interpretive process tracing, the potential of constructivist approaches to address questions often perceived as being at the heart of rationalist approaches was explored. The application of interpretive process tracing enabled a detailed account of how institutional developments play out on the level of agents at different points in time. It was shown that institutions at times constitute self-understandings, while at other points in time act as possibilities and constraints on agents who have developed specific preferences in relation to a particular issue. The benefits with this slightly more open-ended conceptualization of institutions and agents helped identify the two mechanisms. Both mechanisms relied on this duality of institutions and the concomitant shifts in the logics of social interaction on the agent level. This also demonstrates the more general point regarding the usefulness of a framework for institutional analysis that relies on dynamic rather than static analytical categories.

The use of interpretive tools is not only a viable alternative, but also essential to explain the outcomes of specific processes. The commitment to interpretive modes of inquiry is based on the notion that if we do not understand how agents understand themselves in particular contexts, we will have little basis on which to draw out insights as to why they act in specific ways. The analytical framework permitted strategic and intentional action to remain one of several possible logics. Shifts between logics of social interactions are crucial to understand to be able to produce explanations regarding social and political processes.

## Mechanisms of institutional conflict

Both the *rupture* mechanisms and *discursive lock-in* mechanisms are at the heart of explaining the process outcomes analyzed here. More generally, they present an addition to the theoretical toolbox which can be used to approach future cases. As was argued above, mechanisms can be reformulated as analytical tools that are portable across contexts. As such, they can potentially shed light on social and political phenomena that exhibit analogous social dynamics, even in cases that are apparently rather different from those discussed here. The formulation of specific mechanisms is a way to pare down the messy process and unpack the macro-micro-macro relations that provide explanations. It provides us with a model that reduces the findings to their bare essentials and enables them to travel to other similar or dissimilar empirical settings.

Together these two mechanisms point to the central characteristics of the European Union as an international political order. As the respective typologies in which the mechanisms were situated indicate, there are different ways to approach how such tensions become explicit. Mechanisms differ regarding at which level explanatory power should be placed and how we should conceptualize the extent to which institutions produce, enable and constrain specific ways of acting. In this sense, the two mechanisms speak to the broader theoretical field of constructivist research on international political orders and the EU. In particular, they serve as potentially useful tools to help counter criticisms regarding the inability of constructivist research to conceptualize instances of sudden institutional change. That is, these two mechanisms serve to further our understanding of the irregular, tension-laden dynamics of such political orders.

The *rupture mechanism* offered one way to theorize how agents can develop widely conflicting positions on issues which have previously been the object of widespread consensus. The mechanism thus helps us make sense of how processes that exhibit broadly defined socialization dynamics can be halted and even reversed. It helps identify the breaking point at which the institutionalized roles of the Commission and the Council snap agents back into place, without necessarily positing the existence of generally formulated, pre-existing preferences. As such, the *rupture mechanism* also serves as a response to critique often levelled against constructivists, and sometimes more generally historical institutionalists and their supposed inability to explain rapid institutional change and breakdowns in social institutions. This critique has served to reinforce the largely unfounded division of work between rationalists and constructivists in EU studies and IR, often identifying institutional conflict and change as the province of rationalist analysis. The *rupture mechanism* thus supplies an opening to an under-explored area of research for constructivist approaches to institutional analysis. Such analyses need not necessarily be confined to studies of the EU.

In situations where there are constitutional uncertainties, as is the case in the EU, there is a considerable risk that substantial policy issues will become mixed with constitutional ones. In contrast, a system where the constitution is stable and well institutionalized can plausibly harbour considerable tensions on substantial issues, since actors generally will not perceive their fundamental rights as being threatened by such tensions. Thus, conflict on substantial issues, even if fierce, will not activate conflicts on higher-order issues in which actors are recognized as competent to take decisions in particular policy areas. However, when such constitutional issues are made explicit, as was the case in the processes analyzed here, fundamental and unbridgeable conflict is a more likely outcome.

This study was divided analytically in order to capture the two mechanisms. However, as was discussed in relation to the *discursive lock-in mechanism*, these mechanisms were clearly interlinked. The notion of lock-in, whether in the historical institutionalist or the more constructivist sense, presupposes circumstances that are latent or manifestly conflictual. For the mechanism to be applicable one or more agents must experience a specific social setting in terms of constraints. Such constraints in the historical institutionalist tradition concern the persistence of sub-optimal arrangements due to mechanisms of increasing returns and the considerable costs associated with comprehensive institutional reform. Furthermore they assume bounded rational agents. It also presupposes an ability of the researcher to establish an objective reference point in relation to which inefficiency can be understood. The *discursive lock-in mechanism*, however, relies on the idea that lock-in can only occur when agency, as an emergent property of agents, has been produced through processes that have already unfolded. The notion of discursive lock-in is thus inseparable from an understanding of prior processes through which social institutions have been established. These mechanisms highlight patterns regarding the character of the relations between institutional processes and agent-level dynamics. They place attention to intersubjective institutions such as identities, norms and practices front and center within studies of the EU.

## JHA and CFSP after Lisbon

The findings in the policy areas studied must invariably be read in light of the rather far-reaching expansion of the EU's membership that has occurred in the last ten years, as well as in light of the changes brought about by the Lisbon Treaty that entered into force in 2009. When the *environmental crimes* court case was brought to the Luxembourg Court in 2003, the EU was only composed of fifteen Members. Thus, almost half of today's Member States came into the process when important parts were already over and done with. In a similar way, the ECOWAS case, initiated in 2005, was not driven by the current EU twenty-eight Member States. The actual court proceedings, being only the tip of the iceberg, were only initiated the year after the EU expanded from fifteen to twenty-five Member States. So what does the study tell us about present conditions?

The formal institutional issue underlying the conflict in the *environmental crimes* case has in many formal aspects been surpassed by the constitutional changes brought about by the Lisbon Treaty. The competencies fought for by the Commission regarding criminal sanctions as an implementation tool for ordinary EU legislation are now formally enshrined in the Treaty of the Functioning of the European Union (TFEU) and are henceforth regulated through the normal decision-making procedures of the EU. Through article 83 of the TFEU, decision making on criminal sanctions to ensure effective implementation was brought within the 'normal' legislative procedures of the Union, with Commission initiative,[1] QMV in the Council, jurisdiction of the Court, and full involvement of the European Parliament. However, the formal shift in competencies has not necessarily made the policy field of European criminal law less sensitive. Criminal law remains imbued with symbolic overtones and is often connected to prevailing conceptions of national identity and the purported systems of norms that specific societies are thought to abide by.[2] The complicated and, at the time of writing, still ongoing negotiations on the establishment of a European Public Prosecutors Office is a clear manifestation of such sensitivities.[3] Thus, even if the formal constitutional landscape has changed, the area of EU criminal law is an area where it is likely that the kind of tensions discussed here will arise again in the future.

Regarding the issue of proliferation of small arms and light weapons, and external action in the EU more generally, the Lisbon Treaty also brought with it some important changes. This was perhaps most clearly manifested by the European External Action Service (EEAS), an organization cohabited by national diplomats and former officials of the Commission and the Council Secretariat, responsible for the management of the EU's external relations. The EU's High Representative for Foreign Affairs and Security Policy is not only head of the EEAS, but also Vice President of the Commission (Denza 2012). In addition to this, the Commissioner for Development heads the development part of the EEAS. Thus, the institutionally defined self-understandings among Commission officials and officials of the Council Secretariat have arguably given way to new and, one would suspect, less ingrained ones. However, while the establishment of the EEAS entailed the creation of an organization which is tasked to handle both security and development policies, the formal separation between these fields of policymaking was left very much intact (Wessels 2012).

Furthermore, as concerns the specific area of SALW, the ruling in the *small arms* court case did not necessarily contribute much clarity regarding delimitation between the CFSP and EU cooperation on development. In the RELEX group where the issue had first arisen, the Commission did not exploit the ruling in the years that followed.[4] The representatives of the Council, and more specifically its Legal Service, emphasized that the Court case in itself was a 'dead letter' after the entry into force of the Lisbon Treaty, and that it could not in any circumstances be referred to as a precedent in future cases.[5] Indeed, an opinion that was released by the Council Legal Service after the Court ruling stressed as its main point that the word 'development' should from now on never figure in any part of a CFSP measure (Council 2008).[6] That is, many seemed to argue that important legal aspects of the case would not be applicable after Lisbon.[7]

However, for officials working on the issue of SALW in the Council Secretariat, the Commission, and further on, in the EEAS, the case remained very much alive. The feeling communicated by respondents was that the conflict had been generally unproductive.[8] With the competence issue pushed to the extreme, participants in the policy process had become more cautious. As one respondent stated, when setting up new instruments in the field of SALW, they constantly felt the need to go back and see how the instruments related to the ruling, as well as informing new colleagues of the case and how to interpret it.[9] Thus, the fact that the Court stated that there is a Community competence in SALW acts as an important precedent.[10] In this sense, the assertions among the lawyers of the Council Legal Service to the effect that the ruling is a dead letter after Lisbon is perhaps more a continuation of its legalistic defence in front of the Court rather than a clear assessment of how the ruling has and will continue to play out in practice.

Studying the EU is always to some extent the study of a moving target. However, the relevance of the mechanisms identified is not confined to the pre-Lisbon era. It is important, especially from a legal standpoint, to be aware of changes in the formal institutional set-up of the EU. However, the analysis of the cases also indicated that interpretations often travelled across such changes in the formal rules. The *discursive lock-in mechanism* pointed specifically to how rulings and legislative measures that were adopted under completely different constitutional conditions and for different purposes came to shape the outcome of conflicts in the *environmental crimes* case and the *small arms* case. In light of this we should not discount the possibility that these Court rulings, and the mechanisms that produced them, will continue to feed into processes of reinterpretation through which the scope of the JHA and the CFSP are redefined in the future. The development of professional practices in particular policy areas seldom line up neatly with the often inflexible formal rules in place. This suggests that the approach to the EU's institutional dynamics offered here, and the mechanisms of institutional conflict suggested in this book can serve as useful points of departures for future studies of the EU and international political orders more generally.

## Notes

1 Under the Lisbon Treaty, the Member States retain the possibility to table initiatives in JHA. While some had predicted this to become a dead letter, the first legislative proposals after the Lisbon Treaty were Member State initiatives. Commission officials working in the field generally argue that this is transitory (interview with Commission official, Cabinet Reding, Respondent 46); interview with Commission official, Cabinet Reding, Respondent 4); interview with Commission official, Legal Service, Respondent 33). Member States and Council officials tend to emphasize that the Member State initiative will be an enduring part of policymaking in this area.

2 Indeed, the so-called 'emergency brake' provision that opens up for individual Member States to refuse to agree to the criminalization of certain acts on the grounds that it affects 'fundamental aspects of its criminal justice system' (Article 83[3] TFEU) points in this direction.

3 The Commission presented a proposal for the establishment of a European Public Prosecutor's Office in 2013 (Commission 2013a).

4 Interview with Member State representative of Italy to the RELEX working group (Respondent 3).

5 Interview with official of Council Secretariat, Legal Service (Respondent 23); interview with official of Council Secretariat, Legal Service (Respondent 18); interview with official of Council Secretariat, Legal Service (Respondent 21). This is in particular in view of the fact that Article 47 of the old TEU has been revised. The old article

was formulated as protecting the *acquis communautaire* and the scope of the TEC against encroachments on its competencies. The new article (art 40 TEU) goes both ways, which means that it is formulated as also protecting policies under the new TEU from encroachment.

6 Interview with Czech RELEX Counsellor (Respondent 39), interview with French RELEX Counsellor (Respondent 37), interview with official of the Council Secretariat, Legal Service (Respondent 23).

7 Interview with Commission official, DG RELEX (Respondent 52), interview with official of the European Court of Justice (Respondent 30), interview with French RELEX Counsellor (Respondent 37).

8 Interview with EEAS official (Respondent 43); interview with EEAS official (Respondent 48).

9 Interview with EEAS official (Respondent 48).

10 Interview with official of Council Secretariat (Respondent 15); interview with Commission official, DG RELEX (Respondent 52); interview with Commission official DG DEV, formerly DG RELEX (Respondent 17).

# Bibliography

Adler, Emmanuel and Haas, Peter (1992) Conclusion: Epistemic Communities, World Order, and the Creation of a Reflective Research Program. *International Organization*, 46(1): 367–390.

Adler, Emmanuel and Pouliot, Vincent (2011) International Practices. *International Theory*, 3(1): 1–36.

Allison, Graham and Zelikow, Philip (1999) *Essence of Decision: Explaining the Cuban Missile Crisis.* (2nd ed.) New York: Longman.

Alter, Karen J. (2009) *The European Court's Political Power*. Oxford: Oxford University Press.

Alter, Karen J. and Helfer, Laurence R. (2010) Nature or Nurture: Judicial Law Making in the European Court of Justice and the Andean Tribunal of Justice. *International Organization*, 64(4): 563–592.

Apps, Katherine M. (2006) Case C-176/03, Commission v. Council. Pillars Askew: Criminal Law EC-Style. *Columbia Journal of European Law*, 12: 625–637.

Arthur, Brian W. (1989) Competing Technologies, Increasing Returns, and Lock-in by Historical Events. *Economic Journal*, 99(1): 116–131.

Arts, Karin (2004) 'Changing Interests in EU Development Cooperation: The Impact of Membership and Advancing Integration', in Arts, K and Dickson, A. K. (eds.) *EU Development Cooperation: From Model to Symbol*, Manchester: Manchester University Press, pp. 101–112.

Arts, Karin and Dickson, Anna K. (eds.) (2004) *EU Development Cooperation: From Model to Symbol*. Manchester: Manchester University Press.

Bachrach, Peter and Baratz, Morton, S. (1962) Two Faces of Power. *American Political Science Review*, 56(4): 947–952.

Baldwin, David A. (1995) Security Studies and the End of the Cold War. *World Politics*, 48(1): 117–141.

Balzacq, Thierry (2008) The Policy Tools of Securitization: Information Exchange, EU Foreign and Interior Policies. *Journal of Common Market Studies*, 46(1): 75–100.

Barnett, Michael and Finnemore, Martha (2004) *Rules for the World: International Organizations in Global Politics*. Ithaca: Cornell University Press.

Baumgartner, Frank R. and Jones, Bryan D. (1993) *Agendas and Instability in American Politics*. Chicago: The University of Chicago Press.

Beach, Derek (2004) The Unseen Hand in Treaty Reform Negotiations: The Role and Impact of the Council Secretariat. *Journal of European Public Policy*, 11(3): 408–439.

Beach, Derek and Pedersen, Rasmus Brun (2013) *Process-Tracing Methods: Foundations and Guidelines*. Ann Arbor: University of Michigan Press.

Béland, Daniel and Cox, Robert Henry (2010) 'Introduction: Ideas and Politics', in Béland, D. and Cox, R. H. (eds.) *Ideas and Politics in Social Science Research*, Oxford: Oxford University Press, pp. 1–25.

Bennett, Andrew (2010) 'Process Tracing and Causal Inference', in Brady, H. E. and Collier, D. (eds.) *Rethinking Social Inquiry: Diverse Tools, Shared Standards* (2nd ed.), Lanham: Rowman and Littlefield, pp. 207–220.

Bennett, Andrew (2013) The Mother of all Isms: Causal Mechanisms and Structured Pluralism in International Relations Theory, *European Journal of International Relations*, 19(3): 459–481.

Bennett, Andrew (2014) 'Appendix: Disciplining our Conjectures: Systematizing Process Tracing with Bayesian Analysis', in Bennett, A. and Checkel, J. (eds.) *Process Tracing: From Metaphor to Analytical Tool*. Cambridge: Cambridge University Press, pp. 276–298.

Bennett, Andrew and Checkel, Jeffrey T. (2014) Process Tracing: From Philosophical Roots to Best Practices, in Bennett, A. and Checkel, J. T. (eds.) *Process Tracing: From Metaphor to Analytical Tool*, Cambridge: Cambridge University Press, pp. 3–37.

Bennett, Andrew and George, Alexander L. (2004) *Case Studies and Theory Development in the Social Sciences*. Cambridge: MIT Press.

Benson, David and Jordan, Andrew (2011) What Have We Learned from Policy Transfer Research? Dolowitz and Marsh Revisited, *Political Studies Review*, 9(3): 366–378.

Beyer Jan (2005) Multiple Embeddedness and Socialization in Europe: the Case of Council Officials. *International Organization*, 59(4): 899–936.

Beyer, Jan (2010) Conceptual and Methodological Challenges in the Study of European Socialization. *Journal of European Public Policy*, 17(6): 909–920.

Bicchi, Federica (2011) The EU as a Community of Practice: Foreign Policy Communications in the COREU Network. *Journal of European Public Policy*, 18(8): 1115–1132.

Blauberger, Michael (2014) National Responses to European Court Jurisprudence. *West European Politics*, 37(3): 457–474.

Blom-Hansen, Jens and Brandsma, Gijs Jan (2009) The EU Comitology System: Intergovernmental *and* Deliberative Supranationalism. *Journal of Common Market Studies*, 47(4): 719–740.

Booth, Ken (1991) Security and Emancipation. *Review of International Studies*, 17(4): 313–326.

Bremberg, Niklas (2015) *Diplomacy and Security Community-Building: EU Crisis Management in the Western Mediterranean*. London: Routledge.

Bueger, Christian and Gadinger, Frank (2015) The Play of International Practice. *International Studies Quarterly*, 59(3): 449–460.

Burley, Anne-Marie and Mattli, Walter (1993) Europe Before the Court. *International Organization*, 47(1): 41–76.

Büthe, Tim (2002) Taking Temporality Seriously: Modeling History and the Use of Narratives as Evidence. *American Political Science Review*, 96(3): 481–493.

Buzan, Barry (1983) *People States and Fear: The National Security Problem in International Relations*. Brighton: Weatsheaf Books.

Buzan, Barry, De Wilde, Jaap and Waever, Ole (1998) *Security: A New Framework for Analysis*. Boulder: Lynne Rienner.

Call, Charles T. (2008) The Fallacy of 'Failed States'. *Third World Quarterly*, 29(8): 1491–1507.

Carbone, Maurizio (2007) *The European Union and International Development: The Politics of Foreign Aid*. London: Routledge.

Carbone, Maurizio (2010) The European Union, Good Governance and Aid Co-ordination. *Third World Quarterly*, 31(1): 13–29.

Carstensen, Martin B. and Schmidt, Viviene B. (2016) Power through, over and in Ideas: Conceptualizing Ideational Power in Discursive Institutionalism. *Journal of European Public Policy*, 23(3): 318–337.

Checkel, Jeffrey T. (2005) Socialization in the European Union. *International Organization*, 59(4): 801–826.

Checkel, Jeffrey T. (2006) Tracing Causal Mechanisms. *International Studies Review*, 8(2): 362–370.

Checkel, Jeffrey T. (2012) 'Theoretical Pluralism in IR: Possibilities and Limits', in Carlsnaes, W., Risse, T. and Simmons, B. (eds.) *Sage Handbook of International Relations* (2nd ed.), London: Sage, pp. 220–241.

Checkel, Jeffrey T. (2014) Socialization Ain't Always Nice: Cooperation and Conflict in the Post-Cold War World. *Working Paper* available at www.sfu.ca/content/dam/sfu/internationalstudies/checkel/Soc-WorkshopII-JCPaper-1014.pdf

Checkel, Jeffrey T. and Zürn, Michael (2005) Getting Socialized to Build Bridges: Constructivism and Rationalism, Europe and the Nation-State. *International Organization*, 59(4): 1045–1079.

Christiansen, Thomas (2002) The Role of Supranational Actors in EU Treaty Reform. *Journal of European Public Policy*, 9(2): 33–53.

Christiansen, Thomas and Tonra, Ben (eds.) (2004) *Rethinking European Union Foreign Policy*. Manchester: Manchester University Press.

Clayes, Anne-Sophie (2004) '"Sense and Sensibility": The Role of France and French Interests in European Development Policy since 1957', in Arts, K. and Dickson, A. K. (eds.) *EU Development Cooperation: From Model to Symbol*, Manchester: Manchester University Press, pp. 113–132.

Coleman, James S. (1986) Social Theory, Social Research, and a Theory of Action. *American Journal of Sociology*, 91(6): 1309–1335.

Coleman, James S. (1990) *Foundations of Social Theory*. Harvard: Harvard University Press.

Collier, David (2011) Understanding Process Tracing. *PS: Political Science and Politics*, 44(4): 823–830.

Conant, Lisa (2007) Review Article: The Politics of Legal Integration. *Journal of Common Market Studies*, 45(s1): 45–66.

Corbet, Richard, Jacobs, Francis and Shackleton, Michael (2011) *The European Parliament* (8th ed.). London: John Harper Publishing.

Cram, Laura (1994) The European Commission as a Multi-Organisation: Social Policy and IT Policy in the EU. *Journal of European Public Policy*, 1(2): 195–217.

Crawford, Neta (1991) Once and Future Security Studies. *Security Studies*, 1(2): 283–316.

Crawford, Sue and Ostrom, Ellinor (1995) A Grammar of Institutions. *American Political Science Review*, 89(3): 582–600.

Da Conceicão-Heldt, Eugénia (2011) Variation in Member States' Preferences and the Commission's Discretion in the Doha Round. *Journal of European Public Policy*, 18(3): 403–419.

Dahl, Robert, A. (1957) The Concept of Power. *Systems Research and Behavioural Science*, 2(3): 201–215.

Daugbjerg, Carsten and Swindbank, Alan (2004) The CAP and EU Enlargement: Prospects for an Alternative Strategy to Avoid the Lock-in of CAP Support, *Journal of Common Market Studies*, 42(1): 99–119.

David, Paul (1985) Clio and the Economics of QWERTY. *American Economic Review*, 75(2): 332–337.

Davidson, Donald (1963) Actions, Reasons, and Causes. *The Journal of Philosophy*, 60(23): 685–700.

Dawes, Anthony and Lynskey, Orla (2008) The Ever Longer Arm of EC Law: The Extension of Community Competence into the Field of Criminal Law. *Common Market Law Review*, 45(1): 131–158.

Delmas Marty, Mireille (1997) *Corpus Juris: Introducing Penal Provisions for the Purpose of the Financial Interests of the European Union*. Paris: Editions Economica.

Denza, Eileen (2012) 'The Role of the High Representative of the Union for Foreign Affairs and Security Policy', in Blanke, H. J. and Mangiameli, S. (eds.) *The European Union after Lisbon: Constitutional Basis, Economic Order and External Action*. Heidelberg: Springer, pp. 481–493.

Dijkstra, Hylke (2010) Explaining Variation in the Role of the Council Secretariat in First and Second Pillar Policy Making. *Journal of European Public Policy*, 17(4): 527–544.

Dimier, Véronique (2006) Constructing Conditionality: The Bureaucratization of EC Development Aid. *European Foreign Affairs Review*, 11(2): 263–280.

Dimier, Véronique and McGeever, Mike (2006) Diplomats without a Flag: The Institutionalization of the Delegations of the Commission in African, Caribbean and Pacific Countries. *Journal of Common Market Studies*, 44(3): 483–505.

Duffield, John (2007) What Are International Institutions? *International Studies Review*, 9(1): 1–22.

Duina, Francesco and Kurzer, Paulette (2004) Smoke in Your Eyes: The Struggle over Tobacco Control in the European Union. *Journal of European Public Policy*, 11(1): 57–77.

Dür, Andreas and Elsig, Manfred (2011) Principals, Agents, and the European Union's Foreign and Economic Policies. *Journal of European Public Policy*, 18(3): 323–338.

Edelman, Murray (1977) *Political Language: Words That Succeed and Policies That Fail*. New York: Academic Press.

Egeberg, Morten (2006) Executive Politics as Usual: Role Behaviour and Conflict Dimensions in the College of European Commissioners. *Journal of European Public Policy*, 13(1): 1–15.

Egeberg, Morten (2012) Experiments in Supranational Institution-Building: The European Commission as a Laboratory. *Journal of European Public Policy*, 19(6): 939–950.

Elinas, Antonis and Suleiman, Ezra (2011) Supranationalism in a Transnational Bureaucracy: The Case of the European Commission. *Journal of Common Market Studies*, 49(5): 923–947.

Elman, Colin (2005) Explanatory Typologies in Qualitative Studies of International Politics, *International Organization*, 59 (2): 293–326.

Elster, Jon (1989) *Nuts and Bolts for the Social Sciences*. Cambridge: Cambridge University Press.

Elster, Jon (1998) 'A Plea for Mechanisms' in Hedström, P. and Swedberg, R. (eds.) Social Mechanisms. Cambridge: Cambridge University Press.

Elster, Jon (1999) *Alchemies of the Mind: Rationality and the Emotions*. Cambridge: Cambridge University Press.

Elster, Jon (2007) *Explaining Social Behaviour: More Nuts and Bolts for the Social Sciences*. Cambridge: Cambridge University Press.

Eriksson, Johan and Rhinard, Mark (2009) The Internal-External Security Nexus: Notes on an Emerging Research Agenda. *Cooperation and Conflict*, 44(3): 243–267.

Farquharson, Karen (2005) A Different Kind of Snowball: Identifying Key Policymakers. *International Journal of Social Research Methodology*, 8(4): 345–353.

Farrell, Henry and Héritier, Adrienne (2003) Formal and Informal Institutions Under Codecision: Continuous Constitution-Building in Europe. *Governance: An International Journal of Policy, Administration, and Institutions*, 16(4): 577–600.

Farrell, Henry and Héritier, Adrienne (2007a) Introduction: Contested Competences in the European Union. *West European Politics*, 30(2): 227–243.

Farrell, Henry and Héritier, Adrienne (2007b) Conclusion: Evaluating the Forces of Interstitial Institutional Change. *West European Politics*, 30(2): 405–415.

Fearon, James and Alexander Wendt (1999) 'Rationalism v. Constructivism: A Skeptical View', in Carlsnaes, W., Risse, T. and Simmons, B. (eds.) *Handbook of International Relations*, London: Sage, pp. 52–72.

Fieretos, Orfeo (2011) Historical Institutionslism in International Relations, *International Organization*, 65(2): 367–399.

Fijnaut, Cyrille (2001) 'Transnational Organized Crime and Institutional Reform in the European Union: The Case of Judicial Cooperation', in Williams, P. and Vlassis, D. (eds.) *Combating Transnational Crime- Concepts, Activities and Responses*. London: Frank Cass, pp. 276–302.

Finnemore, Martha (1996) Norms, Culture, and World Politics: Insights from Sociology's Institutionalism. *International Organization*, 50(2): 324–347.

Finnemore, Martha and Sikkink, Kathryn (1998) International Norm Dynamics and Political Change. *International Organization*, 52(4): 887–917.

Fletcher, Maris and Lööf, Robin (2008) *EU Criminal Law and Justice*. Cheltenham: Edward Elgar Publishing.

Forwood, Genevra (2001) The road to Cotonou: Negotiating a Successor to Lomé. *Journal of Common Market Studies*, 39(3): 423–442.

Garrett, Geoffrey (1992) International Cooperation and Institutional Choice: The European Community's Internal Market. *International Organization*, 46(2): 533–560.

Garrett, Geoffrey, Kelemen, Daniel R. and Schulz, Heiner (1998) The European Court of Justice, National Governments, and Legal Integration in the European Union. *International Organization*, 52(1): 149–176.

Garrett, Geoffrey and Tsebelis, George (2001) The Institutional Foundations of Intergovernmentalism and Supranationalism in the European Union. *International Organization*, 55(2): 357–390.

Geertz, Clifford (1973) *The Interpretation of Cultures*. New York: Basic Books.

Gerring, John (2008) The Mechanismic Worldview: Thinking inside the Box. *British Journal of Political Science*, 38(1): 161–179.

Gibert, Marie V. (2009) The Securitization of the EU's Development Agenda in Africa: Insights from Guinea-Bissau. *Perspectives on European Politics and Society*, 10(4): 621–637.

Gofas, Andreas and Hay, Colin (2010) 'Varieties of Ideational Explanation', in Gofas, A. and Hay, C. (eds.) *The Role of Ideas in Political Analysis*, Oxon: Routledge, pp. 13–55.

Goldstein, Judith and Keohane, Robert O. (1993) 'Ideas and Foreign Policy: An Analytical Framework', in Keohane, R. and Goldstein, J. (eds.) *Ideas and Foreign Policy: Beliefs, Institutions and Political Change*, Ithaca: Cornell University Press, pp. 3–30.

Gosalbo-Bono, Ricardo (2006) Some Reflections on the CFSP Legal Order. *Common Market Law Review*, 43(2): 337–394.

Gross, Neil (2009) A Pragmatist Theory of Social Mechanisms. *American Sociological Review*, 74(3): 358–379.

Gryzmala-Busse, Anna (2011) Time Will Tell? Temporality and the Analysis of Causal Mechanisms and Processes. *Comparative Political Studies*, 44(9): 1267–1297.

Guzzini, Stefano (1993) Structural Power: The Limits of Neorealist Power Analysis. *International Organization*, 47(3): 443–478.

Guzzini, Stefano (2012) *The Return of Geopolitics in Europe? Social Mechanisms and Foreign Policy Identity Crises*. Cambridge: Cambridge University Press.

Haas, Ernst B. (1964) *Beyond the Nation State: Functionalism and International Organization*. Stanford: Stanford University Press.

Haas, Peter M. (1992) Epistemic Communities and International Policy Coordination: Introduction. *International Organization*, 46(1): 1–35.

Haas, Peter M. (2004) When does Power Listen to Truth? A Constructivist Approach to the Policy Process. *European Journal of Public Policy*, 11(4): 569–592.

Hacker, Jacob S. (1998) The Historical Logic of National Health Insurance: Structure and Sequence in the Development of British, Canadian, and U.S. Medical Policy. *Studies in American Political Development*, 12(1): 57–130.

Hacking, Ian (2000) *The Social Construction of What?* Cambridge, MA: Harvard University Press.

Hall, Peter A. (2003) 'Aligning Ontology and Methodology in Comparative Research', in Mahoney, J. and Rueschemeyer, D. (eds.) *Comparative Historical Analysis in the Social Sciences*. Cambridge: Cambridge University Press, pp. 373–404.

Hall, Peter A. (2010) 'Historical Institutionalism in Rationalist and Sociological Perspective', in Mahoney, J. and Thelen, K. (eds.) *Explaining Institutional Change: Ambiguity, Agency and Power*. Cambridge: Cambridge University Press, pp. 204–223.

Hall, Peter A. (2013) Tracing the Progress of Process Tracing. *European Political Science*, 12(1): 20–30.

Hansen, Peo and Jonsson, Stefan (2014) *Eurafrica: The Untold History of European Integration*. London: Bloomsbury.

Hansen, Susanne Therese (2016) Taking Ambiguity Seriously: Explaining the Indeterminacy of the European Union Conventional Arms Export Control Regime, *European Journal of International Relations*, 22(1): 192–216.

Harvey, William S. (2011) Strategies for Conducting Elite Interviews. *Qualitative Research*, 11(4): 431–441.

Hedström, Peter and Swedberg, Richard (1998) 'Social Mechanisms: An Introductory Essay', in Hedström, P. and Swedberg, R. (eds.) *Social Mechanisms: An Analytical Approach to Social Theory*, Cambridge: Cambridge University Press, pp. 1–31.

Hedström, Peter and Yliksoski, Petri (2010) Causal Mechanisms in the Social Sciences. *Annual Review of Sociology*, 36: 49–67.

Héritier, Adrienne (2007) *Explaining Institutional Change in Europe*. Oxford: Oxford University Press.

Héritier, Adrienne and Moury, Catherine (2012) Shifting Competences and Changing Preferences: The Case of the Delegation to Comitology. *Journal of European Public Policy*, 19(9): 1316–1335.

Herlin-Kernell, Ester (2007) Commission v. Council: Some Reflections on Criminal Law in the First Pillar. *European Public Law*, 13(1): 69–84.

Hettne, Björn (2010) Development and Security: Origins and Future. *Security Dialogue*, 41(1): 31–52.

Hewitt, Adrian (1989) 'ACP and the Developing World', in Lodge, J. (ed.) *The European Community and the Challenge of the Future*, London: Pinter, pp. 285–300.

Hewitt, Adrian and Whiteman, Kaye (2004) 'The Commission and Development Policy; Bureaucratic Politics in EU Aid: From the Lomé Leap Forward to the Difficulties of

Adapting to the Twenty-First Century', in Arts, K. and Dickson, Anna, K. (eds.) *EU Development Cooperation: From Model to Symbol*, Manchester: Manchester University Press, pp. 133–148.

Hillion, Christophe and Wessels, Ramses, A. (2009) Competence Distribution in EU External Relations after ECOWAS: Clarification or Continued Fuzziness? *Common Market Law Review*, 46(2): 551–586.

Hoffmann, Stanley (1982) Reflections on the Nation State in Western Europe Today. *Journal of Common Market Studies*, 21(1): 21–38.

Hoffmann, Stanley (1995) *The European Sisyphus: Essays on Europe 1964–1994*. Boulder: Westview Press.

Hooghe, Liesbeth (2012) Images of Europe: How Commission Officials Perceive Their Institutions. *Journal of Common Market Studies*, 50(1): 87–111.

Hopf, Ted (2002) *Social Construction of Foreign Policy: Identities and Foreign Policies, Moscow, 1955 and 1999*. Ithaca, NY: Cornell University Press.

Hopf, Ted (2010) The Logic of Habit in International Relations. *European Journal of International Relations*, 16(4): 539–561.

Hopf, Ted (2012) *Reconstructing the Cold War: The Early Years, 1945–1958*. New York: Oxford University Press.

Howorth, Jolyon (2007) *Security and Defence Policy in the European Union*. London: Palgrave Macmillan.

Huysmans, Jef (2000) The European Union and the Securitization of Immigration. *Journal of Common Market Studies*, 38(5): 751–777.

Immergut, Ellen M. (2005) 'Historical-Institutionalism in Political Science and the Problem of Change', in Wimmer, A. and Kössler, R. (eds.) *Understanding Change: Models, Methodologies, and Metaphors*. Houndmills: Palgrave Macmillan, pp. 237–259.

Jackson, Patrick Thaddeus and Nexon, Daniel, H. (2013) International Theory in a Post-Paradigmatic Era: From Substantive Wagers to Scientific Ontologies, *European Journal of International Relations*, 19(3): 543–565.

Jacobs, Allan M. (2009) How Do Ideas Matter? Mental Models and Attention in German Pension Politics. *Comparative Political Studies*, 42(2): 252–279.

Jacobs, Alan M. (2014) 'Process Tracing the Effects of Ideas', in Bennett, A. and Checkel, J. (eds.) *Process Tracing: From Metaphor to Analytical Tool*, Cambridge: Cambridge University Press, pp. 41–73.

Joerges, Christian and Neyer, Jürgen (1997) Transforming Strategic Interaction into Deliberative Problem-Solving: European Comitology in the Foodstuffs Sector. *Journal of European Public Policy*, 4(4): 609–625.

Johnson, James (2002) How Conceptual Problems Migrate: Rational Choice, Interpretation, and the Hazards of Pluralism. *Annual Review of Political Science*, 5: 223–248.

Jupille, Joseph (2007) Contested Procedures: Ambiguities, Interstices and EU Institutional Change, *West European Politics*, 30(2): 301–320.

Jupille, Joseph, Caporaso, James A. and Checkel, Jeffrey T. (2003) Integrating Institutions: Rationalism, Constructivism, and the Study of the European Union. *Comparative Political Studies*, 36(1–2): 7–40.

Kassim, Hussein and Menon, Anand (2003) The Principal-Agent Approach and the Study of the European Union: Promise Unfulfilled? *Journal of European Public Policy*, 10(1): 121–139.

Kaunert, Christian (2011) *European Internal Security: Towards Supranational Governance in the Area of Freedom Security and Justice?* Manchester: Manchester University Press.

Kelemen, Daniel R. (2012) The Political Foundations of Judicial Independence in the European Union. *Journal of European Public Policy*, 19(1): 43–58.

Keohane, Robert O. (1984) *After Hegemony: Cooperation and Discord in the World Political Economy*. Princeton, NJ: Princeton University Press.

Kingdon, John, W. (1995) *Agendas, Alternatives and Public Policies*. New York: HarperCollins.

Krasner Stephen D. (1995) 'Power Politics, Institutions, and Transnational Relations', in Risse-Kappen, T. (ed.) *Bringing Transnational Relations Back In: Non-State Actors, Domestic Structures and International Institutions*. Cambridge: Cambridge University Press, pp. 257–279.

Krause, Keith and Willliams, Michael C. (1996) Broadening the Agenda of Security Studies: Politics and Methods. *Mershon International Studies Review*, 40(2): 229–254.

Krook, Mona Lena and True, Jacqui (2012) Rethinking the Life Cycles of International Norms: The United Nations and the Global Promotion of Gender Equality, *European Journal of International Relations*, 18(1): 103–127.

Lebow, Richard Ned (2009) Constitutive Causality: Imagined Spaces and Political Practices. *Millennium: Journal of International Studies*, 38(2): 1–29.

Leech, Beth L. (2002) Asking Questions: Techniques for Semi structured Interviews. *Political Science and Politics*, 4: 665–668.

Lewis, Jeffrey (2005) The Janus Face of Brussels: Socialization and Everyday Decision Making in the European Union. *International Organization*, 59(4): 937–971.

Lindberg, Leon N. (1963) *The Political Dynamics of European Economic Integration*. Stanford, CA: Stanford University Press.

Mahoney, James (2012) The Logic of Process Tracing Tests in the Social Sciences. *Sociological Methods and Research*, 41(4): 570–597.

Mahoney, James and Thelen, Kathleen (2010) *Explaining Institutional Change: Ambiguity, Agency and Power*. New York: Cambridge University Press.

Mangenot, Michel (2006) Jeux Européens et Innovation Institutionnelle: Les logiques de Création d'Eurojust (1996–2004). *Cultures et Conflits*, 62: 1–16.

March, James G. and Olsen, Johan P. (1989) *Rediscovering Institutions: The Organizational Basis of Politics*. New York: The Free Press.

March, James G. and Olsen, Johan P. (1998) The Institutional Dynamics of International Political Orders. *International Organization*, 52(4): 943–969.

Marcussen, Martin, Risse, Thomas, Eneglmann-Martin, Daniela, Knopf, Hans Joachim, Roscher, Klaus (1999) Constructing Europe? The Evolution of French, British, and German Nation-State Identities, *Journal of European Public Policy*, 6(4): 641–633.

Mattli, Walter and Slaughter, Anne-Marie (1998) Revisiting the European Court of Justice. *International Organization*, 52(1): 177–210.

Mayntz, Renate (2004) Mechanisms in the Analysis of Social Macro-Phenomena. *Philosophy of the Social Sciences*, 34(2): 237–259.

Mearsheimer, John J. (1995) The False Promise of International Institutions. *International Security*, 19(3): 5–49.

Meyer, John W. and Rowan, Brian (1977) Institutional Organizations: Formal Structure as Myth and Ceremony. *American Journal of Sociology*, 83(2): 340–363.

Michalski, Anna and Norman, Ludvig (2015) Conceptualizing European Security Cooperation: Competing International Political Orders and Domestic Factors. *European Journal of International Relations*. doi:10.1177/1354066115602938.

Mitsilegas, Valsamis, Monar, Jörg and Rees, Wyn (2003) *The European Union: Guardian of the People?* Basingstoke: Palgrave Macmillan.

Mitzen, Jennifer (2006) Ontological Security in World Politics: State Identity and the Security Dilemma. *European Journal of International Relations*, 12(3): 341–370.

Monar, Jörg (2001) The Dynamics of Justice and Home Affairs: Laboratories, Driving Factors and Costs. *Journal of Common Market Studies* 39(4): 747–764.

Moore, Barrington (1966) *Social Origins of Dictatorship and Democracy*. Boston: Beacon Press.

Moravcsik, Andrew (1998) *The Choice for Europe: Social Purpose and State Power from Messina to Maastricht*. Ithaca: Cornell University Press.

Morin, Jean-Frédéric and Gold, Richard E. (2010) Consensus-seeking, Distrust and Rhetorical Entrapment. *European Journal of International Relations*, 16(4): 563–587.

Mörth, Ulrika (2000) Competing Frames in the European Commission: The Case of the Defence Industry and Equipment Issue. *Journal of European Public Policy*, 7(2): 173–189.

Mörth, Ulrika (2003) *Organizing European Cooperation*. Oxford: Rowman and Littlefield.

Müller, Harald (2004) Arguing, Bargaining and All That: Communicative Action, Rationalist Theory and the Logic of Appropriateness. *European Journal of International Relations*, 10(3): 395–435.

Naurin, Daniel, Hayes Renshaw, Fiona and Wallace, Helen (forthcoming) *The Council of Ministers* (3rd ed). Basingstoke: Palgrave Macmillan.

Nay, Oliver (2012) How Do Policy Ideas Spread Among International Administrations? Policy Entrepreneurs and Bureaucratic Influence in the UN response to Aids. *Journal of Public Policy*, 32(1): 53–76.

Neumann Iver, B. and Pouliot, Vincent (2011) Untimely Russia: Hysteresis in Russian-Western Relations over the Past Millennium. *Security Studies*, 20(1): 105–137.

Neyer, Jürgen (2006) The Deliberative Turn in Integration Theory. *Journal of European Public Policy*, 13(5): 779–791.

Nilsson, Hans G. (1991) The Council of Europe Laundering Convention: A Recent Example of a Developing International Criminal Law. *Criminal Law Forum*, 2(3): 419–441.

Nilsson, Hans G. (2004) 'The Justice and Home Affairs Council', in Galloway, D. and Westlake, M. (eds.) *The Council of the European Union* (3rd ed.), London: John Harper, pp. 113–142.

Norman, Ludvig (2015a) When Norms and Rules Collide: The Social Production of Institutional Conflict in the European Union. *Journal of European Public Policy*, 22(5): 630–649.

Norman, Ludvig (2015b) Interpretive Process Tracing and Causal Explanations. *Newsletter of the American Political Science Association Organized Section for Qualitative and Multi-Methods Research*, 13(2): 4–9.

North, Douglas C. (1990) *Institutions, Institutional Change, and Economic Performance*. Cambridge: Cambridge University Press.

Nugent, Neil and Rhinard, Mark (2015) *The European Commission*. Basingstoke: Palgrave Macmillan.

Occhipinti, John D. (2002) *The Politics of EU Police Cooperation: Toward a European FBI?* Boulder: Lynne Rienner.

O'Mahoney Joseph (2014) Rule Tensions and the Dynamics of Institutional Change: From 'to the Victor go the Spoils' to the Stimson Doctrine. *European Journal of International Relations*, 20(3): 834–857.

Ostrom, Elinor (1986) An Agenda for the Study of Institutions. *Public Choice*, 48(1): 3–25.

Parsons, Craig (2010). "How—and How Much—Are Sociological Approaches to the EU Distinct?" *Comparative European Politics*, 8(1): 143–159.

Parsons, Craig (2016) Ideas and Power: Four Intersections and how to Show them, *Journal of European Public Policy*, 23(3): 446–463.

Peterson, John and Shakleton, Michael (eds.) (2012) *The Institutions of the EU*. Oxford: Oxford University Press.

Pierson, Paul (1996) The Path to European Integration. *Comparative Political Studies*, 29(2): 123–163.

Pierson, Paul (2000) Increasing Returns, Path Dependency and the Study of Politics. *American Political Science Review*, 94(2): 251–267.

Pierson, Paul (2004) *Politics in Time: History, Institutions, and Social Analysis*. Princeton: Princeton University Press.

Pollack, Mark A. (1994) Creeping Competence: The Expanding Agenda of the European Union. *Journal of Public Policy*, 14(2): 95–145.

Pollack, Mark A. (2003a) *The Engines of European Integration: Delegation, Agency and Agenda Setting in the EU*. Oxford: Oxford University Press.

Pollack, Mark A. (2003b) Control Mechanism or Deliberative Democracy? Two Images of Comitology. *Comparative Political Studies*, 36(1–2): 125–155.

Pouliot, Vincent (2008) The Logic of Practicality: A Theory of Practice of Security Communities. *International Organization*, 62(2): 257–288.

Pouliot, Vincent (2014) 'Practice Tracing', in Bennett, A. and Checkel, J. T. (eds.) *Process Tracing in the Social Sciences: From Metaphor to Analytical Tool*, Cambridge: Cambridge University Press, 237–259.

Powell, Walter W. (1993) 'Expanding the Scope of Institutional Analysis', in Powell, W. and DiMaggio, P. (eds.) *The New Institutionalism in Organizational Analysis*, Chicago: Chicago University Press, pp. 183–203.

Powell, Walter W. and DiMaggio, Paul (eds.) (1993) *The New Institutionalism in Organizational Analysis*. Chicago: Chicago University Press.

Princen, S. and Rhinard, M. (2006) Crashing and Creeping: Agenda-Setting Dynamics in the European Union. *Journal of European Public Policy*, 13(7): 1119–1132.

Quaglia, Lucia (2010) Completing the Single Market in Financial Services: The Politics of Competing Advocacy Coalitions. *Journal of European Public Policy*, 17(7): 1107–1023.

Radaelli, Claudio M. (1999) The Public Policy of the European Union: Whither the Politics of Expertise? *Journal of European Public Policy*, 6(5): 757–774.

Radaelli, Claudio M. (2000) Policy Transfer in the European Union: Institutional Isomorphism as a Source of Legitimacy. *Governance: An International Journal of Policy and Administration*, 13(1): 25–43.

Rawls, John (1955) Two Concepts of Rules. *The Philosophical Review*, 64(1): 3–32.

Rees, Wyn (2008) Inside Out: The External Face of EU Internal Security Policy. *Journal of European Integration*, 30(1): 97–111.

Reckwitz, Andreas (2002) Towards a Theory of Social Practices: A Development in Culturalist Theorizing. *European Journal of Social Theory*, 5(2): 243–263.

Rein, Martin and Schön, Donald (1994) *Frame Reflection: Toward the Resolution of Intractable Policy Controversies*. New York: Basic Books.

Rhinard, Mark (2010) *Framing Europe: The Policy Shaping Strategies of the European Commission*. Dordrecht: Martinus Nijhoff Publishers.

Richards, David (1996) Elite Interviewing: Approaches and Pitfalls. *Politics*, 16(3): 199–204.

Ripoll Servent, Ariadna (2013) Holding the European Parliament Responsible: Policy Shift in the Data Retention Directive from Consultation to Codecision. *Journal of European Public Policy*, 20(7): 972–987.

Risse, Thomas (2000) Let's Argue! Communicative Action in International Relations. *International Organization*, 54(1): 1–39.

Risse-Kappen, Thomas, Ropp, Stephen C. and Sikkink, Kathryn (1999) *The Power of Human Rights: International Norms and Domestic Change*. Cambridge: Cambridge University Press.

Rittberger, Berthold and Schimmelfennig, Frank (2006) Explaining the Constitutionalization of the European Union. *Journal of European Public Policy*, 13(8): 1148–1167.

Rittberger, Berthold and Stacey, Jeffrey (2003) Dynamics of Formal and Informal Institutional Change in the EU, *Journal of European Public Policy*, 10(6): 858–883.

Rochefort, David A. and Cobb, Roger W. (1994) *The Politics of Problem Definition: Shaping the Policy Agenda*. Lawrence: University of Kansas Press.

Ross, George (1995) *Jacques Delors and European Integration*. New York: Oxford University Press.

Ruggie, John Gerard (1998) *Constructing the World Polity: Essays on International Institutionalization*. London: Routledge.

Ryland, Diane (2009) The Protection of the Environment through Criminal Law: A Question of Competence Unabated. *Energy and Environmental Law Review*, 18(2): 91–111.

Sabatier, Paul A. (1998) The Advocacy Coalition Framework: Revisions and Relevance for Europe. *Journal of European Public Policy*, 5(1): 98–130.

Sandholtz, Wayne (2008) Dynamics of International Norm Change: Rules Against Wartime Plunder, *European Journal of International Relations*, 14(1): 101–131.

Saurugger, Sabine (2013) Constructivism and Public Policy Approaches in the EU: From Ideas to Power Games, *Journal of European Public Policy*, 20 (6): 888–906.

Schafer, Jerome (2014) European Commission Officials' Attitudes. *Journal of Common Market Studies*, 52(4):911–927.

Scharpf, Fritz (2006) The Joint-Decision Trap Revisited. *Journal of Common Market Studies*, 44(4): 845–864.

Scharpf, Fritz (2012) Perpetual Momentum: Directed and Unconstrained?. *Journal of European Public Policy*, 19(1): 127–139.

Schattschneider, Elmer, E. (1960) *The Semisovereign People: A Realist View of Democracy in America*. New York: Holt, Rinehart, Winston.

Schimmelfennig, Frank (2001) The Community Trap: Liberal Norms, Rhetorical Action, and the Eastern Enlargement of the European Union. *International Organization*, 55(1): 47–80.

Schimmelfennig, Frank (2014) Efficient Process Tracing: Analyzing the Causal Mechanisms of European Integration, in Bennett, A. and Checkel, J.T. (eds.) *Process Tracing: From Metaphor to Analytical Tool*, Cambridge: Cambridge University Press, pp. 98–125.

Schmidt, Susanne K. (2004) 'The European Commission's Powers in Shaping European Policies', in Dimitrakopoulos, D. (ed.) *The Changing European Commission*, Manchester: Manchester University Press, pp. 105–120.

Schmidt, Susanne K. (2012) Who Cares about Nationality? The Path-Dependent Case Law of the ECJ from Goods to Citizens. *Journal of European Public Policy*, 19(1): 8–24.

Schmidt, Vivien, A. (2008) Discursive Institutionalism: The Explanatory Power of Ideas and Discourse, *Annual Review of Political Science*, 11: 303–326.

Searle, John R. (1995) *The Construction of Social Reality*. New York: Free Press.

Sending, Ole Jacob (2002) Constitution, Choice and Change: Problems with the 'Logic of Appropriateness' and Its Use in Constructivist Theory. *European Journal of International Relations*, 8(4): 443–470.

Skocpol, Theda (1973) A Critical Review of Barrington Moore's Social Origins of Dictatorship and Democracy. *Politics and Society*, 4(1): 1–34.

Smith, Michael E. (2004) *Europe's Foreign and Security Policy: The Institutionalization of Cooperation*. Cambridge: Cambridge University Press.

Spencer, John R. (1998) 'The Corpus Juris and the Fight against Budgetary Fraud', in Dashwood, A. and Ward, A. (eds.) *Cambridge Year Book of European Legal Studies, Vol. I*, Oxford: Hart, pp. 77–106.

Steele, Brent J. (2008) *Ontological Security in International Relations: Self-Identity and the IR State*. Oxon: Routledge.

Stein, Arthur A. (2008) 'Neo-Liberal Institutionalism', in Reus-Smith, C. and Snidal, D. (eds.) *The Oxford Handbook of International Relations*. Oxford: Oxford University Press, pp. 201–221.

Stetter, Stefan (2007) *EU Foreign and Interior Policies: Cross-Pillar Politics and the Social Construction of Sovereignty*. Oxon: Routledge.

Stillhof Sörensen, Jens and Söderbaum, Fredrik (2012) Introduction: The End of the Development-Security Nexus? *Development Dialogue*, 58: 7–19.

Stinchcombe, Arthur L. (1991) The Conditions of Fruitfulness of Theorizing About Mechanisms in Social Science. *Philosophy of the Social Sciences*, 21(3): 367–388.

Stone, Diane (2004) Transfer Agents and Global Networks in the 'Transnationalization' of Policy. *Journal of European Public Policy*, 11(3): 545–566.

Stone Sweet, Alec and Sandholtz, Wayne (1998) *European Integration and Supranational Governance*. Oxford: Oxford University Press.

Stone Sweet, Alec, Sandholtz, Wayne and Fligstein, Neil (2001) 'The Institutionalization of European Space', in Stone Sweet, A., Sandholtz, W. and Fligstein, N. (eds.) The Institutionalization of Europe, Oxford: Oxford University Press, pp. 1–28.

Tallberg, Jonas (2000) The Anatomy of Autonomy: An Institutional Account of Variation on Supranational Influence. *Journal of Common Market Studies*, 38(5): 843–864.

Tallberg, Jonas (2002) Delegation to Supranational Institutions: Why, How and with What Consequences? *West European Politics*, 25(1): 23–46.

Tansey, Oísin (2007) Process-Tracing and Elite Interviewing: A Case for Non-Probability Sampling. *PS: Political Science and Politics*, 40(4): 765–772.

Thelen, Kathleen (2004) *How Institutions Evolve: The Political Economy of Skills in Germany, Britain, the United States and Japan*. New York: Cambridge University Press.

Thomson, Robert (2008) National Actors in International Organization: The Case of the European Commission. *Comparative Political Studies*, 41(2): pp. 169–192.

Tilly, Charles (1996) 'Citizenship, Identity and Social History', in Charles, T. (ed.) *Citizenship, Identity and Social History*, Cambridge: Cambridge University Press, pp. 1–18.

Tilly, Charles (2001) Mechanisms in Political Processes. *Annual Review of Political Science*, 4: 21–41.

Tonra, Ben (2000) 'Committees in Common: Committee Governance and CFSP', in Christiansen, T. and Kirchner, E. (eds.) *Committee Governance in the European Union*, Manchester: Manchester University Press, pp. 145–60.

Van Ooik, Ronald (2008) Cross-Pillar Litigation before the ECJ: Demarcation of Community and Union Competences. *European Constitutional Law Review*, 4: 399–420.

Waever, Ole (1995) 'Securitization and Desecuritization', in Lipschutz, R. (ed.) *On security*. New York: Columbia University Press, pp. 46–86.

Waldner, David (2010) What Are Mechanisms and What Are They Good For? *QMMR Newsletter*, 34(2): 30–34.

Waldner, David (2012) 'Process Tracing and Causal Mechanisms', in Kincaid, H. (ed.) *The Oxford Handbook of Philosophy of Social Science*, Oxford: Oxford University Press, pp. 66–84.

Waldner, David (2014) What Makes Process Tracing Good? Causal Mechanisms, Causal Inference, and the Completeness Standard in Comparative Politics, in Bennett, A. and Checkel, J. T. (eds.) *Process Tracing: From Metaphor to Analytical Tool*, Cambridge: Cambridge University Press, pp. 126–152.

Wasmeier, Martin and Thwaites, Nadine (2004) The 'Battle of the Pillars': Does the European Community Have the Power to Approximate National Criminal Laws? *European Law Review*, 29(5): 613–635.

Weiler, Joseph H. H. (1991) The Transformation of Europe. *Yale Law Journal*, 100(8): 2403–2483.

Weiler, Joseph H. H. (1999) *The Constitution of Europe*. Cambridge: Cambridge University Press

Weiss, Moritz and Dalferth, Simon (2009) Security Re-Divided: The Distinctiveness of Policy-Making in ESDP and JHA. *Cooperation and Conflict*, 44(3): 268–287.

Wendon, B. (1998) The Commission as Image-Venue Entrepreneur in EU Social Policy. *Journal of European Public Policy*, 5(2): 339–353.

Wendt, Alexander (1998) On Constitution and Causation in International Relations. *Review of International Studies*, 24(5): 101–118.

Wendt, Alexander (1999) *Social Theory of International Relations*. Cambridge: Cambridge University Press.

Wessels, Ramses E. (2012) Initiative and Voting in Common Foreign and Security Policy: The New Lisbon Rules in Historical Perspective', in Blanke, H. J. and Mangiameli, S. (eds.) *The European Union after Lisbon: Constitutional Basis, Economic Order and External Action*, Springer: Heidelberg, pp. 495–515.

Whitford, Josh (2002) Pragmatism and the Untenable Dualism of Means and Ends: Why Rational Choice Does Not Deserve Paradigmatic Privilege. *Theory and Society*, 31(3): 325–363.

Wiener, Antje (2004) Contested Compliance: Interventions on the Normative Structure of World Politics, *European Journal of International Relations*, 10(2): 189–234.

Wight, Colin (2004) Theorizing the Mechanisms of Conceptual and Semiotic Space. *Philosophy of the Social Sciences*, 34(2): 283–299.

Williams, David and Young, Tom (1994) Governance, the World Bank and Liberal Theory. *Political Studies*, 42(1): 84–100.

Wonka, Arndt (2008) Decision Making Dynamics in the European Commission: Partisan, National or Sectoral? *Journal of European Public Policy*, 7(2): 173–189.

World Bank (1989) *Sub-Saharan Africa, From Crisis to Sustainable Growth*. Washington DC: The World Bank.

Yanow, Dvora (2006) 'Thinking Interpretively: Philosophical Presuppositions and the Human Sciences', in Schwartz-Shea, P. and Yanow, D. (eds.) *Interpretation and Method: Empirical Research and the Interpretive Turn*, New York: Armonk, pp. 5–26.

Ylikoski, Petri (2013) Causal and Constitutive Explanation Compared, *Erkenntnis*, 78(2): 277–297.

Youngs, Richard (2008) Fusing Security and Development: Just Another Euro-platitude? *European Integration*, 30(3): 419–437.

Zarakol, Ayse (Forthcoming) States and Ontological Security: A Historical Rethinking. *Cooperation and Conflict*.

## Official documents and legislation

Commission of the European Communities (1976a) Draft for a Treaty Amending the Treaties establishing the European Communities so as to permit the Adoption of Common Rules on the Protection under Criminal Law of the Financial Interests of the

Communities and the Prosecution of infringements of the Provisions of the said Treaties. *Official Journal of the European Communities*, C 222, 22.9.1976, p. 2.

Commission of the European Communities (1976b) Draft for a Treaty Amending the Treaty Establishing a Single Council and Single Commission of the European Communities so as to permit the Adoption of Common Rules on the Liability and the Protection under Criminal Law of Officials and other Servants of the European Communities. *Official Journal of the European Communities*, C 222, 22.9.1976, p. 13.

Commission of the European Communities (1989) *Legal Protection of the Financial Interests of the Community*, Proceedings of the Seminar Organized by the Directorate-General for Financial Control and the Legal Service of the Commission of the European Communities on the 27, 28, 29 November 1989 in Brussels. *Luxembourg: Office for Official Publications of the European Communities*, 27.11.1989.

Commission of the European Communities (1990) Proposal for a Council Directive on Prevention of use of the Financial System for the Purpose of Money Laundering, COM (90) 106 Final. *Official Journal of the European Communities*, C 106, 28.04.90, p. 6.

Commission of the European Communities (1991) Commission Communication to the Council and the Parliament. Human Rights, Democracy and Development Cooperation Policy, SEC (91) Final, 25.03.91.

Commission of the European Communities (1992a) Development Cooperation Policy in the Run-Up to 2000: The Consequences of the Maastricht Treaty. SEC (92) 915 Final, 15.05.1992.

Commission of the European Communities (1992b) Communication from the Commission to the Council and the European Parliament. The Operation of the Community's Internal Market After: Follow-Up to the Sutherland Report, 1992 SEC (92)2277 Final, 02.12.1992.

Commission of the European Communities (1993a) Commission Staff Working Paper, SEC (93)1172, 16.07.1993.

Commission of the European Communities (1993b) Communication from the Commission to the Council: Making the Most of the Internal Market: Strategic Program, COM (93) 632 Final, 22.12.1993.

Commission of the European Communities (1994a) Communication to the Council and the European Parliament on the Development of Administrative Cooperation in the Implementation and Enforcement of Community Legislation in the Internal Market, COM (94) 29 Final, 16.02.1994.

Commission of the European Communities (1994b) Proposal for a Council of the European Union Act for the Establishment of a Convention for the Protection of the Communities' Financial Interests, COM (1994) 214 Final, 15.06.1994.

Commission of the European Communities (1995) Communication from the Commission to the Council and the European Parliament on the Role of Penalties in Implementing Community Internal Market legislation, COM (95) 162 Final, 03.05.1995.

Commission of the European Communities (1996) Green Paper on Relations between the European Union and the ACP Countries on the Eve of the 21st Century: Challenges and Options for a New Partnership, COM (96) 570 Final, 20.11.1996.

Commission of the European Communities (2001a) *Small Arms and Light Weapons: The Response of the European Union*. Brussels: Office for Official Publications of the European Communities.

Commission of the European Communities (2001b) Proposal for a Directive of the European Parliament and of the Council on the Protection of the Environment through Criminal Law, COM (2001)139 Final. *Official Journal of the European Communities*, C 180/E 238, 26.06.2001, pp. 238–243.

Commission of the European Communities (2003a) Requête Contre le Conseil de l'Union Européenne, JURM (2003) 6006 JFP/fag, 14.04.2003.

Commission of the European Communities (2003b) Mémoire en réplique dans l'affaire 176/03. JURM(2003) 6032 JFP/fag, 18.09.2003.

Commission of the European Communities (2003c) Communication from the Commission to the Council and the European Parliament: Towards the Full Integration of Co-operation with ACP Countries in the EU Budget, COM (2003) 590 Final, 08.10.2003.

Commission of the European Communities (2004) Observations de la Commission sur les Mémoires en Intervention Présentés par les États Membres dans l'Affaire C-176/03, JURM (2004)6023 JFP/nf, 21.06.2004.

Commission of the European Communities (2005a) Application to the Court. D (2005), JURM 10007, 14.02.2005.

Commission of the European Communities (2005b) Reply in Case 91/05, JURM (2005) 10025, 04.07.2005.

Commission of the European Communities (2005c) Communication from Commission to the European Parliament and the Council on the Implications of the Court's Judgement of 13 September 2005 (Case C-176/03 Commission v Council), COM (2005) 583 final, 24.11.2005.

Commission of the European Communities (2006a) *The European Union Mine Actions in the World.* Luxembourg: Office for Official Publications of the European Communities.

Commission of the European Communities (2006b) Observations on the Statements in Intervention in Case 91/05, JURM (2006) 10012, 13.03.2006.

Commission (2012) 29th Annual Report on Monitoring the Application of EU Law, COM (2012)714 final, 30.11.2012.

Commission of the European Communities (2013a) Statistical Bulletin http://ec.europa.eu/civil_service/about/figures/index_en.htm (Accessed 2 May 2013).

Commission of the European Communities (2013b) Proposal for a Regulation on the Establishment of a European Public Prosecutor's Office, COM (2013) 534 Final, 17.07.2013.

Cotonou Agreement (2000) Partnership Agreement between the Members of the African, Caribbean and Pacific Group of States of the one Part, and the European Community and its Member States, of the other Part, Signed in Cotonou on 23 June 2000. *Official Journal of the European Communities*, L 317/3, 15.12.2000, pp. 3–64.

Council of Europe (1990) Council of Europe Convention on Laundering, Search, Seizure and Confiscation of the Proceeds of Crimes, ETS 141, 08.11.1990.

Council of Europe (1998) Convention on the Protection of the Environment through Criminal Law, ETS 172, 04.11.1998.

Council of the European Union (1987) Council Regulation (EEC) No 2241/87 of 23 July 1987 Establishing certain Control Measures for Fishing Activities, OJ 1987 L 207, 29.7.1987, p. 1.

Council of the European Union (1991a) Council Directive 91/308/EEC on Prevention of the use of the Financial System for the Purpose of Money Laundering. *Official Journal of the European Communities*, OJ L 166, 28.6.1991, pp. 77–82.

Council of the European Union (1991b) Resolution of the Council and the Member States meeting in the Council on Human Rights, Democracy and Development. *Bulletin of the European Communities*, 24(11), pp. 122–123.

Council of the European Union (1992) Council Resolution of 7 December 1992 on Making the Single Market Work. *Official Journal of the European Communities*, C 334, 18.12.92, p. 1.

Council of the European Union (1993) Council regulation (EEC) No 2847/93 of 12 October 1993 Establishing a Control System Applicable to the Common Fisheries Policy. *Official Journal of the European Communities*, L 261, 20.20.1993, pp. 1–16.

Council of the European Union (1994) Council Resolution on the Development of Administrative Cooperation in the Implementation and Enforcement of Community Legislation in the Internal Market. *Official Journal of the European Communities*, C 179, 01.07.1994, p. 1.

Council of the European Union (1995a) Council Resolution of 29 June on the Effective Uniform Application of Community Law and on the Penalties Applicable for Breaches of Community Law in the Internal Market, *Official Journal of the European Communities*, C 188, 22.07.1995, p. 1–3.

Council of the European Union (1995b) Council Act of 26 July 1995 Drawing up the Convention of the Protection of the European Communities' Financial Interests. *Official Journal of the European Communities*, C 316, 27.11.1995, pp. 48–57.

Council of the European Union (1999a) Joint Action of 17 December 1998 Adopted by the Council on the Basis of Article J.3 of the Treaty of the European Union on the European Union's Contribution to Combating the Destabilising Accumulation and Spread of Small Arms and Light Weapons. 1999/34/CFSP, *Official Journal of the European Communities*, L 9/1, 15.01.1999, pp. 1–5.

Council of the European Union (1999b) Council Resolution on Small Arms and Light Weapons, 8435/99, 21.05.1999.

Council of the European Union (1999c) Presidency Conclusions, Tampere European Council, 15–16 October 1999, No 200/1/99, 16.10.1999.

Council of the European Union (1999d) Council Decision of 17 December 1999 Implementing Joint Action 1999/34/CFSP with a View to a European Union Contribution to Combating the Destabilising Accumulation and Spread of Small Arms and Light Weapons in Mozambique, 1999/845/CFSP. *Official Journal of the European Communities*, 1999 L 326, 18.12.1999, p. 73.

Council of the European Union (2000a) Initiative of the Kingdom of Denmark with a View to Adopting a Council Framework Decision on Combating Serious Environmental Crime. 2000/C 39/ 05. *Official Journal of the European Communities*, C 39/4, 11.02.2000, pp. 4–7.

Council of the European Union (2000b) Council Framework Decision of 29 May 2000 on Increasing Protection by Criminal Penalties and other Sanctions against Counterfeiting in Connection with the Introduction of the Euro, 2000/383/JHA. *Official Journal of the European Communities*, L 140, 14.06.2000, pp. 1–3.

Council of the European Union (2001a) Opinion of the Legal Service of the Council on the Draft EU Framework Decision on the Protection of the Environment through Criminal Law, 6793/01, 05.03.2001.

Council of the European Union (2001b) Regulation (EC) 1049/2001 of the European Parliament and of the Council of 30 May 2001 Regarding Public Access to European Parliament, Council and Commission Documents. *Official Journal of the European Communities*, L 145/43, 31.5.2001, pp. 43–47.

Council of the European Union (2001c) Council Framework Decision 2001/413/JHA of 28 May 2001 on Combating Fraud and Counterfeiting of Non-Cash Means of Payment, *Official Journal of the European Union*, OJ L 149, 02.06.2001, pp. 1–4.

Council of the European Union (2001d) Council Framework Decision 2001/500/JHA of 26 June 2001 on Money Laundering, the Identification, Tracing, Freezing, Seizing and Confiscation of Instrumentalities and the Proceeds of Crime. *Official Journal of the European Communities*, L 82/1, 05.07.2001, pp. 1–2.

Council of the European Union (2001e) Regulation (EC) No 1724/2001 of the European Parliament and of the Council of 23 July 2001 Concerning Action against Anti-Personnel

Landmines in Developing Countries. *Official Journal of the European Communities*, L 234/1, 01.09.2001, pp. 1–5.

Council of the European Union (2001f) Council Regulation (EC) No 1725/2001 of 23 July 2001 Concerning Action against Anti-Personnel Landmines in Third Countries other than Developing Countries. *Official Journal of the European Communities*, L 234, 01.09.2001, pp. 6–9.

Council of the European Union (2002a) Joint Action of 12 July 2002 on the European Union's Contribution to Combating the Destabilising Accumulation and Spread of Small Arms and Light Weapons and Repealing Joint Action 1999/34/CFSP, 2002/589/CFSP. *Official Journal of the European Communities*, L 191, 19.07.2002, pp. 1–4.

Council of the European Union (2002b) Council Decision of 21 October 2002 Concerning the Implementation of Joint Action 2002/589/CFSP with a View to a European Union Contribution to Combating the Destabilising Accumulation and Spread of Small Arms and Light Weapons in South East Europe, 2002/842/CFSP. *Official Journal of the European Communities*, L 289, 21.10.2002, pp. 1–2.

Council of the European Union (2002c) Council Framework Decision on the Strengthening of the Penal Framework to Prevent the Facilitation of Unauthorized Entry, Transit, and Residence. 2002/946/JHA. *Official Journal of the European Communities OJ*, L 328, 05.12.2002, pp. 1–3.

Council of the European Union (2002d) Council Directive 2002/90/EC of 28 November 2002 Defining the Facilitation of Unauthorized Entry, Transit and Residence. *Official Journal of the European Communities*, L 328, 05.12.2002, pp. 17–18.

Council of the European Union (2003a) Council Framework Decision on 2003/80/JHA of 27 January 2003 on the Protection of the Environment through Criminal Law. *Official Journal of the European Union*, L 29/55, 05.02.2003, pp. 55–58.

Council of the European Union (2003b) Mémoire en Défense du Conseil dans l'Affaire C-176/03, 01.06.2003.

Council of the European Union (2003c) Council Decision of 21 July 2003 Concerning the Implementation of Joint Action 2002/589 with a View of a European Union Contribution to Combating the Destabilizing Accumulation and Spread of Small Arms and Light Weapons in Latin America and the Caribbean, 2003/543/CFSP. *Official Journal of the European Union*, L 185, 24.07.2003, p. 59.

Council of the European Union (2003d) *A Secure Europe in a Better World: European Security Strategy*, 12.12.2003.

Council of the European Union (2004a) Note from Presidency to COREPER II, 14253/04, 08.11.2004.

Council of the European Union (2004b) Council Decision of 22 November 2004 Extending and Amending Decision 2003/276/CFSP implementing Joint Action 2002/589 with a view to a European Union Contribution to the Destruction of Small Arms and Light Weapons in Albania, 2004/790/CFSP. *Official Journal of the European Union*, L 348, 24.11.2004, p. 45.

Council of the European Union (2004c) Council Decision 2004/791/CFSP of 22 November 2004 Extending and Amending Decision 2002/842/CFSP Implementing Joint Action 2002/589 with a View to a European Union Contribution to the Destabilising Accumulation and Spread of Small Arms and Light Weapons in South East Europe. *Official Journal of the European Union*, L 348, 24.11.2004, p. 46.

Council of the European Union (2004d) Council Decision 2004/792/CFSP of 22 November 2004 Extending and Amending Decision 1999/730/CFSP Implementing Joint Action 1999/34 with a View to a European Union Contribution to Combating the Destabilising Accumulation and Spread of Small Arms and Light Weapons in Cambodia. *Official Journal of the European Union*, L 348, 24.11.2004, p. 47.

Council of the European Union (2004e) Draft Council Decision Implementing Joint Action 2002/589/CFSP with a View to a European Union Contribution in the Framework of the ECOWAS Moratorium for Small Arms and Light Weapons (SALW), 15236/04, 25.11.2004.

Council of the European Union (2004f) Decision 2004/833/CFSP of 2 December 2004 Implementing Joint Action 2002/589/CFSP of 12 July 2002 with a View to a European Union Contribution to ECOWAS in the Framework of the Moratorium on Small Arms and Light Weapons. *Official Journal of the European Union*, L 359, 04.12.2004, pp. 65–66.

Council of the European Union (2005a) The European Consensus on Development. *Official Journal of the European Union*, C 46/1, 24.02.2006, pp. 1–19.

Council of the European Union (2005b) Statement of Defence in Case C-91/05, 12.05.2005.

Council of the European Union (2005c) Rejoinder in Case 91/05. SN 3226/05 EN, 22.09.2005.

Council of the European Union (2005d) Council Framework Decision 2005/667/JHA of 12 July 2005 to Strengthen the Criminal-law Framework for the Enforcement of the Law against Ship-source Pollution. *Official Journal of the European Union*, L 255, 30.09.2005, pp. 164–167.

Council of the European Union (2006a) EU Strategy to Combat Illicit Accumulation and Trafficking of SALW and their Ammunition, 5319/06, 13.01.2006.

Council of the European Union (2006b) Directive 2006/24/EC of the European Parliament and the Council of 15 March 2006 on the Retention of Data Generated or Processed in Connection with the Provision of Publicly Available Electronic Communications Services or of Public Communications Networks and Amending Directive 2002/58/EC. *Official Journal of the European Union*, L 105, 13. 04. 2006, pp. 54–60.

Council of the European Union (2008) Opinion of the Legal Service: Follow-Up to Judgment of ECJ of May 2008 in Case C-91/05 Commission v Council (ECOWAS), Small Arms and Light Weapons, 10986/08, 18.07.2008.

Council of the European Union (2013) List of Council Preparatory Bodies, 5581/13.

De Kerchove, Gilles (2002) Intervention de Gilles de Kerchove, Directeur du Sécretariat Général du Conseil devant la Groupe de Travail X 'Liberté, Sécurité et Justice, 08.10.2002.

European Parliament (2002) Resolution on the Draft Council Framework Decision on the Protection of the Environment through Criminal Law, 09.04.2002.

European Parliament (2005) Mémoire en Intervention dans l'Affaire 91/05. D (2005)52495.

European Court of Justice (1963) Judgment of the Court in Case 26/62, *Van Gend en Loos v. Nederlandse Administratie Belastingen*, 05.02.1963.

European Court of Justice (1964) Judgment of the Court in Case 6/64, *Costa v. ENEL*, 15.07.1964.

European Court of Justice (1979) Opinion 1/78 1979 ECR 2871, 04.10.1979.

European Court of Justice (1989) Judgment of the Court in Case C-68/88, *Commission v. Greece*, 21.09.1989.

European Court of Justice (1990) Order of the Court in case C-2/88, *Zwartfeld and Others*, 06.12.1990.

European Court of Justice (1998) Judgment of the Court in Case C-170/96, *Commission v. Council*, 12.05.1998.

European Court of Justice (1999) Judgment of the Court in case C186/98, *Nunes and Matos*, 08.07.1999.

European Court of Justice (2005a) Opinion of Advocate General Ruiz Jarabo Colomer in case C-176/03, *Commission v Council*, 26.05.2005.

European Court of Justice (2005b) Judgment of the Court in Case C-176/03, *Commission v. Council*, 13.09.2005.

European Court of Justice (2007a) Judgment of the Court in Case C-355/04, *Segi and Others v. Council*, 27.02.2007.

European Court of Justice (2007b) Opinion of Advocate General Mengozzi in case C-91/05, *Commission v. Council*, 19.09.2007.

European Court of Justice (2007c) Judgment of the Court in Case C-440/05, *Commission v. Council*, 27.10.2007.

European Court of Justice (2008) Judgment of the Court in Case C-91/05, *Commission v. Council*, 20.05.2008.

European Court of the First Instance (2004) Order of the Court of First Instance in Case T-338/02, *Segi v. Council*, 7.6.2004.

Federal Republic of Germany (2003) Mémoire en Intervention par l'Allemagne dans l'Affaire C-176/03, 04.12.2003.

House of Lords (1999) Ninth Report of the Select Committee on European Communities, 18.05.1999.

Kingdom of Denmark (2003) Mémoire en Intervention par le Danemark dans l'Affaire C-176/03, 15.12.2003.

Kingdom of the Netherlands (2003) Mémoire en Intervention par les Pays-Bas dans l'Affaire C-176/03, 12.12.2003.

Kingdom of the Netherlands (2005) Statement in Intervention in Case C-91/05, 17.11.2005.

Kingdom of Spain (2003) Mémoire en Intervention par l'Espagne dans l'Affaire C-176/03, 06.11.2003.

Kingdom of Spain (2005) Mémoire en Intervention par l'Espagne dans l'Affaire C-91/05, 22.12.20.

Kingdom of Sweden (2003) Mémoire en Intervention par la Suède dans l'Affaire C-176/03, 12.11.2003.

Republic of Finland (2003) Mémoire en Intervention par la Finlande dans l'Affaire C-176/03, 17.11.2003.

Republic of France (2003) Mémoire en Intervention du Gouvernement de la République Française dans l'Affaire 176/03, 12.12.2003.

Republic of France (2005) Mémoire en Intervention du Gouvernement de la République Française dans l'Affaire C-91/05, 19.12.2005.

Republic of Greece (2003) Mémoire en Intervention par la République Hellénique dans l'affaire C-176/03, 11.11.2003.

Republic of Ireland (2003) Mémoire en Intervention par l'Irlande dans l'Affaire 176/03, 18.11.2003.

Republic of Portugal (2003) Mémoire en Intervention par la République Portugaise dans l'Affaire C-176/03, 17.11.2003.

UNESCO (1998) International Conference on Sustainable Disarmament for Sustainable Development: The Brussels Call for Action, 13.10.1998. www.unesco.org/cpp/uk/declarations/brussels.pdf (Accessed 29 September 2011).

United Kingdom (2003) Mémoire en Intervention par le Royaume-Uni dans l'Affaire C-176/03, 12.12.2003.

United Kingdom (2005) Statement in Intervention by the United Kingdom in Case C-91/05, 08.12.2005.

United Nations (1973) *Declaration on the Establishment of a New International Economic Order*. Resolution 3201(S-VI).

United Nations (1988) United Nations Convention Against Illicit Traffic in Narcotic Drugs and Psychotropic Substances of December 19, 1988, no. 27627, 19.08.1988.

United Nations (2002) Report from the Secretary-General: Relationship between Disarmament and Development. A/57/167, 02.07.2002.

United Nations (2003) Report of the United Nations First Biennial Meeting of States to Consider the Implementation of the Programme of Action to Prevent, Combat and Eradicate the Illicit Trade in Small Arms and Light Weapons in All Its Aspects. A/CONF/BMS/2003/1, 18.07.2003.

United Nations Development Programme (1994) *Human Development Report.* Oxford: Oxford University Press.

United Nations Development Programme (1998) The Oslo Platform for a Moratorium on Small Arms in West Africa. http://legacy.prio.no/nisat/Publications/A-Moratorium-on-Light-Weapons-in-West-Africa/ (Accessed 21 August 2013).

World Bank (1981) *Accelerated Development in Sub-Saharan Africa: An Agenda for Action.* Washington, DC: The World Bank.

# Appendix I

## Data gathering and processing[1]

### Interviews

Interviews were conducted during a three month period in the spring of 2010 and during a shorter follow-up round in the fall of 2012. Interviews lasted between 30 minutes up to an hour and a half, though generally around 40 minutes. The lion part of the interviews (41/54) were taped.

### *Selecting respondents*

Non-probability sampling is intimately connected to process tracing as an approach to analyze the particular processes that led to more or less well-defined events (Tansey 2007). This implies that the analyst must seek to identify the relevant 'population' defined by their importance for the particular process (Tansey 2007: 769). This also means that not all interviews contributed in equal amount to answering the research questions. As Bennett has argued, 'not all data are created equal' (2010: 209). Respondents were selected strategically with the view of conducting interviews with as many of the officials as possible who had been directly involved in the drafting and discussions of the central legislative measures. The Commission officials who had been involved in the initiation of the legal action against the Council were of central importance as they were positioned in close proximity to the events that the book aims to explain. Officials in the corresponding services of the Council Secretariat were also of central importance for mapping the processes.

More generally, the interview data in combination with the textual material serve as proxies for more unwieldy and time consuming methods of gathering and analyzing the institutionally defined self-understandings of agents. That is, the investigation does not rely on techniques such as participant observation or the deep immersion in the particular social context of the respondents. Such techniques would enable a more thorough, and in that sense reliable, account of the self-understandings and practices governing the actions of these officials (Yanow 2006). The process of gathering and analyzing the material was more structured. Rather than mapping shared understandings among particular officials as an end in itself the purpose of these procedures was to answer the rather distinct research question of why institutional conflict erupted in the specific cases and what explained the redrawing of institutional boundaries in the specific policy areas. The approach chosen sought to strike a reasonable balance between depth of the analysis and the need to operate a manageable research process.

The collection of interview data as a whole started with a very specific focus on the two Court cases and the officials who had been primarily involved in the run-up to the outbreak of conflict. This included officials who had been involved in the preparation of the legislative acts that became the object of the institutional conflict. In the *environmental crimes* case, these were officials in the substantive Directorates-General of the Commission who had been directly involved in drafting the proposal for a Directive on the protection of the environment through criminal law, DG Environment (DG ENV) (Commission 2001a).[2] In the *small arms* case, this concerned the official from DG RELEX (Relations Extérieurs), who acted as the Commission representative in the so-called RELEX working party in which the Council decision on SALW was discussed (Council 2004d).[3] Apart from those directly involved in the preparation of these legislative acts, several interviews were also conducted with officials working in the same parts of the Commission. In the *environmental crimes* case, these were officials from DG Environment,[4] DG for Justice Liberty and Security (JLS),[5] and officials in the cabinets of the two JHA Commissioners at the time, Viviane Reding and Cecilia Malmström.[6] In the *small arms* case, respondents were drawn from DG RELEX[7] and later the European External Action Service (EEAS)[8] as well as the DG for Development (DG DEV).[9]

Interviews also covered the representatives from the Commission, Council and Parliament who had been directly responsible for the preparation, drafting and pleading of the respective cases to the Court. These respondents were very important for the analysis, since they were situated close to the point in the process at which the decision was taken to formally instigate the legal action against the Council in the European Court of Justice. In the *environmental crimes* case this included officials of the JHA units of the respective legal services[10] and in the *small arms* case officials from the CFSP units of the respective legal services.[11] In particular those involved in the actual legal actions were easily identified, since the documents from the Court proceedings in these cases list all those who have acted as agents for the respective institutions, and often those who have been responsible for the drafting of the arguments.[12] In other cases I relied on recommendations from respondents regarding key officials. In several cases this helped me to identify important respondents of whom I had been previously unaware. As Tansey has argued, such 'snow-ball techniques' are particularly useful 'when the population of interest is not fully visible' (Tansey 2007: 770; cf. Farquharson 2005). Recommendations by other respondents are of course not a foolproof way of identifying the totality of those respondents who played an important role in the processes. However, the fact that several respondents recommended me to interview the same officials was taken as an indication that such respondents were commonly recognized as having played an important role in particular events. In both cases Member State representatives within the substantive areas concerned were interviewed. In the *environmental crimes* case these included councillors in the field of substantive criminal law.[13] In the *small arms* case respondents were drawn among representatives to the Council RELEX working party.[14]

The interview data were also crucial for establishing the broader institutional developments in the selected policy fields. Some respondents were thus located who had either worked for a long time in the bureaucratic machinery of the EU or who had been present in the formative periods of these policy fields. These respondents often also gave important clues that helped contextualize specific pieces of legislation or jurisprudence.[15] In relation to the *environmental crimes* case, such contextualizing respondents included officials in the Council Secretariat[16] and the Parliament and Commission.[17] In relation to the *small arms* case, such bearers of the 'institutional memory' of the policy field proved more difficult to locate. Rather, bits and pieces were recovered across several interviews,[18] which were then complemented with secondary literature on the early developments in the field of development cooperation policy. Secondary sources were also cross-checked with other primary data, such as official documents. In most cases secondary sources have been used to establish specific chronologies or the factual intricacies of organizational developments.

### Interview questions and interpretation

Due to the central aim of the study to analyze the process leading to events, no set questionnaire was established. Rather, depending on the interviewee and his or her position in relation to the process studied, questions, while corresponding to the general themes of the study, were adapted for each interview. Oftentimes interviews evolved by way of a more open-ended discussion which sometimes involved confronting interviewees with official documents or with statements of other interviewees who had given sometimes contradictory interpretations of the process.

Themes around which interviews with respondents in the Commission revolved were:

- What, in your view, prompted the decision to take the Council to Court in this particular case?
- What was the role of your unit in relation to other parts of the Commission in this process?
- Were there other units/DGs involved? If so, which were they?
- Which parts of the Commission were less active, or perhaps even in opposition to challenging the Council in this area?
- What in their view was the fundamental issue at stake in this conflict?
- Were your perceptions of the issues at stake shared by others? If not, how did they differ?

Interviews with key officials of the Council Secretariat revolved around the actual process but were also instrumental in mapping the longer-term developments of the policy field, especially since several senior officials in the Secretariat had worked in this particular area for longer periods of time. Interviews with these respondents were thus connected to immediate events in relation to the process, but also to a longer temporal perspective.

- What in your view provoked conflict in this case?
- Why, in your view, did the Commission act in this case as opposed to previous similar cases?
- Why from your perspective was the case controversial?
- How would you perceive Council statements that point to broad agreements regarding these issues?
- What was the primary issue at stake in this conflict?
- How did you choose what arguments to level in front of the Court?

Interviews with national representatives were used as a way to contextualize the institutional conflict as well as provide an understanding of their views of the conflict, and what in their view made it controversial or not. These interviews revolved around questions such as:

- How would you describe the process through which the contested legislative act was adopted?
- How were the legal actions of the Commission perceived by you and your government?
- What was the primary issue at stake in this conflict?
- What was the primary reason for the outbreak of the conflict?
- What prompted your government to intervene in the proceedings?
- Why did you formulate your arguments before the Court in that particular way?
- What in your view made the Commission's actions controversial?

In general, interviews were geared towards tapping into respondents' perceptions of themselves and their role in the actual processes that led to the institutional conflict. They were also used as a way of identifying lines of conflict *within* their particular organization. This was especially the case with interviews with Commission officials. The aim of this was to capture the internal dynamics that feed into the decision to take legal action against the Council. This understanding was used to draw inferences regarding what motivates the Commission to initiate institutional conflict.

Interviews contributed in different ways to the investigation. Some interviews contributed primarily by confirming, for instance, that a particular unit in the Commission had *not* been involved in the decision-making process. Others indicated important aspects of the processes I had previously not been aware of. While some interviews opened doors by revealing previously unknown aspects of the cases, others served to close doors. Thus, interviews sometimes served the crucial purpose of closing avenues of the investigation and helping to narrow down the analytical scope of the study.

An example of this was how the investigation of the *environmental crimes* case was initially focused on the Commission Directorate General for Justice Liberty and Security (DG JLS). Since this is the DG responsible for questions of criminal law, it was initially assumed it had been officials from this DG who had driven the process through which institutional conflict had broken out in this case. As more interviews were performed it became clear that this DG had actually played a less important role than expected in comparison with the Commission Legal Service and DG Environment (DG ENV). This allowed me to further delimit the focus of the investigation, while also supplying important information regarding why a particular Commission DG comes to participate in the initiation of institutional conflict, while another would take a more passive role, or even resist.

Respondents who were farther removed from actual events would sometimes give key insights that would help contextualize what others had said. What Leech calls 'grand tour questions' (Leech 2002: 667) were often useful. These are open-ended questions regarding, for instance, the working procedures that the respondent normally engages in or the tasks that his/her specific unit regularly performs. Thus, apart from the questions presented above, geared towards mapping the process immediately leading up to the institutional conflicts, some interviews focused more on general insights in the evolution of the particular policy area.

The interview material was collected, analyzed and interpreted in relation to the broader institutional context in which respondents were situated. In line with the interpretive variant of process tracing used, the analysis went constantly back and forth between the collection and analysis of textual material in the form of official documents and the collection and analysis of interview data.[19] The analysis of official documents in light of interviews and vice versa resulted in a growing familiarity with the general context in which respondents acted. Since the processes took place in the highly structured and well-documented setting of the EU, there were often opportunities to back up (or refute) statements regarding the intricacies of the process with official documents.

There were sometimes sharply contrasting views among Commission officials themselves regarding the actorness of the Commission and why some action had been taken in a certain context. In one case a respondent described a rather complex process through which a Member State government had actively convinced the Commission to enact a Directive,[20] rather than a third pillar instrument in the form of a Framework Decision on data retention (Council 2006a).[21] Another official working in the very same Commission DG described the same process in a radically different way:

> To speak frankly, on the part of the Commission the most important thing in this context was to prevent the Member States from tabling the proposal. You could say it was about protecting turf; to not allow for a precedent where Member States would be dealing with this.[22]

However, while some respondents seemed more eager to highlight their role or the role of their specific unit in a specific process, others reacted to questions regarding differing opinions across the Commission directorates, or the role of a specific part of the Commission with quick answers like "it was a consensual decision" or as one respondent formulated, the process through which the decision was taken to bring the Council to Court in one of the cases:

> There was a long standing discussion about how to go about it. It was not an easy decision. Definitely not. But all the interventions, hesitations at some point were overruled by . . . not overruled, sorry. There was a consensual decision about how to go along, but it was not taken light heartedly. It was very much discussed.[23]

The internal conflicts of the Commission are not only a well-documented aspect of this specific multi-organization. It can also be argued that to describe *any* organization of that size in terms of more or less complete consensus is by definition misleading.[24] However, respondents are not neutral vessels of information. Indeed, an important point of conducting interviews at all was precisely to tap into their contextually defined self-understandings. Thus, rather than discarding statements by respondents that seemed factually misleading, such statements proved important to understand how they viewed themselves and the institutional environment in which they worked.

## Textual data

Textual material such as policy documents, legislation and case law, and in some cases secondary material, was used to map the evolution of how the questions of sanctions and more particularly criminal sanctions had been dealt with on the EU level. This mapping of the evolution of the policy field was not just a descriptive exercise. It served the purpose of debunking alternative explanations by identifying very similar instances where existing theories would have expected institutional conflict to break out but where it did not. Similar legislative acts were identified and by engaging in within-case comparisons, also in combination with the interview material, the underlying social mechanism that led to the final outcome could be chiselled out in more detail.

The collection and processing of textual material, similar to the selection of respondents, combined explorative and more systematic methods. When important points in the process had been identified as a result of the explorative approach, more systematic methods were employed for uncovering all relevant sources in relation to that particular point. The collection of textual data took the documents produced in relation to the Court cases as its point of departure. This initial body of material included the Court's judgment, the opinions of the Advocate General and the complete submissions of the Commission, Council and intervening Member States in these proceedings. The references made to existing legislation, policy documents and jurisprudence in this body of material made up the preliminary 'population' of textual material, which was then analyzed with the goal of mapping the broader, macro-level institutional developments through which the issues of criminal law and SALW and their relation to the institutional structure of the EU had evolved over the years.

It is important to point out that all documents do not have the same status, either formally or in relation to the analysis. Firstly, the category of official documents includes formal legislation and agreements with third parties as well as the jurisprudence of the Court. These are obviously important as they, together with the treaty texts, supply the more concrete institutional structure in the sense of institutional rules with which agents operate.[25] Secondly, it contains policy documents such as green papers and communications from the Commission. These are often more generally formulated and draw out the contours on how the Commission intends to continue its work on particular issues. Such documents can also emanate from the Council and take the form of resolutions or general strategies on particular issues or policy fields more broadly. These types of documents supply important indicators as to how issues are understood and the assumptions that underlie how they are formulated. They can thus be treated as a way to tap in to broadly defined conceptions of policy issues. Thirdly, the overarching category of official documents contains the range of documents that are produced as part of the working process of the Commission and the Council. These include working documents of the Commission that are primarily for the use of the internal process of intra-service consultations between different parts of the Commission. This also includes official summaries of meetings of Council working parties and opinions of the Council's Legal Service on particular issues.

Obviously, the process of selecting which documents to include in the analysis was not an *a priori* decision but evolved gradually in a movement back and forth between theory and the empirical material analyzed. Similar to the sampling of respondents, parts of the relevant material were initially hidden. When theoretically significant discrepancies were identified, the mode of analysis shifted and became more systematic. For instance, during the course of the investigation legislative measures were identified that were very similar to either the Framework Decision on the Protection of the Environment through Criminal Law or the Council Decision on the contribution to ECOWAS in the field of SALW. However, around these measures there had been no indications of institutional conflict. After the identification of such measures, the analysis could proceed systematically by seeking to identify the entire 'population' of legislative measures that fit this category. This allowed me to home in on the factors that had actually triggered the mechanism and explained the eventual outbreak of conflict. Thus, even if the approach here has an important inductive element, the open-ended exploration was also combined with more systematic techniques once particularly important steps in the process had been identified.

The European Court of Justice (ECJ),[26] in contrast to several of the other bodies of the EU, remains somewhat enigmatic. As a Court it is not bound by the legislation that regulates transparency of the European Parliament, the Commission and the Council. The deliberations of the members of the Court are confidential, and the Court passes its judgments without revealing any of the elements of discussion that led up to a specific ruling. All that remains is the final ruling of the Court with the formal motivations of why it had ruled in a specific way. The internal dynamics of the Court are largely inaccessible to scholars. This obviously presents a problem for any investigation that is interested in finding out why the Court reasoned in a certain way in a specific case.

As the analysis progressed, the process of both gathering and analyzing data to answer the question of why the Court ruled as it did became highly enmeshed with the analysis of why the institutional conflict erupted in the first place. As the theoretical chapter sought to demonstrate, the system of rules in place did not adequately explain the controversial rulings of the Court. That is, the formal legal rules in place did not adequately explain the final decisions of the Court in the *environmental crimes* and *small arms* court cases. This notion was further strengthened through the identification of other cases where the Court could indeed have furthered European integration in these intergovernmental areas, but where it had refrained from doing so.

## Notes

1  Parts of this appendix can be found in the supplemental file to Norman (2015a) available at www.tandfonline.com/doi/suppl/10.1080/13501763.2014.982155
2  Respondents 11 and 31.
3  Respondent 17.
4  Respondent 1 and 28.
5  Respondents 9, 12, 35, 42, 50.
6  Respondents 4, 5, 45, 46, 54. One interview was also conducted with an official of the JHA unit of the Secretariat of the European Parliament (Respondent 24).
7  Respondents 2, 7, 52, 53.
8  Respondents 16, 43, 48.
9  Respondents 6, 41, 47.
10  Respondents 8, 22, 40, 44, 49.
11  Respondents 18, 19, 21, 23, 29, 32, 38, 40. One single official of the European Court of Justice agreed on being interviewed. The respondent had been partially responsible in the drafting of the opinion of the Advocate General in the *small arms* court case (Respondent 30).
12  In the *environmental crimes* case, the Director-Generals of the respective legal services of the Commission and the Council were listed as agents. However, it became clear to the Council that it was not primarily the Director Generals who had actually drafted the arguments, but officials in the relevant units of the respective legal services.
13  Respondents 10, 20, 25, 26, 34.
14  Respondents 3, 37, 39. One respondent was also drawn from the CODEV working party (Respondent 27).
15  Richards (1996) specifically notes this as a benefit with conducting elite interviews (Richards 1996: 200).
16  Respondents 14, 36, 44.
17  Respondents 13, 31, 33, 38.
18  Respondents 7, 15, 17, 23, 47.
19  See Harvey (2011: 434) for a discussion on the problems and benefits of using recording devices when conducting elite interviews.

20　This account was also corroborated by another, high-ranking official in the Council Secretariat (Respondent 14).

21　Interview with Commission official, DG JLS (Respondent 50). In the interest of making the analysis more transparent, references to the interview material will figure in footnotes throughout the book.

22　Interview with Commission official, DG JLS (Respondent 9).

23　Interview with Commission official, DG RELEX (Respondent 17).

24　It can be noted that the Commission currently employs about 33,000 officials, of which approximately 21,000 are stationed in Brussels (Commission 2013a).

25　EU legislative acts are also a differentiated category of documents, as they have different formal status and are adopted through different procedures. For instance, in the pre-Lisbon era in which most of the analysis is located, Framework Decisions were an intergovernmental instrument that was used under the JHA. Joint Actions, Council Decisions, and Council Common Positions were also intergovernmental, used under the CFSP. These legislative instruments can be contrasted with Community instruments (presently instruments adopted under the TFEU) such as Directives and Regulations which are adopted through the 'normal' legislative procedures of the EU. While Directives have to be transposed into national legislation, Regulations are binding in their entirety as soon as they enter into force on the EU level.

26　Or, as it is formally known after the entry into force of the Lisbon Treaty, the Court of Justice of the European Union (CJEU).

# Appendix II

## List of respondents

1 Commission official, Policy officer, DG ENV, European Commission, interview, Offices of DG ENV, Brussels, April 28, 2010.
2 Commission official, Head of Unit, DG RELEX, European Commission, interview, Charlemagne building, Brussels, June 8, 2010.
3 Italian Government official, CFSP Counsellor, Permanent representation of Italy to the European Union, interview, Italian representation, Brussels, June 8, 2010.
4 Commission official, Member of Cabinet of Commissioner Reding, European Commission, interview, Berlaymont building, Brussels, May 6, 2010.
5 Commission official, Member of Cabinet of Commissioner Reding, European Commission, interview, Berlaymont building, Brussels, November 28, 2012.
6 Commission official, Legal Advisor, DG DEV, European Commission, interview, Offices of DG DEV, Brussels, June 22, 2010.
7 Commission official, Deputy Head of Unit, DG RELEX, European Commission, interview, Offices of DG RELEX, Brussels, May 28, 2010.
8 European Parliament official, Head of Unit, Legal Service of the Parliament, European Parliament, Parliament building, Brussels, interview, June 3, 2010.
9 Commission official, Head of sector, DG JLS, European Commission, interview, Café, Brussels, April 22, 2010.
10 Italian Government official, Counsellor JHA, Permanent representation of Italy to the European Union, interview, Italian representation, Brussels, June 17, 2010.
11 Commission official, Head of Sector, DG JLS, (formerly DG ENV), European Commission, interview, Offices of DG JLS, Brussels, May 5, 2010.
12 Commission official, Head of unit, DG JLS, European Commission, interview, Offices of DG JLS, Brussels, April 22, 2010.
13 Former Commission official, former Director, DG for Financial Control, European Commission, Café, Brussels, November 27, 2012.
14 Council Secretariat official, Counter-Terrorist Coordinator (former Director of DG JHA), Council Secretariat, interview, Justus Lipsius building, Brussels, June 9, 2010.
15 Council Secretariat official, Member of the Council Secretariat, SALW desk, Council Secretariat, interview, Justus Lipsius building, Brussels, June 21, 2010.

16  Official of the EEAS, Chairperson COARM, interview, European External Action Service, EEAS building, Brussels, November 26, 2012.

17  Commission official, DG DEV (formerly DG RELEX), European Commission, interview, Offices of DG DEV, Brussels, April 19, 2010.

18  Council Secretariat official, Member of the Council Legal Service, Council Secretariat, interview, Justus Lipsius building, Brussels, May 31, 2010.

19  Commission official, Member of the Commission Legal Service, European Commission, interview, Berlaymont building, Brussels, May 25, 2010.

20  Polish Government official, Counsellor for Criminal Law, Representation of Poland to the European Union, interview, Restaurant, Brussels, May 11, 2010.

21  Council Secretariat official, Member of the Council Legal service, Council Secretariat, interview, Café, Brussels, June 17, 2010.

22  European Parliament official, Member of the Parliament legal service, interview, European Parliament, Parliament building, Brussels, June 4, 2010.

23  Council Secretariat official, Member of the Legal Service, Head of CFSP Unit, Council Secretariat, interview, Justus Lipsius building, Brussels, May 27, 2010.

24  European Parliament official, Administrator, Secretariat of the Committee on Civil Liberties, Justice and Home Affairs, European Parliament, interview, Parliament building, Brussels, June 22, 2010.

25  Swedish government official, Home Affairs Counsellor, Permanent representation of Sweden to the EU, Swedish Representation, Brussels, 19 April, 2010.

26  German government official, Counsellor substantial criminal law, Permanent representation of Germany to the EU, interview, restaurant, Brussels, 29 April, 2010.

27  Swedish government official, Development Counsellor and CODEV representative, Permanent Representation of Sweden to the European Union, Swedish representation, Brussels, November 27, 2012.

28  Commission official, Case handler, DG ENV, European Commission, interview, Offices of DG ENV, Brussels, April 28, 2010.

29  Commission official, Member of the legal service, Commission Legal Service, European Commission, interview, Berlaymont building, Brussels, April 27, 2010.

30  Official of the European Court of Justice, Legal Secretary, Cabinet of Advocate General Mengozzi, European Court of Justice, Luxembourg, June 7, 2010.

31  Former Commission official, Former Head of Unit, DG ENV, European Commission, interview, Offices of ClientEarth, Brussels, June 10, 2010.

32  Former Commission official, former member of the Legal Service, European Commission, interview, Restaurant, Brussels, June 4, 2010.

33  Commission official, assistant to the Director-General of the Legal Service, European Commission, interview, Berlaymont building, Brussels, May 18, 2010.

34 Dutch Government official, Counsellor JHA, Permanent representation of the Netherlands to the European Union, interview, Dutch Representation, Brussels, 31 May, 2010.

35 Commission official, legislative officer, DG JLS, European Commission, Offices of DG JLS, Brussels, April 20, 2010.

36 Council Secretariat official, Head of Unit, DG JHA, Council Secretariat, interview, Justus Lipsius building, Brussels, June 18, 2010.

37 French Government official, Counsellor CFSP, Permanent Representation of France to the European Union, interview, French representation, Brussels, May 20, 2010.

38 European Parliament official, Member of Parliament Legal service, European Parliament, Brussels, interview, June 22, 2010.

39 Czech Government official, Counsellor CFSP, Permanent Representation of the Czech Republic to the European Union, interview, Czech representation, Brussels, 18, May, 2010.

40 Former Commission official, former Director-General of the Legal Service, European Commission, Offices of Clifford Chance law firm, Brussels, November 28, 2012.

41 Commission official, Deputy Head of Unit, DG DEV, European Commission, Offices of DG DEV, Brussels, May 31, 2010

42 Commission official, Director, DG JLS, European Commission, interview, Offices of DG JLS, Brussels, April 28, 2010.

43 EEAS official, Administrator, Security Policy and Sanctions Division, European External Action Service, EEAS building, Brussels, 26 November 2012.

44 Council Secretariat official, Member of Council Legal Service, Council Secretariat, interview, Justus Lipsius building, Brussels, June 16, 2010.

45 Commission official, Member of Cabinet of Commissioner Cecilia Malmström, European Commission, interview, Berlaymont building, Brussels, May 3, 2010.

46 Commission official, Head of Cabinet of Commissioner Reding, European Commission, interview, Berlaymont building, Brussels, May 19, 2010.

47 Commission official, Policy officer, DG DEV, European Commission, interview, Offices of DG DEV, Brussels, May 20, 2010.

48 EEAS official, Political Desk Officer, European External Action Service, EEAS building, Brussels, November 30, 2012

49. Commission official, Member of Legal Service, JLS Team, European Commission, interview, Berlaymont building, Brussels, April 14, 2010.

50 Commission official, Policy officer, DG JLS, European Commission, interview, DG JLS building, Brussels, April 28, 2010.

51 Swedish Government official, Counsellor criminal law, Permanent Representation of Sweden to the European Union, interview, Swedish representation, Brussels, May 10, 2010.

52 Commission official, Policy officer, DG RELEX, European Commission, interview, Charlemagne building, Brussels, June 2, 2010.

53 Commission official, Director, Crisis Platform-Policy Coordination, DG RELEX, European Commission, interview, Charlemagne building, Brussels, June 23, 2010.
54 Commission official, Head of Cabinet of Home affairs Commissioner Cecilia Malmström, European Commission, interview, Berlaymont building, Brussels, 20 April 2010.

# Index

Figures are indicated by page numbers in italics.